Program Guide for Infants and Toddlers with Neuromotor and other Developmental Disabilities

D1417712

Program Guide for
INFANTS AND TODDLERS
with
NEUROMOTOR
and other
DEVELOPMENTAL
DISABILITIES

Frances P. Connor
G. Gordon Williamson
John M. Siepp

IN COOPERATION WITH
United Cerebral Palsy Association, Inc.

TEACHERS COLLEGE PRESS
Teachers College, Columbia University
New York and London

Published by Teachers College Press, Columbia University, 1234 Amsterdam Avenue, New York, NY 10027.

This work was developed under a grant from the U.S. Office of Education, Department of Health, Education, and Welfare. However, the content does not necessarily reflect the position or policy of that Agency, and no official endorsement of these materials should be inferred.

The Program Guide for Infants and Toddlers with Neuromotor and Other Developmental Disabilities has been developed as a product of the United Cerebral Palsy Nationally Organized Collaborative Project to Provide Comprehensive Services for Atypical Infants and Their Families, supported by grants No. 0-71-4492 and 0-74-1443 USOE (Bureau of Education of the Handicapped). The points of view expressed herein are those of the individual authors and editors.

Library of Congress Cataloging in Publication Data
Main entry under title:

Program guide for infants and toddlers with neuromotor and other developmental disabilities.

Includes bibliographical references and indexes. 1. Developmentally disabled children—Care and treatment. 2. Developmentally disabled children—Education. I. Connor, Frances P. II. Williamson, G. Gordon. III. Siepp, John M. IV. United Cerebral Palsy Associations.
RJ138.P67   362.7'8   77-28188
ISBN 0-8077-2546-3

Manufactured in the U.S.A.

98 97 96   15 14 13 12 11 10

ACKNOWLEDGMENTS

In this collaborative effort, national in scope, there were innumerable people who gave unselfishly of their time and talent. We only regret that each cannot be recognized here individually. Foremost, however, we wish to thank the thousands of young children and their families who taught us so much. We are totally indebted to the staffs of the 49 participating centers, the contributing writers, and the reviewers for their innovative ideas, methods, and programs, but particularly for their willingness to share.

The National Collaborative Infant Project was sponsored by United Cerebral Palsy Associations, Inc. (UCPA), under the direction of Una Haynes, and partially funded by the Bureau of Education for the Handicapped, United States Office of Education. The interest and support provided by Mrs. Haynes and the project's Advisory Council were consistently helpful. UCPA's Professional Services Program Department, originally directed by Sherwood A. Messner and currently directed by Ethel Underwood, administered the grant. The Technical Assistance Development System under the leadership of David Lillie at the University of North Carolina generously offered needed consultation in the preparation of this guide. Likewise, gratitude is expressed for the support of the United Cerebral Palsy Research and Educational Foundation under the leadership of Leon Sternfeld.

Evelyn Katrak provided a great service in preparing the manuscript for publication. Barbro Šálek drew the original sketches. Barbara Sheets, Pat Carter, Lee Jackson, and Barbara Kolucki helped in organization and typing. To them, we are deeply appreciative.

F.P.C.
G.G.W.
J.M.S.

CONTRIBUTIONS BY

Maureen Keenan Abell
Judy Johnson Ayers
Ellis I. Barowsky
Adrienne Bergen
Lois L. Bly
Gloria Boylan
Molly Brickenstein
Linda Buch
Susan Collins
Maxine Conway
Leslie Faye Davis
Eric Denhoff
Sylvia Brooklyn Denhoff
Helen Bee Douglas
Lynn Freer
Sue Gelber
Donna Hanson

Una Haynes
Helen Hoffman
Carol Hosaka
Margaret H. Jones
Shari Stokes Kieran
Nancy Kinney
Claire Lapidakis
Shirley Joan Lemmen
Billie Levine
Sharon McDermott
Laureen B. Place
Claire Salant
Barbro Šálek
Margaret Schilling
Lillian Shapiro
Dorothy M. Smith
Jerry Staller

in collaboration with

Ellen Anderson
Kathryn E. Barnard
Frances Berko
Lee Ann Britain
Nancy D'Wolf
Bruce Ettinger
Mary Garrigan
Elsie D. Helsel
Ann Johnson
Patricia Keesee
Mark Leventhal
Elaine Lieberman

Miriam Lowry
Joan Meisel
Sherwood A. Messner
Joan Day Mohr
Gary Nielsen
Carol Porter
Sylvia O. Richardson
Leon Sternfeld
Janice Tessier
Ethel Underwood
Doris Woodward

Illustrations by
Carol Fortunato and Barbro Šálek

CONTENTS

FOREWORD

This remarkable documentation of ten years of service and experience in intervention for atypical children and their families deserves the recognition it will undoubtedly receive. It is a remarkable collection of the United Cerebral Palsy Associations, Inc.'s practical experience in program planning, in implementation, and in individualization of programs for children with handicaps. Forty-nine centers, over six years, and 4,000 children have contributed to the wisdom in this document. I am impressed with the enormously practical advice, all aimed at "mainstreaming" or helping handicapped children toward the ultimate goal of as normal and healthy development as they can achieve. I am also in agreement with the authors when they state that this can only be used as a "guide," *not* as a definitive curriculum for any individual child or program—for each is, indeed, too individual. Unfortunately, no written document can or will replace a demonstration program, but this book comes as close as one might hope —for it contains a wealth of information.

The idea that an atypical child can achieve his/her optimal level of function by the same processes as do normal children appeals to me. Whether the handicap may delay, deter, or decrease this potential is far too well known by parents and professionals who deal with such children; they are all too burdened by the handicap and aberrant functioning in the child. But the energizing that can come from an awareness of and attention to normal developmental processes is greater than many of us have been aware. In our Down's syndrome program at Children's Hospital in Boston, the most exciting aspect to me is to watch delayed children as they are motivated by their mothers' optimistic enthusiasm to learn a task in the same way and with the same reinforcement that would provide the background for a normal child's learning. So a positive model for approaching such children is more likely to engender a positive approach in their parents, and they will inevitably sense and respond to their feelings of optimism.

I am sure that the most serious handicap with which atypical children are burdened is their own poor self-image. The inevitable result of failure in developmental achievement, which naturally follows a handicapping condition, will result in children's having an expectation for failure even before they start a task. This expectation for failure engenders a feeling of hopelessness that de-energizes them and interferes with the duration of attention and the motivation that fuels attention to the task. So the chance of failure is redoubled at every turn. We see poor self-image haunting children with even a mild learning disability long after the specific disability is dispelled.

It is a monumental task to change the self-destructive image that repeated failures have engendered. We can see how important it is to follow the suggestions of this document and couple them with an optimistic, encouraging atmosphere that says to such a child, "You *can* do it, and when you do, we shall both be *so* proud!" A child with handicaps needs a constant source of such encouragement and proud expectancy for success even when accomplishments are limited. The difficulties are in providing encouragement without too much pressure and avoiding a kind of chauvinism that conveys the feeling that failure is really the expectancy. In order to do that one must *really* identify with the child as she or he is. Few of us are really ready for that. Hence, the experience and the suggestions accumulated in this book can become a valuable source of information to try to relate to handicapped children.

I wish more attention in this document had been paid to work with parents. However, materials on parent involvement developed by the National Collaborative Infant Project are companion pieces to this program guide. These products, available through United Cerebral Palsy Associations, Inc., include: slide/tape modules *(Parents Are Teachers Too, Sharing Ideas of Family Involvement in Programs for Atypical Infants)*; audiotapes *(Teaching*

Styles and Parent-Child Interactions, The Effect of the Infant on the Caregiver); and monographs *(Programming for Atypical Infants and Their Families; Interviews with Parents of Atypical Infants and Parent Teaching Styles).*

Work with parents is necessary and valuable if one wants to provide the most optimal environment for an atypical child. For, as the book says repeatedly, the home environment is the best source of encouragement and learning in a child's development. Most parents do need and can utilize the encouragement of a supportive single professional or team of professionals. I agree that one or two caring professionals can get to know the mother, and the father too, as individuals and incorporate them into a helpful team rather than a large overpowering group of specialists.

Implicit in helping such a mother or father is a deep understanding of the inevitable grief reaction that burdens parents of a handicapped child. Lindemann (1944) described the grief reactions that accompanied the losses to loved ones by death or damage in the Cocoanut Grove fire in Boston in the 1940's. This concept seems equally applicable to parents who produce a damaged or handicapped child. At the base of their adjustment to such a child is their own feeling of having been responsible for the handicapping condition. Whether there is reality in this or not, a parent *inevitably* feels it. Along with this feeling of responsibility goes an overwhelming sense of guilt and of hopeless inadequacy to the child and his or her condition. So overwhelming are these feelings in grieving parents that they must build up defenses to protect themselves from severe depression. The most common defenses we see around hospitalized, ill children are: (1) denial—masked often as an unwillingness or inability to face a child's problems, and (2) distancing from the children—as if in their minds having damaged the children already, they feel that they would be better off without them. This latter defense mechanism can be the most serious over the long run, for then parents may indeed feel that anyone else can do better than they can. Implicitly, they withdraw from their children's care and turn it over to others. Even though they may continue to receive adequate attention and therapy, their reaction to their desertion is likely to be that of self-devaluation. Any team or center that has as its goal preserving the parent-child bond must realize that such distancing, negative behavior toward atypical children is more likely based on a damaged self-image in the parents than on simply not caring about them. When this understanding is coupled with assistance in dealing with *natural* grief reactions, many more apparently rejecting parents can be reached and cemented into an intervention program.

Of course, my bias is for early intervention—as early as possible in infancy—long before the parents' lowered self-esteem and grieving can convey hopelessness and a poor self-image to the infant. Certainly, there is rapidly increasing evidence that early intervention programs can effect remarkable development of function, even in severely damaged babies. It makes me feel that there is often more acquisition of function available in the immature organism than later, when complete maturation and secondary complications, such as spasticity, have occurred. Can we all begin to fight for earlier and earlier intervention approaches? I think parents are aware of and are seeking help for delayed children long before we professionals are ready to face the diagnoses of retardation or cerebral palsy. This book should go a long way toward reassuring such professionals and presenting them with programming suggestions for parents and atypical children. And this volume offers all of us—caring parents and committed professionals—a valuable source of experience and ideas on which to build programs for children.

T. Berry Brazelton, M.D.
Children's Hospital Medical Center
Boston, Massachusetts

INTRODUCTION

In 1967 and 1968 the United Cerebral Palsy Associations, Inc. (UCPA), held a series of hearings across the country attended by state and local affiliates of UCPA, disabled individuals, and representatives of governmental and voluntary agencies serving the handicapped. The purpose of these meetings was to review the current program of services delivered by UCPA and to make recommendations for the future. One of the top priorities that surfaced was the need to provide comprehensive programs for infants at risk or known to be disabled—and for the families of such children. In the ensuing 18 months, UCPA's Task Force on Prevention and Early Care initiated a variety of activities, including the preparation of an annotated bibliography on the early identification of and intervention in developmental disabilities, the preparation and distribution of audiovisual materials, and the organization of a national conference on interdisciplinary programming.

The task force soon recognized that comprehensive services for atypical children under 3 years of age, and their families, could not be supported by UCPA alone. Federal monies were required to promote the endeavor. Thus, the National Collaborative Infant Project was launched, sponsored by UCPA under the direction of Una Haynes and partially funded by the Bureau of Education for the Handicapped of the United States Office of Education. The original grant was for a 3-year period, July 1971 to July 1974, with a 3-year extension available for dissemination of the findings.

This program guide for curriculum development has been based primarily on the experience and insight gained by those involved in the 49 participating centers of the National Collaborative Infant Project (see Appendixes B and C). The project began with 5 centers, all of which had acquired considerable experience in serving the young handicapped population: Agency for Infant Development, Kentfield, California; Meeting Street School, Providence, Rhode Island; Program for Infants and Young Children with Developmental Disabilities, University of California Medical Center, Los Angeles; United Cerebral Palsy of Greater New Orleans, Inc.; and University Hospital School, Iowa City, Iowa. During the second phase of the project, 13 additional centers joined the consortium. A further 31 centers were added in the third phase; they were centers that had expressed interest in being involved in the project and that met the criteria for selection (i.e., quality of program, adequate funding, and commitment to staff development).

Over 4000 children* up to 3 years of age participated in the project. They were referred to one of the 49 centers by parents, physicians, or others, as having a possible problem in development. For the most part, the children were moderately to severely handicapped; most evidenced major motor problems. Approximately one-half of the children were diagnosed as cerebral palsied. Of this cerebral palsied group, more than one-half were identified as spastic; 20 percent as hypotonic; and 18 percent as athetotic. Visual problems were diagnosed or suspected in 38 percent of all the children, and hearing deviations were noted or suspected in 11 percent. Convulsions were reported for 17 percent. Oropharyngeal abnormalities were identified in 32 percent of the children, with such disorders suspected in an additional 8 percent; of these children, 83 percent presented speech difficulties and 17 percent had major feeding problems. The behavior of 28 percent of all the children was deemed either socially or emotionally atypical; over 50 percent were said to be unresponsive to social stimuli or to show behavioral control problems. While resistance to attaching such labels or categories to the children was strong among the centers, completely ignoring groups of pathologies or atypicalities was viewed as illogical and unprofessional.

*Does not represent the total number of children and families served during the 6 years of the project.

The Curriculum Task Force (see Appendix D), composed of representatives from the original five centers, requested the staffs of the participating centers to develop individual program plans for each child, with stated goals and objectives in five overlapping developmental areas—movement, pre-speech, language, cognition, and social–emotional well-being. The baby's functional assets, not just his/her deficits, were to be recorded. The infant was to be seen as a total being, and answers sought to such questions as: What can he do now? What can he learn next? What should he learn next? How can that learning be facilitated? In other words, the child was viewed as having the right to be who he is—and become what he is able to become—in the ways in which he is capable of developing.

The information relating to each child and his family was systematically recorded on curriculum sheets (see Appendix E), and copies were forwarded to the task force. Though varying in format, they usually included the child's strengths and weaknesses, goals and objectives stated in behavioral terms, a listing of materials and techniques employed, the person(s) designated to work with the child and/or the caregiver, the time spent (both frequency and duration) on each intervention, and the degree to which the specified objectives were met through the intervention. This program guide represents the information gleaned from over 1200 such curriculum sheets and incorporates interventions and activities effectively employed in the 49 centers.

A professional seminar was held at Teachers College, Columbia University, to sift and collate the material. The first task was to develop a series of statements as to what, in each area, was generally considered to be normal growth and development. Next, efforts were made to identify the most critical or the most frequently occurring developmental problems encountered. Comprehensive intervention approaches were then formulated. When questions arose, or information was considered to be inadequate, a member of the writing team would visit or communicate with center personnel. In addition, individuals with specialized skills were recruited to contribute their expertise to various sections of the book. A comprehensive list of contributing writers and reviewers is found in Appendix F.

Upon completion of the preliminary draft of the program guide, reactions and suggested revisions were sought from the 49 centers. The final meeting of the Curriculum Task Force included members of the participating centers, and it provided ex post facto validation and acceptance of the written material by those who had actually carried out the interventions over the past 3 to 4 years. Thus, the therapeutic and educational interventions incorporated in this text have been employed with recorded clinical success.

Lastly, a national network of four transdisciplinary work conferences was set up to demonstrate and further field test the usefulness of the material. The 3-day meetings were held in San Raphael, California; Kansas City, Kansas; Pittsburgh, Pennsylvania; and Commack, New York. The 40 persons participating in each conference—all professionals involved in atypical infant programs—were divided into teams, which rotated through comprehensive sessions on cognition, language, movement, and prespeech and feeding. Each session centered around a mother and her baby, and an advocate—either a disabled adult or the parent of a child who had been through an infant program. These target sessions consisted of an introductory discussion, a demonstration with the atypical infant and his mother, and the development of a transdisciplinary, individualized program plan based on the information obtained. In addition to these small group sessions, there were general meetings on the foundational material related to health factors, evaluation techniques, family involvement, and community organization.

This program guide is just that—a guide! It cannot be considered a definitive curriculum for a particular child or even for a specific group of children. While most of the children in the project had neuromuscular involvement, the guide does not take into full account the physical uniqueness of such special groups as those with spina bifida or those with primary sensory impairment or major health problems. However, because emphasis is directed toward normal growth and development, the material presented has relevance to the wider population of atypical infants.

The book is intended for knowledgeable professional and paraprofessional personnel who have additional staff resources available to them. Although an effort has been made to render it easily readable by all those concerned with young children having developmental disabilities, the use of these curriculum materials for planning and evaluation purposes requires the involvement of at least one representative from each of the fields—medical, educational, and psychosocial. The employment of an integrated transdisciplinary approach appears critical to the planning and execution of an effective program for atypical infants and toddlers who require comprehensive and diversified services on a regular basis. Although the book is written for team personnel, it is felt that parents and other caregivers may gain a better understanding of their developing handicapped baby by reading it. For practical application or intervention, however, parents as well as professionals need the guidance of the whole team.

The guide is intended as an evolving, fluid source book. It represents broad brush-stroke outlines for interactional study. It is designed to foster more intensive individualized curriculum development, as knowledge is generated about the integration of the maturational and learning processes of moderately to severely disabled and developmentally delayed babies. It is expected that the specialized materials presented here will be used in conjunction with the many other curriculum designs emerging from other nationally supported studies, most of which have emphases different from this one.

The text is divided into three parts. Part One is devoted to the basic foundations for a program serving atypical young children and their families. It comprises a chapter on the operational assumptions upon which this curricular approach is grounded, and chapters on important aspects of assessment, nutrition, and health. That is, Part One represents what are considered to be the essential components of a sound developmental program. These components provide the frame of reference for evaluation and intervention but, in addition, emphasize the primary health needs of the child as learner.

Part Two of the guide presents narrative and summary presentations of the developmental program in five major curriculum areas—movement, pre-speech, language, cognition, and social–emotional. Each of the chapters devoted to these five areas includes the normal developmental sequence, development in atypical children, and interventions that proved in this project to be effective for the populations served and the staffs involved. Since the majority of the children were physically handicapped, the chapter on movement (Chapter 5) is the longest and includes separate sections based on the various types of abnormal muscle tone—spastic diplegia (and quadriplegia), hemiplegia, athetosis, ataxia, and hypotonia.

Part Three deals with the curriculum in action—its practical application. The first chapter of this part (Chapter 10) presents sample program plans tailored to the needs of particular children and their families. The plans are presented here to illustrate the complexity of the problems present in individual instances, the use of the transdisciplinary approach to programming, and the cross-categorical, integrative nature of the child's growth and development. Chapter 11 discusses various models for the delivery of services. It outlines formats that can be used in the structuring of programs. Brief illustrations of the interactional models are offered.

Appendix A, a discussion on adaptive equipment, describes modified materials and furniture that have proved beneficial in the field, as well as a list of sources for commercially available equipment.

PART ONE

PROGRAM FOUNDATIONS

CHAPTER 1

OPERATIONAL ASSUMPTIONS

Т HE statements that follow reflect the core around which have evolved programs of early intervention for young children with neuromuscular and related disabilities and their families. The first six assumptions are general in nature. The last one, dealing with play, introduces the reader to the approach employed throughout the developmental program outlined in Part Two.

The Right to Optimum Development

Every child has a right to life with a caregiver
who can facilitate the child's early development
to the upper levels of the child's ability.

The notion of the right to education has been recognized in the courts of almost every state (Abeson, 1973). It is reflected in legislation initiating or upgrading programs for children living in residential facilities for the severely and multiply disabled and in proposals to improve the services of public and private health agencies concerned with the handicapped. The right to education as applied to handicapped infants assumes (a) that no child is too disabled to respond in some way to carefully selected stimuli; (b)

The major contributor to this chapter is Frances P. Connor.

that the stimuli and the child's responding behaviors should be appropriate to promote development in a wide range of areas; and (c) that atypical babies need specialized interventions that will assist them in closing the gap between their levels of functioning and those of their chronological age peers and help prevent their developing secondary and tertiary disabilities.

This program guide is based on an additional premise—the right of parents and other caregivers to know what they can do to help their child. This right assumes the availability of supportive and specialized help when needed. Under no circumstances is the complexity or severity of the infant's disability to preclude or limit service to the child or his family.

The Need for Early Intervention

Children learn at a very early age and will attend and respond to selected stimuli.

Support for early intervention programs for infants and toddlers with severe neuromuscular involvement and developmental lags is inherent in much of the research on general early childhood development. The early responses of infants reflect their efforts to explore and control their environment. Brazelton (1962, 1966) demonstrated that a baby during the third day of life turned her head in the direction of his softly spoken, repeated command, "Look over here, baby." And the infant visually tracked a red ball across her midline. Lipsitt (1967) has noted that newborns will suck harder and faster—or kick harder and faster—in an attempt to regulate the brightness of a picture projected on the wall.

It appears that infants actually seek out pleasurable stimulation of many kinds; they do not limit their responses to seeking satisfaction of such physiological needs as hunger, thirst, or pain. The newborn's natural curiosity can be exploited to encourage his use of body parts in a manner that will promote the response desired by the therapeutic staff.

For example, a baby can be encouraged to move his affected leg in an appropriate pattern to achieve the ringing of a bell or the moving of a mobile placed at his side. When his position is appropriate and the stimuli are designed and placed so that he can control them, he will move correctly. The action will be self-initiated and will be reinforced by the responses the baby achieves from the play object and by encouragement from his caregiver.

The attention of very young children to stimuli is the critical factor in cognitive development. Sustained attention requires the presence in the environment of stimuli that will attract, hold, and extend the baby's interest. Under usual conditions, such attention is strengthened over time. Kagan and Lewis (1965) conducted a longitudinal study of attention, cognition, emotion, and temperament in 180 infants at 4, 8, 13, and 27 months of age. They concluded that a developmental sequence governs attention. For example, objects and strategies that are primary attention gainers in the first few weeks differ from those that succeed in gaining attention in the later months. Major stimuli that attract the attention of the newly born are black-and-white contrasting patterns, rather than the solid pastel colors of the traditional nursery environment. Later, less dramatic stimuli attract attention.

As early as 1902, Dewey pointed out that while a child's development depends upon his experiencing responses to his felt needs and desires, it is the adult who selects the stimuli. Thus, it is the adult-controlled factors in the environment that control the direction of the child's learning. The more opportunities a child has to apply feasible behaviors (that is, behaviors that are feasible for *him*), the more he will be enabled to modify his own actions and cope with his environment. The critical factor in programming for physically limited babies is to enable them to experience multiple stimuli that result in satisfying social interaction and decision making. If, as Bloom (1964) concluded, 50 percent of all growth in intelligence takes place between birth and 4 years of age, the responsibilities of early childhood specialists are great. Awareness of this responsibility and of its disturbing corollary—that vast numbers of very young children are still being unwarrantedly written off as nonresponsive or untreatable—calls for a systematically developed program with these children in mind.

The Parent as Primary Programmer

The parent is the primary programmer for the baby.

Establishment of a positive interactional relationship between the child and his/her caregivers underlies the twin concepts of the parent or caregiver as the primary programmer and the use of the transdisciplinary approach.

Erikson (1963) pointed to the importance of trust between the infant and his mother or caregiver. Bell (1970) related infant–caregiver attachment to facilitation of the baby's concept development. By approximately 9 months of age, the infant has usually developed a strong attachment to his caregiver. He experiences anxiety each time he is separated from his caregiver and is fearful of strangers.

Ainsworth and Bell (1970) suggest that mothers who can see things from the baby's point of view tend to adopt infant care practices that lead to harmonious interaction. Sears, Maccoby, and Levin (1957), among others, also indicate that the direction of impact is not one-way and that infants who manifest irritability and are hyperkinetic have mothers who are relatively more anxious, protective, and dominant.

Normal attachment patterns are hard to maintain or develop in families under stress (Rutter, 1972). In order to foster attachment patterns and avoid their disruption (e.g., by invoking fear of strangers and separation anxiety), sustained parental involvement in the therapeutic work undertaken with handicapped infants is seen as a basic element in programming. Since the strength of the mother–child (or caregiver–child) relationship is critical to the child's development, every effort must be made to strengthen the mother's ability to help her disabled baby.

It is also generally accepted that infants and toddlers need to be fondled and that fondling should take place in an environment of trust. Such handling has been noted as an important factor in physical, cognitive, linguistic, social, and emotional development. Solkoff, Yaffe, Weintraub, and Blase (1969) report that premature infants who were handled and stimulated were healthier and more active, brighter and more demanding of stimulation than those who were not. The effects were stable over time.

Increased visual attentiveness in babies who were handled was reported by Brody as early as 1951. Subsequently, White (1967) related increased handling and increased mobility in a prone position to the onset of hand regard, visually directed reaching, and growth in visual attention.

Parents or other caregivers are in a position to foster such experiences as part of the infant's life at home and with his family in a variety of settings. A baby's cognitive and language development is related to the amount and quality of stimulation through play and the use of toys. If, in addition, the caregiver labels objects and actions or talks to the child about his behavior and interactions, development is noted to be much greater (Yarrow, Rubenstein, Pedersen, & Jankowski, 1972; Rubenstein, 1967).

Yarrow and his colleagues provide details about kinds of cognitive development in relation to various types of stimulation. For example, 5-month-old babies whose homes provided many and varied play objects scored better in a number of cognitive areas. Early vocalization and early language development were found to be related to the frequency of social and verbal stimulation provided in the home, especially by the principal caregiver.

However, according to the findings of Tulkin and Kagan (1972), a mother's attitude toward her children is not independent of social and economic conditions, and professionals should realize the futility of attempts to change maternal behavior patterns without regard to the sources of those patterns.

The Transdisciplinary Approach

The number of adults actually relating to the atypical infant is to be limited, even in face of his need for the professional services of a variety of disciplines.

While the infant's relationship to his principal caregiver is crucial to his optimum development, children can develop multiple attachments, especially in relating to more than one caregiver, and their attachment can be strong (Schaffer & Emerson, 1964a; Caldwell, 1970). The important factors in establishing attachment appear related to the consistency and quality of the relationship between the baby and his caregivers.

The atypical infant is usually in need of the services offered by a variety of specialists, including the nurse, physician, and teacher, and the physical, occupational, and speech therapist. Yet it is essential that the number of these supplementary caregivers be limited in order to foster a familiar and trusting relationship. Moreover, evidence suggests that too much stimulation in the early development of children is counterproductive. Cronbach (1969), among others, points to the confusion that results when a child cannot process the excess of visual and auditory stimuli that are introduced into his environment. For the same reason, Caldwell (1970) urges that children not be subjected to the booming, buzzing confusion that constitutes the environment of some babies.

What appears to be called for is the careful selection of equipment and materials, so placed for the individual baby as to promote the integration of his learning. Numerous well-meaning professional workers each performing designated and traditional roles are possibly working to the child's detriment. Instead, a transdisciplinary approach is recommended.

The transdisciplinary approach, which evolved from the more traditional medical–psychosocial team planning and action on behalf of the ill and the physically disabled, demands new behaviors on the part of members of such teams. While there continues to be multiprofessional representation, the roles have new dimensions and carry with them new professional responsibilities.

The transdisciplinary approach is built on the assumption that, in providing the necessary services, one person will carry out several professional roles under the supervision of his/her colleague specialists from the other fields involved. For this modus operandi, several basic elements obtain:

1. Each professional worker continues to increase his knowledge and skill in his own field.
2. The professional worker releases his role to another who appears to be (a) in a better position, physically or psychologically, to work effectively with the baby and/or his parents or (b) better able to integrate the program interventions in two or more areas into a single activity.
3. Each member of the team is to extend his own role to incorporate the traditional roles of his colleagues.
4. Regardless of who provides the instruction to the child and his parents, the specialist does not relinquish his accountability for superior intervention in areas related to his specialized field.

Under such program operation, a teacher, for example, with instructions from the physical therapist, may assume responsibility for positioning a severely physically involved child or, with the guidance of the occupational therapist, instruct a parent or other caregiver in the use of materials that will increase a baby's visual attentiveness or his understanding of means and ends in causal relationships.

Exploring Options and Providing Variety

The disabled infant's development can be facilitated both quantitatively and qualitatively through alteration of the physical environment and/or of the child's physical position.

The gradual increase in intellectual function of a child is not solely attributable either to environmental factors or to inherent maturational processes. Rather, it is due to the continuous interaction between the two.

Jenson (1969), in highlighting genetic factors and questioning the environmentalists, indicated that the only supportable upward shifts in IQ associated with environmental factors were related to "young children whose initial social environment was deplorable to a greater extent than can be found among any children who interact with other people or are able to run about out of doors." For such socially deprived children, he suggested, a shift to good average environmental circumstances could boost the IQ by 20 or 30 points and, in extremely rare cases, by as much as 60 or 70 points. Such a conclusion would seem to have major programming implications for children with disabilities, particularly when it is borne in mind that a child's disabilities may extend beyond his own physical limitations to the negative reactions of his family.

All infants need stimulation from the environment, particularly interaction with other human beings. Where a child's parents are greatly upset or disappointed by his condition, or experience guilt as a result of it, their social relationships with the child are likely to be distorted. Thus, he experiences social–emotional deprivation in addition to his physical limitations.

The severely disabled infant who is without adult understanding of his uniqueness and his need for highly specialized intervention will be further disadvantaged in early development. The baby whose asymmetrical tonic neck reflex fails to be integrated within his first 4 months of life can be helped by well-placed physical support. For example, a bolster under his chest as he lies prone will facilitate freer exploratory activities; functional use of his hands in manipulative play can thus be increased.

Research suggests that mere visual experiences with objects, even when accompanied by verbalization, may not be sufficient for perceptual sensory learning. For example, some children were shown objects as they were named; others were shown objects and encouraged to handle them at the same time; total times of experience with the objects were the same for both groups. The children who handled the objects learned much more and at a more rapid rate (Razran, 1961).

However, even for the most severely disabled, options exist. The child might be able to learn—even at a very early age—without actually touching the object. For example, Weiner and Goodnow (1970) noted that when a shape was enclosed in an eye-catching plastic globe, the baby remembered it equally well when he just looked at it as when he looked at and handled it. They conclude that the contribution of motor action is not essential, that substitutions are possible. In other words, for some of the babies with severe cerebral dysfunction for whom the usual very early motor action may not be possible, learning can still take place. Nor is the nature of the contribution of motor activity constant. It interacts with the resultant response. Weiner and Goodnow question the modality hierarchy and stress that individual differences point up the advantage of employing particular methods for particular children.

Judicious positioning can affect the development of visual and auditory tracking skills, as well as everyday feeding and toileting activities. It can also foster an awareness of environmental relationships and a sense of their constancy. Being able to view his world from a variety of perspectives is critical to the baby's expanding cognitive ability. For this, many severely disabled babies need adaptive equipment and careful positioning. Lying on his back, the baby might be hyperextended and unable to view anything but the ceiling. This position limits eye contact with other humans and the opportunity to participate in or even observe ordinary home activities, while at the same time fostering physical deformities and an incapacity for more normal movements.

This program guide is designed to counter the inaction and deprivation of children with abnormal movement. Not all such children have the capacity to develop normal sensorimotor and concomitant social or communication skills, but those who eventually do so will first have had to experience normal body postures and movements.

The Need for Nurturance

*Principles of nurturance apply to all who are concerned with the atypical infant.**

Nurturing is a lifelong interactive process between persons. It involves trust, attachment, awareness of one's own needs, adaptation on the part of others to those needs, and reciprocal gratification. The process suggests personal closeness, intimacy, communication, and mutual responsibility to foster mutual growth and development. There are several factors to consider in the nurturance of the atypical infant. How, in responding to a disabled child, does one promote rest, comfort, and wellness? How does one best facilitate the mastery of skills in movement, cognition, and language? How does one foster the social–emotional development that leads to independence? Are there cricital periods when nurturing is most important?

Nurturing occurs primarily within the family. The totalness of human experience may be attained with confidence in a healthy family environment. It is within this environment that a child first experiences the nurturing that is important to all parameters of his development: the growth of trust, attachment, and feelings of self-worth; the acquisition of skills and emergence of a feeling of competence; and the ability to cope with everyday stress.

However, the tasks of the family are varied and complex. The development of its members does not flow evenly, and one aspect may take priority over another, depending upon individual and group need. For instance, at times it may be the health and well-being of one or all of its members that is given priority, at other times the upward mobility of the breadwinner.

In order to be nurturing, parents need to have a high regard for themselves and each other and to utilize sound child-rearing practices. Moreover, they need to be aware of the supplementary

*The major contributors to this section are Shirley Joan Lemmen, Judy Johnson Ayers, Maxine Conway, Lynn Freer, Una Haynes, and Dorothy M. Smith.

nurturing role of the supportive systems that intermesh with the family—the extended family, health care systems, and religious or other organizations. They need to be able to use the services within the society to enhance the growth of each family member and actualize their ideas and goals for their children and themselves. This is especially true for the family that includes an atypical child. Yet, the impact on a family of the advent of an atypical child is such that the links with supportive systems are often disrupted, at times not visible at all.

For specialists who choose to be involved with the families of atypical children, it is necessary to be aware of the extent to which the family has or does not have the capacity to nurture and be nurtured. Specialists need to be aware of the parents' strengths, resources, and ability to fill the parental role; they need to be able to assess the indicators of a nurturing environment.

The *health of the parent,* which includes genetic factors and current state of wellbeing, is a vital factor in the will and ability to nurture and be nurtured. To what extent have the parents utilized health resources on their *own* behalf?

An important aspect of health is *nutrition* (see Chapter 3) , which, in turn, is directly influenced by socioeconomic patterns. However, any effort to improve nutritional intake must take into account the dietary habits, idiosyncrasies, and culture preferences of the family. There are also other environmental factors that affect health, such as habitation.

Another aspect of health is how the parent feels about him/ herself. Many authors have suggested that positive feelings of *self-worth* are essential in meeting the expectations and goals that are important to an individual and his family. Erikson (1963) suggests a rate and sequence of development that helps a person to achieve ego integrity and the ability to meet the variety of responsibilities and experiences with which an adult is confronted. Thus, ego integrity and positive feelings of self-worth can help the individual to meet life experiences with confidence and competence and to see him/herself as a capable caregiver.

Satir, in *People Making* (1972) , defines four aspects of nurturing in life: (*a*) self-worth (positive) ; (*b*) communication (clear, direct, specific, and honest) ; (*c*) function and roles (flexible, appropriate, and responsive to change) ; and (*d*) linkage to society (hopeful and open) . Interaction with society exists regardless of the family construct; whether the setting is the nuclear family, the single-parent family, the institutional setting, or the modern-day commune, the same forces are operative.

In addition to individual strengths and how the family inter-acts to provide nurturing, other factors influence how a child will grow within a family. The parents' perception of the birth process and of their individual roles once they have become parents affects the step-by-step experience that parent and child share. Also, the birth order of the child may determine the parents' ability to cope with the newborn, particularly the disabled baby.

Several studies (Leifer, Leiderman, Barnett, & Williams, 1972; Klaus & Kennell, 1970) have shown that changes occur in the parents' attachment to their newborn as a result of initial separation, which may affect their behavior toward their infant for months or even years after birth. Where the separation is due to prematurity, disability, or serious illness, parents experience grief in addition to the disruption of the early attachment process. To a greater or lesser extent, their expectations, perceptions, and capabilities tend to be thrown into a state of confusion, disbelief, and shock.

Moreover, in the case of the atypical child, specialists fre-quently make extra demands on the family for assessment and treatment of the child—often entailing further separation from the family for periods of time.The parents need guidance in de-fining their expectations for the child and initiating a direction for themselves. It is necessary for them, even while grieving over their lost hopes for a healthy child, to nurture this baby who demands special attention.

The Role of Play

The opportunity to play as freely as possible in
an independent way is essential for the
*optimum development of the child.**

Children's play has been the subject of much analysis, obser-vation, and, to a more limited extent, meaningful research. Much of the literature justifies and accepts play in the belief that it is "the work of children." But, more recently, writers have been

*The major contributor to this section is Claire Salant.

taking a deeper and different look at the play of young children. Increasingly, it is viewed as an essential component of a child's life, affected by and affecting his or her uniqueness, development, and environmental interaction. White (1959) suggests that play satisfies the child's intrinsic need to deal with the environment through such exploratory activities as grasping, banging, or investigating objects. The motivation for a child's play, according to Piaget (1963), is the joy of mastery, and he sees cognitive and play behaviors as a means through which the child learns to adapt to his environment. The nature of play is distorted and even destroyed when goals are overly set, expectations of accomplishment overly emphasized, and play turned into work (Herron & Sutton-Smith, 1971).

Self-initiated play is spontaneous in nature. It is limited only by the child himself, reflecting his own interests and imagination, providing an outlet for the free expression of his emotions (Freud, 1955; Erikson, 1963). In play, the child can make things come out the way he wants or act out his worst fears. He can be whatever he desires. He can control material things and make them do whatever his competence allows. As his competence develops, so does the content and scope of his play.

The value of adult-directed play lies in the ability of the adult to provide the child with the opportunities, equipment, experiences, and encouragement appropriate to his abilities and interests, but *without* imposing adult standards upon him. Both forms of play are important to the child's total development, and in many ways they are intertwined.

But above all, play belongs to the child! It gives him pleasure, satisfaction, and the opportunity to develop into a vital, motivated, creative human being. Through an understanding of the developmental nature and changing levels of play during the first 3 years of life, the infant's caregiver can provide the optimum space, materials, situations, and interaction for the fullest benefit to baby and family.

Play begins from the moment that an infant enjoys sensation (Major, 1906; Waddle, 1918). One of the earliest spontaneous play experiences is evident when, with his hunger satisfied, the baby rolls the nipple around on his tongue, providing a richer awareness of the nipple and his own mouth. This act may entail the earliest perception of self. It is the adult who provides the material and whose responses to the infant's exploration are important. Eating and play are often combined in this way, because it is usually during feeding time that newborns are most awake and responsive.

There is general agreement on the need for a physical environment far different from the sterile white or bland pastels of the traditional nursery, to provide the infant with the earliest opportunities for play. Babies regard ceiling, walls, and the sides of the crib. They pay attention to sound and are responsive to touch. Mobiles or metal spoons hung over the crib, musical sounds, normal household noises, the soothing voice of the caregiver, and periodic affectionate fondling all combine to set the environmental stage for play in the earliest months.

In planning the baby's environment, the caregiver also needs to take care not to confuse and overstimulate the baby. At every age the child provides clues to his likes and dislikes. The perceptive caregiver can provide the baby with familiar sights and sounds while gradually introducing new and more varied stimuli that are appropriate to his unique needs and abilities.

The caregiver is of prime importance in the play of the young baby. Murphy (1972) points to "active, mutual mother–baby play" as a prerequisite for the development of cognitive structuring. The baby's initial reflexive smile is usually a response to human eyes, though sometimes also a response to shiny movable objects. The smile of the caregiver responding to the smile of the baby sets in motion a cyclical process that aids development of the baby's social smile and is continued throughout the child's life as the need for continual, responsive human contact and interactions. As the baby grows older, his responsive smile is less quickly forthcoming. He needs to see the other's face and body for longer periods before he smiles.

It must be stressed that babies experience their own impact on the environment well before they can play with objects. The kind of feedback infants receive determines and influences their motivation to explore. In this early period, being-done-to and doing-to are intermeshed. The baby cries to express his more obvious needs, such as hunger or discomfort; response to his crying represents the earliest interaction between caregiver and baby. Thus encouraged, the infant eventually learns that he can affect his environment. While the infant's needs should not be ignored, neither should they be constantly anticipated. Hovering over the baby trying to anticipate his every need deprives the infant of the opportunity to influence his environment. Rather, the sensitive adult will take cues from the baby and respond appropriately.

The caregiver can encourage the baby's waving and pushing of his arms and legs in random play by keeping him free from tight clothing as well as by providing short periods in larger areas of space, such as a large bed or a mat—which also offers a beneficial change of surroundings from the crib. Leaving him for long periods in the same place with minimal stimulation may result in a passive baby who chooses to lie quietly and unresponsively. Even the 2- or 3-month-old infant needs to be moved from room to room, dandled on laps, or held against shoulders, so that he can look around and widen his world.

While the caregiver handles the baby (stroking, kissing, cuddling, bathing), he/she is providing enjoyable sensations and increasing body awareness. This gradually leads to the infant reciprocally patting, stroking, and pushing the arms and body of the caregiver. These natural play times come when the baby's physical needs have been met by his being fed, burped, and diapered, and they provide invaluable opportunities to promote his physical development and emotional well-being. Learning at all ages is enhanced by pleasurable interaction involving both verbal and body language between caregiver and baby.

At about 4 months of age, the hands have become very important and bring a new dimension to play. The baby learns about the world through using his hands and mouth, finding out that fingers in the mouth are different from a rattle in the mouth. Cradle gyms with balls to make noise provide the baby with practice in using both hands and mouth. Three-dimensional toys, such as brightly colored, soft rubber toys with projecting limbs, are safe, fun, and easy to grab.

The 4- to 6-month-old is a more sociable person, crying more often for attention. He will respond with enjoyment when a ball is rolled or a toy pulled in front of him. A primitive form of hide-and-seek usually gets enthusiastic response, with baby sitting on someone's lap and finding his mother visually when she calls his name.

The baby without serious motor impairment is generally able to spend some time in a playpen squirming about and exploring soft, washable toys with his mouth. Such activity fosters teething, oral stimulation, motor activity, and fun. Physical, intellectual, social, and emotional growth are all taking place through play and through interaction with the caregiver. All these aspects are important; to be deprived in one area may mean deprivation in all other areas.

Beginning with 6 to 9 months of age, the normally developing baby is increasingly involved in manipulative and active play. As control of fine muscles increases, objects can be picked up at will. The baby is interested in small blocks, metal spoons, and plastic bowls, all of which can be banged or put in his mouth. Eye–hand coordination is developing, and the transferring of objects from one hand to the other is enjoyed. Although initially not ready to find toys when they fall out of reach, the baby is on the verge of independence. He is beginning to sit independently and about to enter the creeping stage. Emerging independence makes for a somewhat more demanding baby, because he wants to do just a little more than he is capable of doing.

Since the baby's estimation of space is still inaccurate, he knocks objects out of his reach time and time again. Confusion between two- and three-dimensional objects still exists. Attaching small toys by means of string to the side of the carriage, crib, or high chair saves the caregiver much effort; while the baby cannot yet retrieve his own toys, the caregiver can pull them up quite easily, ameliorating frustration and impatience for all. Round nesting blocks, and pots or cups into which the baby can drop small toys or cubes promote further experiences in spatial relationships and object permanence.

Social play becomes a priority as the baby begins to enjoy games like being swung in the air, bounced on a lap, or gently roughhoused. He wants to be where people are, but he is wary of strangers at this age and needs support and understanding from caregivers. Games such as pat-a-cake, peek-a-boo, and other time–motion–vision sequences delight the baby and encourage social interaction.

The first year of life is full of new discoveries for the baby (Hutt, 1971). He has achieved mastery over his hands and can release and grasp at will. His home must now be made safe as he crawls around exploring; electric cords, knickknacks that can be knocked over, and tablecloths that can be tugged at represent dangers to watch for. It is time for wheel toys and baby's first book—made of heavy board and nontoxic materials and containing bright, familiar pictures. As the baby is now sitting independently, the bath continues to provide new play opportunities—floating toys to grasp and water to splash. Rhythmic words, simple songs, and nursery rhymes are fun for the caregiver and easy for baby to recognize and memorize.

The baby reaches another important milestone during the 12- to 18-month period, when walking independently is learned. Much of the play at this time seems to be basically motor activity —exploration through climbing and running, and discovery of the larger environment (Berlyne, 1970). When the baby falls, as he will repeatedly, he needs the smile and comfort of the caregiver for encouragement. Sand, mud, and water are inviting and important playthings at this time.

The child is persistent, running for help when he cannot accomplish a task and satisfied only on its completion. Helping the toddler to accomplish simple tasks is now important. The adult should provide equipment like pegboards and simple puzzles of one to three pieces, and unobtrusively guide the baby's hand so that he is able to accomplish the task. Encouragement of the child at this time is very important to the development of self-esteem and perseverance.

The world is much more active than it is passive, and the toddler enjoys imitating daily routines. Shaving and hairbrushing, dusting and cleaning are fine imitative play situations. This active parent–child interplay is important for the continued development of constructive play and encourages independence in self-care. The baby's efforts need to be rewarded and praised as accomplishments.

When the toddler becomes a climber (18 to 24 months), large low blocks or planks provide fun and the opportunity for exploration. Maximum supervision with minimum interference is required. It is the time to introduce animals into the toddler's life if he is not yet acquainted with any. Fear of animals is less likely to result if he can become familiar with them at this age.

Color cones, hammer toys, rubber dolls and animals, safe cars and trucks, and noise-making pull toys encourage motor exploration. Praise and approval by elders plus adult–child cooperation in cleanup set the pattern for the future as well as for the present.

Large storage cartons or low shelves encourage replacing things after use. Large, clear picture books, with the caregiver in close contact to name and identify, provide satisfying play experiences for the 2- to 3-year-old, a precursor of later academic efforts. It is the age for crayons, finger paints, and other art materials. Large painting surfaces encourage large body movements. Children need the opportunity to mess and smear such materials as paint, clay, or homemade dough.

Many young children like to use their bodies in imitation of animals, cars, or planes, leading to dramatic, imaginative play. They act out daily and special events, from going to the store to the arrival of a new baby in the family. Most young children are excited about the natural world of bugs, grass, trees, and plants, which provides an infinite range of sensory experiences that can either be shared or explored alone.

It is fun for the child to throw a ball; this he can do reasonably well, but he should not be expected to catch it accurately. At all ages children should be encouraged to do what they are able and never urged beyond their individual powers to perform. Mild frustration, leading to several attempts before successful accomplishment, is a part of everyday life; but extreme frustration or thwarting can produce undesirable effects and turn a child off, so that he is unwilling to experiment and stops trying.

Children under 3 years of age generally play side by side with other children, rather than together with them. They make their first contacts in this way, leading to good social playing later. In these earliest stages, play may seem overly aggressive. The toddler is still dependent on the caregiver and seems to prefer playing alone. But being in the company of other children is necessary if good relationships are to develop. As with all learning, this may develop more satisfactorily if throughout the early years the child has had contact with other children.

Play with toys enables young children to exercise their muscles and enrich their minds and imagination. The mastery of toys is the vehicle through which children develop understanding of the larger world and their place in it. Thus, playthings and manipulative objects should be provided as being developmentally and socially satisfying, rather than as a reward. The cost of a toy is no criterion of its value. Such objects as regular kitchen equipment, homemade mobiles, and cuddly toys made of old towels stuffed with discarded nylon stockings are minimal in cost but invaluable in the experiences they provide for the child. What is important is that toys be *safe*—that there be no detachable pieces that a baby can swallow; that they be easily grasped and easily washed; that they be able to take hard use and be used in a variety of ways by the baby; that they be multidimensional in color, texture, and/or sound. The most satisfying toys at all ages are those that can be freely handled and manipulated—the nondirective toys like blocks, dolls, simple musical instruments, and unbreakable spoons and bowls.

The first 3 years are a time of vital learning, learning that is best achieved through child-initiated play in an atmosphere of adult approval and support. Piaget (1963), among others, suggests that play becomes a function of cognition and serves ego continuity. Therefore, in programming for the handicapped child, play cannot be considered as an isolated activity. Rather, it should permeate all components of the program. The presence of a handicapping condition makes special demands on the child, the parents, and the family. It is a challenge to staff members to foster a nurturing environment in which play may prosper.

CHAPTER 2

CONSIDERATIONS IN ASSESSMENT

ASSESSMENT of the young child and his family is an ongoing process and forms the basis for individualized program planning. In addition to an initial evaluation, frequent and periodic reevaluations are required in all such areas of development as movement, pre-speech, language, cognition, and social-emotional well-being. A variety of formal and informal assessment procedures are administered by the staff attending the child and his mother at birth, and, where indicated, specialists are consulted as suggested by the special needs of the baby.

Children with suspected or known developmental disabilities are increasingly being referred to infant centers, where a battery of standardized developmental scales are employed. These include *Brazelton's Neonatal Behavioral Assessment Scale,* the *Milani–Comparetti Motor Development Test,* the *Denver Developmental Screening Test,* and the *Bailey Scales of Infant Development.* These tests are supplemented with more detailed examinations in specific areas of concern, whether medical, therapeutic, social–emotional, or cognitive in nature.

Close interaction with the parents (or principal caregiver), siblings, and relatives provides insight into the dynamics of the particular family and the quality of the nurturing environment in

The major contributor to this chapter is Margaret H. Jones.

the home. This information is usually obtained by the center's staff through individual interviews with family members, team discussions on evaluation and planning, and home visits, as the baby and his family become regular participants in the program.

The foundation for any evaluation is a sound knowledge of normal growth and development. It is hoped that this program guide will call attention to the need for a keen awareness of normal development in assessing the deviations in atypical children. Understanding the "how and why" of an infant's deviations from the norm serves as a major guide in curriculum development. However, an in-depth discussion of the issues, tools, and methods of assessment is beyond the scope of this publication. The following outline of the evaluation process is presented to illustrate the multifaceted nature of such assessment. It is not intended to be comprehensive in coverage; rather, it draws attention to the need to focus not only on the newborn or very young infant but also on the family and its nurturing role.

Various attempts to identify a suspect group of infants, based on factors commonly found in the histories of atypical infants, have resulted in so-called high-risk registers (Oppé, 1967; Prechtl, 1965). These registers include possible genetic or hereditary factors in the family history; prenatal illness, accident, or trauma; and abnormalities at delivery or during the perinatal period (birth to 1 month of age). Such registers are useful for overall community planning. In individual cases, however, many of the infants identified by the risk criteria will prove to be normal later; whereas identification of some handicapped children may not be possible in infancy. Risk registers have been found to identify about three-fourths of the infants later showing atypical development. Whether or not the infant falls in a high-risk category, detailed prenatal, natal, and perinatal history are essential for the early detection of atypicality, as are records of subsequent development.

Postnatal records should give special attention to the following factors: feeding problems, visual and auditory function, behavior and attention span, home and other environments in which the child has lived, social-emotional variables, and milestones in developing communication, hand use, and locomotion.

In examining the infant and young child, it is important to observe and report the state (s) of the child during the evaluation. Six states have been outlined (Beintema, 1968; Prechtl, 1965) :

State 1. Eyes closed, regular respiration, no movements
State 2. Eyes closed, irregular respiration, no gross movements
State 3. Eyes open, no gross movements
State 4. Eyes open, gross movements, no crying
State 5. Eyes open or closed, crying
State 6. Other (describe).

Some parts of the evaluation can best be done when the child is relaxed or asleep—for example, those aspects concerned with the degree and type of change in muscle tone or the extent of contractures or deep tendon reflexes. Other evaluation components—such as visual or auditory skills, developmental reflexes and reactions, or tactile and kinesthetic sensory functioning—optimally require an awake, relaxed state.

General Examination

In the general examination it is essential to look for and record all atypical findings, both minor and major (Smith, 1970). Nutritional status and the routine measurements of somatic growth (head and chest measurements, asymmetries in measurement, and the infant's height and weight) should also be recorded. Deviations from the normal provide important clues for the detection of atypical developmental problems. In the neurological evaluation of the newborn and very young infant, special attention needs to be given to oro–pharyngeal development (coordination of suckling–swallowing–breathing), the status of the postural and righting reflexes, and visual and hearing functions.

Observation, in the usual sleeping position, of the infant's head, trunk, arms, hands, legs, and feet provides clues regarding abnormalities related to intrauterine position and neurological deficits. The quality and quantity of spontaneous movement normally varies with the infant's gestational age (Dargassies, 1966), state of alertness, and degree of intactness of his nervous system. The infant who has a strong tendency to extend the trunk and head at birth and in early infancy is suspect for central nervous system abnormality (Jones, Sands, Hyman, Sturgeon, & Koch, 1954). Normally the infant breathes with his or her mouth closed for the first few weeks (Peiper, 1963). The infant who can achieve and tolerate feeding in both supine and lateral positions usually demonstrates adequate oral and pharyngeal function (Logan & Bosma, 1967).

Recent evidence regarding the abilities of newborns to respond to visual (Dayton & Jones, 1964) and auditory (Eisenberg, 1970) stimuli suggests that an evaluation of these sensory functions is needed as early in life as possible. Since the response to stimuli is usually state dependent, it is essential to record the infant's state of alertness at the time of testing. For example, if flicking of the infant's' eyelid results in eye or body movement, this state is termed light sleep; if there is no movement, it is deep sleep (Northern & Downs, 1974). In contrast to the usual technique of undressing an infant prior to examination, Brazelton (1974) prefers to begin with the infant asleep. First he studies responses to sensory stimuli (light, sound, touch, being cuddled, and being gently irritated), and only then does he begin to remove the child's clothing.

Since sensorimotor function in the prematurely delivered infant varies with age of gestation (Dargassies, 1966), knowledge of gestational age as well as the performance to be expected at each age is needed. For example, at 28 weeks of gestational age, one may expect the infant to differentiate clearly touch from pain and to make a taste response suggesting repulsion or attraction.

Paine (1966) lists the following signs as the most important neonatal findings in infants who later evidence signs of cerebral palsy:

1. General depression of all or most of the neonatal reflexes and reactions, including the Moro, blink, rooting and sucking, palmar and plantar grasp, traction from supine, placing, stepping, and supporting
2. Overreaction to a variety of stimuli with excessive jitteriness or tremulousness, whether the stimulus be visual or tactile
3. Convulsions
4. Asymmetry of several neonatal reflexes or responses
5. Motor or sensory neurological signs pointing to localized lesions (such signs are less frequently found than 1 through 4)

The majority of children with abnormality of only one reflex or response develop normally. The absence of abnormal neurological signs make it less likely that cerebral lesions will be followed by residual dysfunction of the brain.

Serial examinations provide much more useful information than single evaluations. Many developmental anomalies of the brain do not produce neurological abnormalities in the newborn period, but deficits become evident as cortical function develops with increasing age. Children having anomalies often show more stereotyped responses and less variation from one examination to another than do normal infants (Andrews, Banks, Blumenthal, Freeman, & Taft, 1972).

Oro-Pharyngeal Evaluation

Evaluation of the oro-pharyngeal area, including feeding, may provide the earliest clues to central nervous system damage (Ingram, 1962). Observation of each of the following should be made when the infant is at rest, during motor activity, and during feeding (Logan & Bosma, 1967; Mueller, 1972, 1975):

1. Customary position of head, trunk, and limbs in supine, prone, vertical, and horizontal suspension
2. Face: expression and movement, symmetry, wetness of chin
3. Lips: open or closed (normally in the newborn period the lips are lightly closed at rest and breathing is through the nose)
4. Mouth: open or closed, movement characteristics
5. Mandible: retrusion, symmetry, size
6. Cry: pitch, strength, movement of mandible and lips
7. Yawn
8. Vocalization: nasality, monosyllabic or polysyllabic, babbling, individual sounds

As discussed in Chapter 6, it is important to test the oral reflexes. In the rooting reflex, if a stimulus touches the lips, the head of the newborn turns to the stimulated side and his tongue extends to the lips and becomes hollow. Normally this reflex is present from birth to around 3 months of age. Sucking may be elicited by offering the finger with the hand held palm upward. Suckle–swallow reflex normally begins at birth and disappears as a reflex sometime between the second and fourth month. The bite reflex is tested with the finger placed between the lateral gums. It is normally present from approximately 1 month to 5 or 6 months of age. The gag reflex is best observed by noting at what point in the entrance of the finger the reflex, if present, is elicited; absence of the reflex should also be noted. It is normally found from birth on but is weaker after the seventh month when chewing begins.

The muscle tone of the lips, cheeks, and tongue should be noted, as well as any asymmetry of tone. The sensory evaluation of infants with swallowing difficulty involves mainly an assessment of the gross response to digital examination. Is the child apathetic, or unusually irritable, with the examiner's finger in the oral area? Where damage by trauma and/or hypoxia (oxygen deficiency) at birth has affected cranial nerves 5, 7, 9, 10, 11, 12, and/or the medulla, it may result in transient or permanent abnormality of oro–pharyngeal function and probably later speech impairment.

Visual Evaluation

Turning to the infant's visual function, contrary to earlier views, the newborn has been shown to be able to fix on slowly moving objects and follow them conjugately (Dayton & Jones, 1964). Brazelton (1966) used a bright red ball. Fantz (1963) found the newborn to be more responsive to the human face than to other stimuli. Kagan (1972) noted that the response to changing stimuli is greater than that to a steady stimulus. Visual tracking skills, which generally develop over a number of months, should be observed first with the infant in the supine then in the sitting position. Assessment should include horizontal, vertical, and diagonal movements, as well as the baby's responses to objects at various distances from him. The Sheridan Tests for Young Children and Retardates (STYCAR) Graded-Balls Vision Test focuses on visual competencies, particularly for distance, for differences between the two eyes tested separately, and for field defects (Sheridan, 1973). For a period after birth that may last up to 4 days, response to both visual and auditory stimuli may be depressed (Stechler, 1964).

Auditory Evaluation

Since the cochlea in the human infant is completely developed and fully functional by 20 weeks of gestational age, hearing experience begins *in utero*. This fact has been demonstrated by an increase in fetal heart rate in response to high frequency pure tones presented through a microphone on the mother's abdomen (Johansson, Wedenberg, & Westin, 1964). At birth, most newborns can distinguish sound on the basis of frequency and intensity. Speechlike signals are remarkably effective in producing responses in the newborn. Even the speed at which unexpected noise reaches its maximum brings about differing responses: if in milliseconds, a defense reaction of closing eyes, startle, and increase in heart rate; if slower (in 2 seconds), the response is by eye opening and looking around and sometimes in decreasing heart rate. The lower the pre-stimulus state, the greater the response; and conversely, the higher the pre-stimulus state, the greater the decrease in response activity (Kearsely, Snider, Richie, Crawford, & Talbot, 1962). At 1 day of age the newborn may make active response, as by changing his rate of sucking, to regulate auditory events (Lipsitt, 1970).

The professional staff caring for the newborn and young child needs to be alerted to high risk factors in relation to hearing. Especially in syndromes associated with mental retardation, hearing impairment is often not detected (Black, Bergstrom, Downs, & Hemenway, 1971). According to Northern and Downs (1974) the criterion for identifying a newborn as at risk for hearing impairment is the presence of one or more of the following factors:

1. A history of hereditary childhood hearing impairment
2. Rubella or other nonbacterial intrauterine fetal infection (e.g., cytomegalovirus infections, herpes infection)
3. Defects of ear, nose, or throat; malformed, low-set, or absent pinnae; cleft lip or palate (including submucous cleft); any residual abnormality of the ororhinolaryngeal system
4. Birthweight less than 1500 grams
5. Bilirubin level greater than 20 mg/100 ml serum

Simple tests can be utilized clinically in the hearing evaluation of the newborn and young child. One such test involves observation of the arousal response—preferably to broad-band noise stimuli (small bell, rattle, squeeze toy, or cellophane paper). In carrying out this test, several important conditions must be observed. First, the room is to be quiet (sound treated). This condition is necessary since, beginning in the newborn period, the normal infant can hear sounds down to 35 decibels, and the usual nursery noise level is 70 to 90 decibels. Second, the stimulus should be held motionless for at least 10 seconds about 3 inches from the ear before making a sound. Third, the state of the baby should be light sleep.

In considering auditory functions in the newborn and young infant, the following points seem helpful:

1. Infants are biologically programmed for language learning in the first 2 years of life. Thus, a knowledge of the development of the auditory behavior that usually precedes linguistic activity is essential for evaluation.
2. Deafness does not keep the infant from very early babbling or vocalizing.
3. Newborn screening, utilizing high-risk detection items in addition to such clinical testing as arousal, identifies a high percentage (75 percent or more) of those with hearing loss.
4. Repeated evaluations are essential, as part of the routine infant follow-up, to detect, for example, hearing loss occurring later or a level of deafness changing with time.

Assessing the Family Context

No assessment of the newborn is complete without considering the baby in the context of his family. Of particular importance is the mother–infant interaction. Interaction between mother and infant is strongly influenced by the baby's behavior, which initiates attention, physical care, and social interaction. Significant in such an evaluation are the mother's impression of the baby and her attention to the infant's signals. The mother's physical and psychological state are also to be considered. At the first moment that baby and mother are together, the opportunity for nurturing begins. This experience produces growth in both mother and infant (Klaus & Kennell, 1970). In large part the newborn does "rule the roost" and set the stage for interaction by his physical appearance, behavior, and immediate needs. It is critical to acknowledge such salient features of the relationship in order to provide adequate support to the mother and foster the nurturing process between her and her child during the first few weeks of life (see Chapter 9).

Why a mother and infant respond to each other in unique ways is not conclusive. The infant's behavior impresses upon the mother that she has a significant and essential role to carry out with him. Four constructs appear to influence the mother–child interaction: (1) biological preference, (2) the primacy of a particular sense modality in influencing the interactive process, (3) the characteristic of the stimulus of change in the dyadic interaction, and (4) the interactive process itself (Lewis & Rosenblum, 1974).

Growth is the result of genetic factors, maternal uterine and systematic environment, postnatal nutritional intake, and the child's ability to assimilate these nutrients in a responsive environment. Newborn infants vary greatly in size, shape, and physical maturity, with noted variation in the advancement or retardation of growth (Tanner, 1974). Sex differences at birth have been documented regarding amount of muscle, size of face and head, skeletal size, and neurological maturity. Although these variations have not been studied empirically as to how they affect the attitude of the mother, possible influences have been discussed (Bell, 1974; Tanner, 1974). For example, the rate of weight gain is critical to the infant physiologically but also may be interpreted culturally as a significant issue of mothering. In addition to weight gain, the amount of muscle or plumpness may affect the caregiver's impression of the infant's masculinity or femininity. Newborn boys are more muscular and have less fat than girls. However, girls are advanced 1 to 2 weeks in neurological maturation and are ahead of boys at birth by about 2 weeks in bone age (Korner, 1973).

There are other differences in healthy full-term babies that may have even more significance in terms of the initial relationship to the mother: color, texture, and opacity of skin; ear form and firmness; presence of edema; amount and appearance of hair, shape of genitalia, breasts, and nipples. These indices have been documented for their significance in determining level of maturity in the newborn. However, they should also be evaluated in terms of how they affect the mother's response to the infant. Physical variation in the infant influences the early caregiving and socialization process.

The healthy baby also has a repertoire of behaviors unique to him that support his individuality and draw responses from his environment. One cannot speak about the growth behavior of babies without also paying attention to the growth and nurturance of the important people in their environments.

During the first 4 weeks, interaction between mother and child centers around feeding and soothing activities. Cyclical interactions involving rest, movement, and consolability occur between mother and child, and, as these become more organized, the opportunity for socialization begins to surface. Thus it is possible for social interaction to develop out of early caregiving (Ainsworth & Bell, 1970; Bell, 1974). The baby is not just a passive recipient; he can initiate activity on the part of the mother by changes in his own behavior. Infant assessment requires knowledge of the mother's awareness of and response to her infant's signals.

In considering the process by which a mother and child "get hooked" on each other, an insight may be gained into how others —such as a therapist, nurse, or physician—can support the early interaction between mother and child by verifying the strengths of each and their attractions to each other. The staff member seeks out infant behaviors that will elicit maternal responses of caregiving or socialization. As in size, shape, and weight, babies differ significantly from one another in the type and amount of attention they provoke (Korner, 1973). The staff should be aware of the subtle differences in the child in order to support the mother or other caregiver in his/her efforts to nurture him. Close cooperation with the family can facilitate the documentation of cycles of interaction. Some of the important activities that may be the focus of attention during the first 4 weeks, and questions relevant to those processes, include the following:

1. *Feeding:* How long are the intervals between feedings? How long does the baby feed and what is the quantity taken each time? How does the feeding activity affect attachment between mother and child? It has been the clinical experience of members of health care teams that indications of disturbance in the mother–child relationship can be recognized during the feeding process.

2. *Alert states:* What is the baby's behavior when he or she is awake? Can the infant spend time alone? It was suggested earlier that some interactions are initiated and sustained by

sensory input. Observation will suggest the sensory stimuli to which the baby is likely to respond and that will sustain his attention (Bell, 1974). The baby's preference for proximal behavior, such as touching, decreases with age, whereas that for distal behavior, such as looking, increases. Maternal behaviors can usually be expected to parallel this shift in the infant's preference.

3. *Sleep cycle:* To what extent is the baby's sleep cycle the source of disruptive changes in the family's life? How does it affect interaction between the infant and other members of the family, especially his mother? The premature infant is likely to exhibit poorly organized sleep patterns (Dreyfus, 1974), as are some atypical full-term infants. Since active sleep and quiet sleep are necessary for the newborn, the pattern of deviation of these states not only has ramifications for caregiving but important implications for the infant's subsequent development.

4. *Level of motor activity:* What degrees and types of movement are associated with the baby's activity during his alert states? The degree, quality, and symmetry of movement are important and are related to the baby's ability to attend to stimuli.

It is one thing for an infant to be assessed as atypical or "at risk." But parents confronted with such an assessment may need help to cope with their feelings toward the child and the reactions of significant others (siblings, relatives, and friends) to the child's exceptionality. It is known that grief and anger on the part of the parents toward the infant affect how they will attend to the task of helping the child thrive (Barnard & Powell, 1972).

There are no standard instruments available for assessing strength or security of attachment, or the child's sense of independence. Such assessment needs to be based on observation of parent–child interactions in the home, during parent–child sessions in a center, or in whatever settings the family may be observed. In these observations particular attention needs to be paid to such indicators as the following:

1. Is there evidence that the child shows a strong attachment to the mother or other caregiver?

2. Is the attachment pattern consistent with the child's chronological or mental age?

3. Does the mother smile at the child? Does the child have an effective social smile?
4. Is there frequent physical contact between mother and child?
5. Is there affectionate contact?
6. Is there eye contact?
7. Is the infant capable of maintaining eye contact in the customary holding positions? During feeding?
8. Does the mother report indifference to or distaste for the child?
9. Is the mother concerned about her inability to feel warm and loving toward this child? Does the father express such feelings?
10. Does the mother treat the child as if he were less capable than he really is?
11. Is the child offered choices? Do the parents follow through on the choices the child makes?
12. Is the child allowed or encouraged to try out new things—new toys, new foods, new playmates, new people? Is the child sheltered from contact with others?

Assessing the Family's Needs

There is frequently a lack of supportive services for the parents of a premature infant whose life is at risk, a baby who is obviously not coping with the extrauterine environment, a baby with dysmorphology, or an infant with Down's syndrome. Parents have reported their feelings of isolation and of helplessness in seeking support for themselves and their child. They are confused about their infant's needs and deprived of the normal informational feedback that would provide them with the knowledge that they are indeed competent and nurturing (Lemmen & Add, 1973).

In addition to the literature dealing with this point, the recorded experiences of parents provide insight into the difficulties facing the caregiver of the exceptional infant:

1. Difficulty in understanding the implications of the infant's disability in terms of knowing what to expect from the child.
2. Lack of specific knowledge about how to carry out such care-

giving activities as feeding, movement, and play stimulation in ways that are appropriate to the child's atypicality.

3. Feelings of inability to meet the child's needs: "Since my infant is different, my ability to care for him is inadequate. It is beyond my ability to take care of him."

4. Doubts and fears about the child's future: "If my baby is retarded or severely handicapped, should I place him in a foster home now or take him home?"

Center staffs as well as parents have tended at times to be overwhelmed by the magnitude of the problems and to overlook the potential strengths that can be used to foster the relationship between the child and his family. For example, in the case of an infant born blind, one of the most powerful modalities during the neonatal period is that of proximal activity—tactile stimulation and response. What better way to foster the first components of nurturing than to assist the mother in the caregiving activities of feeding, holding, and consoling the baby and help her experience the baby's response to the handling? One mother saw the crying of her blind infant as helpful in motivating her to find ways of interacting with him. She especially utilized holding him and talking to him; she taught him to reach for her face for a pat and kiss. She stated, "If he had been a quiet passive baby, I would have left him alone and would have never gotten to know him." It is extremely important to seek out significant components of early attachment and help to define aspects of the atypical infant's behavior that will give gratification to the mother or other caregiver.

Overview

The foregoing presentation of assessment of the needs of the newborn or very young infant and his family functions only as a sample of an evaluative process that varies according to the child (i.e., age, disability) and the family (i.e., health, values, sociocultural factors). The staff's alertness in identifying at an early age deviations from normal development, and their astuteness in diagnosing the possible causes of the problems detected, are essential in planning for the management and guidance of the child and his family. For example, diagnosis of a syndrome may provide information regarding developmental course and outcome. Diagnosis of a metabolic or endocrine deficit may entail specific treatment, which, if initiated early, may change the outlook and outcome. Repeated evaluations are needed, since some conditions that are not evident at birth or in early infancy may develop or become evident later. For professionals responsible for the assessment and management of infants, an index of suspicion may be helpful. Rather than the concept that all babies are "normal" until proven otherwise, constant alertness to various factors that are known to be related to atypical development should be stressed.

The staff members' own approach to the atypical infant, as well as statements about the cause, type, and extent of the exceptionality and proposed management recommendations and prognosis, may make a lasting impression on the minds of the parents. In most instances long-term prognosis is fraught with uncertainties. For most infants, a short-term plan is preferable, with longer-term goals delayed until follow-up evaluations, appropriate consultations, and evidence of response to individualized parent–child intervention can provide a more accurate basis for a prognosis.

CHAPTER 3

CONSIDERATIONS IN NUTRITION

Т HE biblical quotation "Man doth not live by bread alone" applies very literally to children. Findings suggest that a well-balanced diet, with at least a normal complement of protein, eaten by the pregnant mother—especially during the last trimester of pregnancy—and by the infant through the early developing years is necessary for optimal conservation of neurons and consequent healthy brain growth (Rosso & Winick, 1973). When a baby is developmentally disabled, poor nutrition and feeding difficulties further impede growth and development. On the other hand, sound nutrition and successful feeding can enhance well-being and foster higher levels of physical and mental attainment.

Regulatory Brain Systems

Eating

When a baby eats, physiological, social, and emotional needs are fulfilled. But how does the infant's brain, normal or damaged, detect when the body tissues have a need for food? And how does it direct the body to ingest, digest, and eliminate food?

The major contributors to this chapter are Eric Denhoff and Sylvia Brooklyn Denhoff.

Once, it was believed that "hunger pangs" initiated appetite. Now, we recognize that the triggering mechanism for appetite is in the hypothalamus, a deep brain center. The brain center initiates the feeling of hunger and establishes a regularity in feeding schedules. Like all basic drives, this rhythm can be influenced by many variables, including taste, smell, emotional state, and cultural factors (Eyzaguirre, 1969).

Taste is a strong factor affecting appetite. Both animals and humans will consistently choose less nutritious but "good-tasting" food over highly nourishing but "bad-tasting" food. Even "pleasant-tasting" food will be rejected when a child discovers that the food disagrees with him.

A significant portion of food eventually breaks down in the blood plasma into glucose. Neurons, like other living tissue cells, regularly need to receive glucose, as well as oxygen, and they need to metabolize it efficiently if they are to serve as effective information transmitters. The metabolism of glucose depends upon insulin, an important chemical within the pancreas. When the glucose level in the tissue is low (low blood sugar), the hypothalamus signals the baby to eat. When the blood sugar is high, the baby does not experience hunger. In some handicapped infants, the hypothalamus may react or respond inconsistently to the visual or environmental messages it receives because it has been damaged by anoxia (oxygen lack).

Two regions of cells within the hypothalamus specialize in processing information concerning blood sugar level, stomach contractions, taste, smell, and the other factors associated with feeding. These are the "stop eating" center and the "start eating" center. These centers operate reciprocally to help maintain a balanced level of nutrients within the body tissues. The phenomenon is called "body homeostasis" (Winters, 1973).

If the hypothalamic "start" center is functioning inefficiently, the baby will have little desire to eat and forced feedings may be necessary. If the "stop" center is malfunctioning, overeating may result, with consequent obesity. Bad-tasting food can influence the "stop" center. To control obesity, the mother must be persuaded sometimes to serve poor-tasting, unattractive foods that are difficult to chew and swallow, to the accompaniment of noise and commotion. Such a combination is conducive to *not eating*. When one wishes a baby to eat well and gain weight, the reverse applies.

Drinking

The mechanism regulating the intake of liquid is similar to that described for food. The brain detects the need for, and adjusts to, the amount of water needed. With dysfunctioning of the hypothalamus, chronic dehydration due to underdrinking or water poisoning due to overdrinking can occur. A decrease in water intake is accompanied by a decrease in tissue fluid, which is temporarily replenished from the blood stores. The kidneys detect the decrease and secrete a hormone into the bloodstream which signals the hypothalamus to seek out water to replenish the loss (Elliott, 1947; Gardner, 1975). The body's water reserves are not as stable as its food reserves. Thus insufficient water intake is especially dangerous; life is rapidly endangered when the body is deprived of water.

Elements of Nutrition
Calories

Babies usually flourish when their caloric needs are met through a judicious balance of proteins, carbohydrates, fats, vitamins, and minerals. Caloric needs are an individual problem and depend upon the child's metabolic rate, loss in sweat and excreta, growth rate, and activity in play and sleep. A normal newborn requires a daily intake of 100 calories/kg (about 50 calories per pound of body weight) for proper growth, whereas a premature infant needs between 110 and 120 calories/kg per day. At birth, for brain metabolism and growth, 33 calories/kg per day is needed as glucose, requiring an intake of 6 to 8 mg/kg of glucose per day. After the first 6 months, the infant requires 90 to 100 calories/kg per day. A child up to 3 years of age normally needs between 1200 and 2200 calories, depending on his bone size and weight, to grow properly. Each gram of protein and carbohydrates provides 4 calories, while each gram of fat provides 9 calories. During infancy and until the third year, between 30 and 40 grams of protein per day is needed to fulfill daily needs (Silverman, Ray, & Cozzetto, 1971).

The handicapped infant may require as much as 10 to 25 percent more calories per day than a normal baby to maintain himself and to gain weight. This is particularly true in cases of dyskinesias, where excessive body movement increases body energy requirements. Weak or floppy babies also require additional calories, but since such babies can take only small feedings, they need them in a concentrated form and at more frequent intervals. However, care must be taken to avoid overly rich feedings, which often lead to gastroenteritis and chronic diarrhea.

Basic Nutrients

PROTEIN. Protein is the main raw material needed to build body tissue. Only protein contains nitrogen, sulfur, and phosphorus, which are essential ingredients for life. The 20 essential amino acids necessary for body energy and growth are found more in animal than in vegetable proteins. When animal and vegetable proteins are provided in proper combinations and proportions, amino acid requirements are fulfilled.

The best sources of animal protein are meat, poultry, fish, milk, cheese, and egg whites (egg white consists mostly of albumen, a pure protein). The best sources of vegetable protein are legumes (peas, beans, and lentils), nuts and seeds, cereals (whole grain in particular), and cereal-based products. In selecting food for its protein value, the protein content, the caloric, fat, and cholesterol content, and the cost have all to be considered (Food and Agriculture Organization of the United Nations, 1970).

Milk and eggs are the major foods usually given to children for protein value. However, since large quantities of milk depress appetite and too many egg yolks increase the cholesterol content of the blood, these foods should be given in moderation.

Parents and caregivers should be encouraged to be less concerned with weight gain and more concerned with providing proper protein combinations, so as to establish opportunities for long-term health gains (Altschule, 1965).

FAT. Fat is a concentrated source of energy which provides important nutrients. Fat-soluble vitamins and polyunsaturated fatty acids are essential requirements for cellular metabolism. Saturated fat is a fat that is solid at room temperature; unsaturated fat is liquid at room temperature. Unsaturated fats are preferable because they contain less hydrogen than do saturated fats; polyunsaturated fats contain still less. (Hydrogenated fat, which is semisolid, is unsaturated fat hardened by the addition of hydrogen.) Saturated fats are associated with high blood cholesterol and possibly with high blood pressure; the polyunsaturated varieties are therefore generally preferred.

Meat, butter, eggs, milk, cheese, and coconut are high in saturated fat; fish, nuts, olives, and peanuts all contain the unsaturated types of fat; soybean, corn, and safflower oil contain polyunsaturated fats. It should be noted that some vegetable shortenings and margarines are high in hydrogenated fat content.

CARBOHYDRATES. Carbohydrates (starches and sugars) provide the main source of energy and are found in the least expensive foods. Except for lactose, which is found in milk and liver, starches are almost exclusively the product of plants. Rice, potatoes, beets, turnips, and cereal grains (including all foods made with flour, such as bread, cakes, and pasta) are the main sources of starch. Honey, syrup, and table sugar (from sugarcane or beets) are the main sources of sugar.

All sugars—whether white (refined), brown, or raw, and including both honey and maple syrup—are almost pure sucrose without other food value. They provide the energy necessary for metabolism and thus decrease the need to draw upon the body's important protein reserves in the tissues and organs as a source of energy. The brain functions on glucose, which is manufactured within the body from a combination of protein and starch. While most babies and children like sweet foods, too much sugar can cause tooth decay and obesity—and even chronic irritability.

Vitamins and Minerals

Vitamins, in small amounts, are necessary for cellular function. An improper diet, especially one containing too many "empty calories," such as those found in candy, soda pop, and sugar-coated cereals, can produce vitamin deficiency.

Adequate vitamins and minerals are found in a balanced diet; but when there are doubts about the quantity or quality of food intake, synthetic vitamins in the form of pills or liquid can be given. Vitamin supplements do not supplant the vitamins contained in foods, and excesses are eliminated in the urine or feces. However, large doses of some vitamins may be harmful rather than helpful. The use of megavitamins for long periods, as recommended for hyperactive behavior, must be viewed with caution. More than 2000 units of Vitamin D per day is toxic; large doses of Vitamin A can cause convulsions; excessive doses of Vitamin C may produce bladder and kidney irritation (Goodman & Gilman, 1965).

VITAMIN C. Vitamin C is found in orange juice (freshly squeezed or commercially available in bottles, cartons or frozen concentrate form), grapefruit, lemons, limes, green peppers, fresh strawberries, raw cabbage, crisp salad greens, tomatoes, and potatoes boiled or baked in their skins (Guthrie, 1971). While many artificial fruit drink substitutes are fortified with Vitamin C, the natural fruit juices contain more minerals. Parents should look carefully at labels to be sure they are buying pure fruit juice, and not merely water with artificial flavoring and added Vitamin C.

VITAMIN B. The vitamins that make up the Vitamin B complex are all present when the diet is properly balanced with protein, fruits, and vegetables. Enriched flour, breakfast cereals, and bread are "back-up" sources. The important B's are thiamine (Vitamin B1), riboflavin (Vitamin B2), niacin or nicotinic acid, (Vitamin B12), and folic acid (Guyton, 1966).

Among the proteins, meat, poultry, fish, eggs, milk, and cheese supply Vitamin B12, which appears to stimulate appetite. Vegetarians may need Vitamin B12 supplementation.

Pyridoxine (Vitamin B6) may be important for some handicapped children who are prone to convulsions. A lack of Vitamin B6 can precipitate seizures in some children. Cereals are a good source of this vitamin.

VITAMIN A. Vitamin A is necessary for clear vision and for healthy skin. It is found in yellow and green leafy vegetables, such as carrots, pumpkin, corn, broccoli, and lettuce, and in yellow-colored fruits, such as apricots and nectarines. It is also present in eggs, butter, milk, and liver.

VITAMIN D. Vitamin D is essential for bone and tooth growth (Goodman & Gilman, 1965). It is the only vitamin difficult to obtain even in a well-balanced diet. Its best source is fortified milk and margarine, although there are limited amounts of the vitamin to be found in liver, egg yolk, fish, and butter. The best natural source is daily, but not excessive, exposure to the sun.

VITAMIN E. Vitamin E is readily obtainable in all natural foods. It is of value as an antioxidant in maintaining the stability of red cells.

VITAMIN K. Vitamin K is necessary for normal blood clotting. It is plentiful in all green leafy vegetables, liver, egg yolk, cauliflower, and cabbage.

MINERALS. Minerals are needed to strengthen bones and teeth, to build hemoglobin in red cells, and for other tissue-making functions (Guyton, 1966).

Calcium and *phosphorus,* found in milk and milk products, promote healthy bone and tooth growth. Phosphorus is also available in meats and cereals. *Sodium, potassium,* and *magnesium,* essential for body and tissue fluid balance, are present in a well-balanced diet.

Iron prevents anemia. An infant's daily iron requirement depends upon the amount of iron acquired *in utero* and the infant's rate of growth. Severe blood loss will also affect the blood's iron level. The best natural sources of iron are red meats (especially liver and kidneys), eggs, dark whole grains, prunes, raisins, molasses, and green leafy vegetables (Guthrie, 1971). High iron intake, through fortified milk or other iron-rich foods, is necessary during the early years.

Copper, zinc, and *iodine,* necessary only in trace amounts to maintain health, are present in a well-balanced diet. A deficiency in copper causes stunted growth; in zinc, loss of taste and appetite; lack of iodine can cause thyroid deficiency and goiter (Mayer & Ramsey, 1975). Iodized salt is a cheap and readily available source of iodine.

The Seven Major Food Groups

The notion that the "basic four" groups of food will provide a balanced diet is not supported by fact. The basic four—the energy group (cereals and potatoes); the protein group (meat and fish); the milk group (milk, **cheeses, and other** milk products); and fruits and vegetables—do not invariably include the fat, vitamins, and minerals that the body requires (Mayer & Ramsey, 1975).

For a young child to stay healthy, at least one food from each of the following major food groups should be eaten daily:

1. Yellow and green leafy vegetables
2. Citrus fruits, tomatoes, raw cabbage, and salad greens
3. Noncitrus fruits, potatoes, and vegetables not included in Group 1
4. Milk, cheese, and other milk products
5. Meat, poultry, fish, eggs, nuts, dried beans, and peas
6. Bread, whole-grain or enriched flour, and cereals
7. Butter, fortified margarine, or vegetable oils

Children like to eat hotdogs, commercially sold hamburgers, steak, butter, and cream cheese—all high in saturated fat. Instead, they should be encouraged to eat fish, chicken, turkey, nuts, skim milk, and cottage, ricotta, and farmer cheese.

Starting the day with cereal is especially important. Oats, rice, or wheat—served either hot or cold and combined with milk and fruit—will meet every requirement of children and will provide the needed early morning energy source. Bran cereal will provide bulk for bowel regularity and may lessen chances of bowel irritation. For the atypical infant, wheat cereal should be finely ground and combined with ground nuts and chopped dried fruits. Over time, the texture can gradually be coarsened and the pieces made larger. This cereal mixture provides a well-balanced and acceptable food that fulfills many of the basic requirements for growth and development.

Bread is a staple food, but it should be eaten in moderation. The whole-grain breads, which contain bran fiber, B vitamins, and trace minerals, are the most nutritious. White bread is made with refined flour, resulting in loss of vitamins even when enriched. Brown bread may be vitamin-rich or it may be ordinary white bread with coloring added. (Here, again, it is important to read the contents information on the package.) French and Italian breads are the least nutritious. The usual slice of white bread has only 65 calories. However, since children rarely eat bread by itself, watch the calories they add to the bread in the form of peanut butter, jelly, and jam.

Cholesterol is present in many high-protein foods. It is a waxy or fatty substance that tends to deposit itself in the arteries and may eventually cause hardening of the arteries as well as high blood pressure and heart and brain deterioration. While it had long been assumed that such problems start during or after adolescence, more recent evidence suggests that fat cells can be stimulated at quite a young age through overeating or eating the wrong foods (Burch, 1971; Hirsch, 1975; Knittle, 1972).

Diets that include fish as a frequent protein source and that generally emphasize polyunsaturated fats are associated with lower blood cholesterol levels; diets that stress red meat and are high in saturated fats tend to raise blood cholesterol levels. Thus fish (or fish meal) is very good for babies, but it is rarely fed to them. Chicken, turkey, and lamb are all lower in saturated fat content than is beef or pork products. Suggested protein combinations are milk, bread, and cottage cheese; rice and beans served with fish or poultry; milk and whole-grain rice; oat or wheat cereals and fruit; rice and soybean (cereal or Chinese-style curd) served with poultry, fish, or lamb. Since most young children emulate the food habits of the adults around them, an overall change in dietary patterns may be necessary to establish better health for all family members (Lappe, 1971). Food habits, especially likes and dislikes, are established very early in life.

Diet in the Early Years

During the early weeks and months of life, virtually all of the baby's nutrients come from either human breast milk or cow's milk. Breast milk is preferable because it provides immunity against infection, is more readily digested, and has an adequate amount of Vitamin C. Breast feeding also plays a unique role in fostering a close mother–infant bonding. All infants, whether bottle or breast fed, require additional Vitamin D, which can be provided in a fortified form in cow's milk or by means of concentrated supplements.

Between the ages of 3 and 6 months, cereals, vegetables, fruits, and meats, along with natural orange juice, are usually added to the diet (Beal, 1957). Most normal babies start on solid table foods and homogenized cow's milk between 6 and 10 months of age. Easily digested foods like precooked infant cereals are the earliest solids.

Younger children require small and more frequent feedings than older children and adults. They usually need three glasses of milk a day as well as adequate quantities of the seven major food groups.

Malnutrition and Developmental Disabilities
Nutritional Care during Pregnancy

A close relationship exists between the pregnancy–birth processes and the subsequent physical, intellectual, and emotional development of the child (Birch & Gussow, 1970). The nutrition of the mother, particularly during later pregnancy (as well as of the baby during the early years), directly affects neurological outcome. There is thus a clear need for sound maternal nutrition, both to prevent the occurrence of developmental disabilities and to improve the life prospects of those babies that are born handicapped.

In the early weeks of pregnancy, a formal assessment of maternal nutritional practices is necessary. This assessment should include a comprehensive nutritional history, a survey of the mother's daily diet, a thorough physical examination, and basic laboratory tests—including a blood sugar test taken 2 hours after eating (Brasel, 1973). A complete dietary survey should include consideration of the following:

1. Food selection, storage, preparation, and distribution within the household
2. The mother's food allergies or sensitivities, including possible milk intolerance
3. Economic and cultural factors
4. Unusual food habits or practices
5. Medications and/or drug habits
6. Vitamin and mineral intake

Prepregnancy weight, as well as weight gain during pregnancy, may influence the birth weight of the baby. Weight gain restriction during pregnancy to 10 or 15 pounds has not proved necessarily beneficial. An average gain of 24 to 27 pounds is more in keeping with current nutritional knowledge. However, excessive weight gain may present an obstetrical hazard. A sedentary woman may require only 1800 calories per day to gain between 25 and 30 pounds during pregnancy, whereas an active teenager may need up to 3000 calories per day.

A mother with special high-risk problems requires intensive nutritional study and guidance. Such mothers include those from poverty areas, pregnant adolescents, mothers with prepregnancy height or weight disproportions, mothers with chronic illness, and mothers with a poor reproductive history. The poverty populations are especially prone to maternal protein deprivation. High-parity mothers (especially those for whom the intervals between pregnancies have been short), mothers with unusual nutritional practices (e.g., dieters or food faddists), and mothers who are obese or anemic also warrant careful nutritional supervision during pregnancy (Barness & Pitkin, 1975).

Growth Retardation in Utero

Growth retardation *in utero* is responsible for a large proportion of developmentally disadvantaged children. While babies whose growth is retarded *in utero* may appear to have many of the same problems as premature babies—such as a susceptibility to hypoglycemia (low blood sugar)—they are less susceptible to the effects of unstable body temperature and respiratory distress than the premature baby.

Two major causes of growth retardation *in utero* are uterine vascular insufficiency (poor blood supply to the uterus) and maternal undernutrition.

1. *Uterine vascular insufficiency.* When the uterus and placenta receive an insufficient supply of blood, all fetal organs except the brain are growth retarded to about two-thirds of expectancy and are depleted in the normal complement of cells. Consequently, such a baby is small but its brain is relatively large and requires a large amount of glucose to function properly. Postnatally, this glucose cannot be supplied by the small, depleted liver that characterizes prenatal growth disturbance and has to be supplemented (Battaglia, 1970).

2. *Maternal undernutrition.* Malnutrition prior to birth produces a symmetrical growth retardation, with small body size, a small brain, and fewer than the normal complement of brain cells (Winick, 1971). (In contrast, malnutrition experienced after birth—that is, in the early growing years—results in body organs and brain that contain smaller though not fewer cells.)

In animals there are three stages of fetal organ growth (and it is presumed that a similar process occurs in humans). In the first stage, cells increase in number but not in size. The total protein content of the cells increases along with their DNA content, and there is acceleration of cell division. In the second stage, cell number and cell size increase; there is a slowing down of the rate of cellular division (DNA synthesis), but the protein synthesis continues. Finally, in the third stage, DNA synthesis stops while protein synthesis continues, resulting in an increase only in cell size. This three-stage growth process occurs in all organ tissues, including the brain (Manocha, 1972).

Thus there are many different reasons that may account for infants being below average in weight and in size. While small cell size can be modified by a well-balanced protein-enriched diet, retardation of the cell division rate results in permanent stunting regardless of subsequent nutrition.

These findings have tremendous practical implications for the prevention and remedial treatment of disability, including mental retardation. They suggest that proper nutrition before birth and during the first 12 to 18 months of life can help salvage brain cells during the period in which they are dividing, with long-term beneficial effects on the physical, intellectual, and emotional growth of the baby. On the other hand, malnutrition imposed on an infant already physically disadvantaged (e.g., by congenital anoxia) during the weeks after delivery may further interfere with brain development (Rosso & Winick, 1973).

Congenital Abnormalities That May Affect
Nutrition and Growth

Other body systems besides the brain can be affected by genetic deficit as well as by early prenatal viruses. Babies may be born with a short bowel, a malrotation of the intestinal tract, a diaphragmatic hernia, or other malformations that can affect food absorption and excretion.

Metabolic disorders, especially thyroid, parathyroid, adrenal, and pituitary gland dysfunction can contribute to growth failure. Aminoacidurias (disorders in protein metabolism), as well as specific carbohydrate and lipid (fat) malfunction, are a possible source of nutritional difficulty. In some of these cases, dietary manipulation or substitution lessen both the mental and the physical disability (Silverman, Ray, & Cozzetto, 1971). Some inborn errors of metabolism are treatable by removing the offending agent. For instance, in the carbohydrate disorders, the removal of fructose, galactose, or disaccharide may be curative. In defects of lipid metabolism, substituting polyunsaturated fats can be helpful, as can removal of the offending protein. Methionine, phenylalanine, and other amino acids help in the treatment of aminoacidurias (Morrow, 1975).

Brain damage in the area of the hypothalamic growth center is perhaps more responsible for slow linear (height) growth and poor weight gain than is inadequate food intake in cerebral-palsied babies. Poor muscle tone and lack of normal physical activity also contribute to interference with normal long bone growth. Cerebral-palsied children are about 1 to 2 years behind the familial patterns of linear growth, and they rarely catch up in height. However, they may gain weight excessively in the adolescent years. Brain-damaged babies on the average weigh less than nondamaged babies, and, whether from brain damage directly or from associated factors, they continue to remain significantly smaller than their normal peers. Mothers and other caregivers should be alerted that their developmentally disabled children may not grow to normal size even when they are receiving an excellent diet.

Problems in Feeding

As we have seen, sound nutrition during the first 12 to 18 months of life can help salvage brain cells, which in turn can greatly improve the development of atypical infants. However, such children are often likely to be poorly nourished. Among the many reasons that the developmentally disabled infant is prone to undernourishment and malnutrition are the problems associated with feeding, including difficulty with sucking and/or swallowing, hyperactivity or weakness resulting in poor intake of food, and ineffective parenting.

Sucking and Swallowing

Normal babies have little difficulty with feeding because the suckle–swallow reflexes are neurologically mature at birth. Swallowing movements are efficient even in uncomplicated premature infants. However, babies with anoxic complications are prone to feeding problems because involvement of the medulla, the midbrain (including the hypothalamus), and/or the cranial nerves often results in oral impairment.

The most common source of feeding difficulties in the developmentally handicapped baby population is impairment of the suck–swallow mechanism. Less common but nevertheless important are congenital malformations of the palate, pharynx, tongue, or esophagus. Rarely, a primary muscle disorder like myotonia congenita affects the oro–pharyngeal and esophageal mechanism.

Sucking, swallowing, and breathing, including diaphragmatic organization, are integrated under medullary (brain stem) control. Sucking movements are followed by swallowing, which momentarily inhibits breathing. At the start of swallowing, the hyoid bone (Adam's apple) moves forward and upward, the larynx (voice box) becomes elevated, and the laryngeal lumen (voice box cavity) is closed by the epiglottis folding over its entrance. As swallowing nears completion, the cricopharyngeal muscle (the muscle involved in the swallowing mechanism) relaxes and the cricoid cartilage moves forward to allow the bolus (lump of food) to pass through the esophagus on its way to the stomach.

When medullary control is impaired, the muscles involved in sucking and swallowing, which are normally tense, become dystonic or flaccid (i.e., disorganized or floppy). Consequently, liquids may slide down the esophagus prematurely, which results in choking. The infant who can drink without choking while in the lateral, recumbent position, likely has normal oral and pharyngeal functions (Bosma, 1973).

A comprehensive history and a physical examination that includes a demonstration of feeding will often clarify the reasons for suck–swallow difficulties. Asphyxic newborns are often sleepy and refuse to suck or they fail to suck with energy or they frequently interrupt sucking to catch their breath. Nasal regurgitation suggests a cleft palate. Recurrent bouts of pneumonia may indicate a tracheo–esophageal fistula (a passage between the windpipe and the entrance to the stomach, which constitutes a congenital malformation).

During the examination, possible malformation of the nasal passage, mouth, tongue, mandible, palate, and hyoid bone are looked for. The patency of the nasal passages is established by confirming the passage between choanae and oral pharynx. The tone or strength of lip closure is evaluated by encouraging the infant to suck on a finger. Special X-ray procedures and other modes of investigation are additional aids in diagnosis. (Techniques for feeding the atypical infant are discussed in detail in Chapter 6.)

Under- and Overeating

Under- and overeating are common reasons for distress in the feeding of disabled infants and are generally related to an inexperienced mother's inability to interpret correctly the baby's hunger or distress signals. Some hyperactive infants attack a nipple vigorously and then suck excessively, often ingesting more formula than they can tolerate. They become gaseous and distended. On the other hand, a hypoactive (passive) infant will make only feeble attempts to suck, and often the milk he tries to swallow will dribble down the side of his mouth. He becomes underfed and chronically hungry, but is too weak to complain.

Ineffective Parenting

Some mothers and fathers are ineffective in managing feeding because they cannot readjust established family patterns to the demands of a querulous baby. Others lack the time because of overwhelming family pressures or work. Occasionally such ineffectiveness may result from a resistance to assuming a parenting role. All babies are sensitive to their parents' apprehension and inexperience; but developmentally disabled infants are often exceptionally so and may react in an alarming manner, with arching of the body and wailing. They seem to resist being hurried or handled in a mechanical manner, and they respond by rejecting or showing a disinterest in food. Some oversensitive babies withdraw and may be labeled "autistic."

The majority of feeding problems stem from the parental insecurity that arises when young and/or inexperienced parents feel rejected by the baby. After a long stay in an intensive care unit, during which the baby has received little stimulation or loving attention, he is finally united with his parents. At the outset, they are usually quite optimistic about their ability to cope with the stranger in the house. But when the new family member turns out to be querulous and irritable and repeatedly regurgitates or projectively vomits milk, or cries incessantly even after a long feeding, the new parents begin to feel helpless, despairing, and inadequate.

Prompt help must be available to parents of these babies to enable them to establish early workable parenting relationships; a failure to do so may lead to a baby's learning to resist feeding. Thus, in cerebral palsy programs, for example, parent education is considered of critical importance. To ease mealtime frustrations, parents are taught the essential facts about nutrition and are helped to master feeding techniques. Such training increases confidence and invariably results in a strengthening of the mother–father–infant "bonding" that is essential for optimal physical, mental, and emotional growth.

Some Common Nutritional–Gastrointestinal Problems

Food Intolerances and Allergies

Food intolerances occur among both normal and atypical babies. Milk, wheat, or egg allergies are not uncommon. The signs may be a face rash, a rash in the joint areas (eczema), diarrhea, colic, or general irritability. Wheezing or hives may also be allergic symptoms. The treatment is to ascertain which are the offending foods, then remove them from the diet and substitute others. While laboratory tests are useful, maternal intuition is often a better guide in such cases.

If a baby is found to have a sensitivity to milk, a milk substitute such as Nutramagen (a casein hydrolysate with sucrose mixture) or Cho-Free Base formula (a soybean derivative) may be appropriate. Where intolerance of such sugars as disaccharide, lactose, dextrose, or sucrose is detected by laboratory study, one form of sweetening can be substituted for another (Holzel, Schwarz, & Sutcliffe, 1959).

Gluten (wheat) intolerance (celiac or malabsorption syndrome) is occasionally found in developmentally disabled babies. Necrotizing colitis, accompanied by anoxia, in babies that are small for their gestational age can result in intestinal malabsorption (Santulli, Schullinger, Heird, Gongaware, Wigger, Barlow, Blanc, & Berdon, 1975). The substitution of rice cereal or a gluten-free diet can be helpful. Steatorrhea (fat intolerance) can also be a problem; in such cases polyunsaturated fats should be substituted for butter (Schubert, 1973).

Adverse reactions to antibiotics, as well as the ingestion of harmful substances (e.g., lead, iron, organic phosphates), can also produce gastrointestinal complications.

Additives (such as those found in hotdogs, luncheon meats, red colored popsicles, and a variety of other foods), salicylates (found in aspirin and aspirin compounds), and a variety of fruits have been implicated as the cause of hyperactivity (Feingold, 1974); but at this time there is no clear evidence of the validity of this finding.

Intestinal Parasites

Intestinal parasites, such as amoebas, hookworm, roundworm, or Giardia lamblia, irritate the mucosa (lining) of the gastrointestinal tract and are another possible cause of enteric problems. Common symptoms are disturbed sleep, anemia, poor growth, and gastrointestinal complaints (e.g., colicky abdominal pains, diarrhea or constipation, and abdominal distension).

Chronic Diarrhea

Chronic diarrhea is a common reason for the failure of infants to thrive. A careful laboratory search often is necessary to identify the offending agent, whether bacterial, viral, or nonspecific. If indicated, specific antibacterial treatment is initiated, along with the appropriate dietary management. While all babies are susceptible to the effects of diarrhea, those with central nervous system involvement are particularly prone to secondary infection and consequent dehydration.

If loose, watery stools continue and vomiting occurs, milk is usually eliminated from the diet and 1 to 2 teaspoons of coca-cola syrup or honey with 4 ounces of weak tea (or rice or barley water) is substituted, to be given every 1 to 2 hours in teaspoonful doses. To arrest persistent vomiting, one-half of a Tigan rectal suppository may be prescribed. Compazine, paregoric, or sedatives are not usually prescribed because they can camouflage the true status of the handicapped baby, particularly if he is floppy. If there is much fluid loss, either by vomiting or by stool, Pedialyte or Lytren solutions are available for use under medical direction.

Early intravenous therapy is usually considered by the attending physician when vomiting or diarrhea persist. A basic fluid need is 1500 ml per day with an additional 5 percent for mild, 10 percent for moderate, and 15 percent for severe fluid loss. A normal saline solution using 25 ml/kg is indicated. If shock is impending, sodium bicarbonate or blood plasma may be given promptly.

Brain-damaged babies are particularly susceptible to the complications arising from sodium, potassium, or chloride imbalances due to dehydration. Blood chemical studies are helpful in ascertaining the infant's status in this area. With improper handling, central venous thrombosis (blood clotting in the tiny veins of the brain) can result and further complicate the problems of a child already mildly or moderately neurologically impaired (Dekaban, 1959). Special consideration is needed in the case of babies experiencing seizures: too rapid hydration can precipitate status epilepticus, a continuing sequence of seizures; a high dosage of phenobarbital can oversedate and cause further complications.

In some cases of intractable diarrhea, the only alternative is parenteral nourishment. A diet containing the basic food elements in liquid form is given intravenously for 3 to 4 weeks if necessary (Sherman, Hamly, & Khachadurina, 1975).

Constipation

When a baby becomes red in the face, draws up his legs, and strains and grunts, he may be in the act of self-training in bowel control or his anus may be too tight to permit the passage of stool. Excessive straining leads to rectal irritation and fissuring and the resulting pain during the passage of stool is a deterrent to the normal elimination process.

The rectum may be gently stretched with a lubricated gloved finger to lessen the difficulty. The addition of malt soup extract may be recommended to soften the stool and permit easier passage. If a rectal prolapse (extrusion of bowel) occurs from over-straining, it must be gently pushed back into place before edema (swelling) causes further complications.

Rarely, Hirschspring's disease (an absence of or a lesser number of ganglia in a lower bowel segment) will produce abdominal distension and constipation.

The most common cause of constipation is psychogenic (Talbot, Kagan, & Eisenberg, 1971). When bowel training is attempted too early, the baby may resist by holding back feces. As the baby learns to retain the feces, they become larger and harder and may be passed at intervals of 3 or 4 days. While this time period does not appear to bother the baby, parents often become quite distressed and try to encourage regular bowel movements in every imaginable way.

To counter distressful constipation, cleansing with a "Baby Fleet" enema or using digital manipulation to break the impaction is recommended. Administering a stool softener, such as Colace syrup or malt soup extract, and a high bulk diet that includes stewed fruit and Vitamin B complex will often solve the difficulty, especially when positive behavior reinforcement techniques are also incorporated into the training procedure.

Tricks and Treats to Improve Nutrition

Many young children thrive better on frequent, nutritious snacks than when fed only at regularly established mealtimes. Suitable snacks include fresh or canned fruit, fruit juices, peanut butter, nuts, bread, cheese cubes, celery and carrot sticks, or hard-boiled eggs.

The first meal of the day is of great importance because it helps to stabilize the blood sugar. But there is no reason to stick to the traditional breakfast foods. For example, a favorite protein food such as hamburger can replace bacon, and peanut butter and jelly on whole-wheat or enriched bread can replace cereals. Small portions in small plates, followed by second helpings, are better than overpiled adult-sized platters. A water-drinking habit should be established early by providing water before the fruit juice and milk. Finger feeding, finger tasting, and food smelling should not be discouraged, as they help the child to develop an interest in food and improve his motor coordination in bringing his hands to his mouth.

Since many handicapped babies experience feeding difficulty, food needs to be in concentrated form to provide maximum calories, proteins, and other requirements. A basic protein supplement that has been employed effectively is instant nonfat dried milk powder. Instant milk powder may be added to whole milk, pudding, or soup. Three tablespoons of instant nonfat dried milk fortified with Vitamins A and D provides 8 grams of protein, 12 grams of carbohydrates, and 80 calories.

For the handicapped toddler who can chew and swallow well, Cheerios, Rice Crispies, or other popular dry cereals can be mixed with chopped nuts, raisins, and chips of dried apricot; or honey can be added and the mixture baked into fruit squares. These are excellent between-meal snacks.

For the severely handicapped baby who cannot or is unwilling to eat solids, Carnation instant breakfast food mixed with egg, cottage cheese, or strained lamb and served as a milk shake is a smile producer. A less expensive combination can be made by mixing fortified instant nonfat dried milk powder with whole milk, using honey for sweetening.

Using first a clear soup, and then a thickened puree of peas, carrots, or potatoes, it is possible to encourage the intake of coarser foods by immersing pieces of bread in the soup or puree and encouraging the child to suck on the bread pieces. Protein may be added by means of strained lamb or beef, later substituting double-ground meat and then regular ground meat. Small chunks of meat mixed with macaroni and vegetables makes a tasty dish. The addition of a stewed dried fruit makes it tastier and more acceptable to some children.

Macaroni, spaghetti, or rice provide a base for adding protein-rich sauces and gravies. Low-starch pasta is preferred to regular pasta, and brown rice is healthier than white rice, which loses much of its Vitamin B in the refining process (Denhoff, 1976). A number of food product companies have diet plans and suggestions available without charge upon request.

CHAPTER 4

CONSIDERATIONS IN HEALTH

O<small>NE</small> might say of atypical children that they begin the game of life with a relatively poor hand of cards. How successfully they are able to play that hand in the course of life depends very largely on those responsible for their care and development in the early years. It is up to them to help the infants build on their strengths (psychosocial, cognitive, or other) and overcome as far as possible their dysfunctions and disabilities. And this, in turn, depends upon helping the children to achieve and maintain an optimal state of general health.

Many families of disabled infants maintain a routine program of health surveillance, with regularly scheduled visits to a family physician or pediatrician. Others utilize the services of a pediatric nurse practitioner or a public health nurse associated with a group health program, health department, or similar medical resource. However, many families are without such health surveillance, and this is a cause for concern.

Along with the primary health needs shared by all infants, the baby with neuromotor dysfunction faces some special health hazards. This does not mean that these infants tend to be sickly, in the usual sense of the word, nor that they need to be kept in a germ-free environment. But families, together with staff mem-

The major contributor to this chapter is Una Haynes.

bers from a variety of disciplines (including the health professions), can do a great deal to foster optimal health. This can be done in quiet, unobtrusive ways during the course of the normal interactions and activities of daily living—in the home, at school, and in other familiar settings. Developmental disability, usually due to an initial maldevelopment or injury, is only rarely the result of a progressive disease process. It is critical to the child's developing self-image and to the perceptions of relevant others that the presence of developmental disability *not* be equated with the presence of disease.

Hopefully, no program of early childhood education, day care, or other group service for atypical infants will be organized or operated without a physician who serves at least in a part-time capacity as a consultant and as a liaison with the medical community. A nurse who is knowledgeable about developmental approaches to service is a necessary member of the staff. The interactive role of health professionals with other members of the team, in providing direct service to children and families and in liaison relationships with health professionals in the community, is among the recurring themes of this chapter.

Problems Related to Life Support Systems

Attention has been called in the preceding chapters to the way in which abnormal muscle tone and function can influence basic life support systems as well as the infant's ability to move in space. One example is the compromising effect on hydration and nutrition that can occur in the presence of serious problems in the infant's ability to suck, chew, and swallow effectively and to coordinate these behaviors. Speech-producing problems can also occur among children who have difficulty in achieving smooth exhalation.

Abnormal tone and muscle function may affect respiration in other ways, too. Many atypical infants do not have adequate respiratory exchange, and it is generally agreed that a baby requiring support in order to sit upright should not be constricted around the chest or abdomen by binders or strap supports. Therapists can be very helpful in suggesting the use of such devices as cutout trays, support at shoulder level or in the pelvic area, or some combination of these, so that respiratory exchange is not further impeded.

Neuromotor impairments often make it hard for a child to blow the nose effectively or to cough up mucus. The common cold may thereby cause uncommon difficulties. Similarly, atypical infants are often at special risk when unprotected by prophylactic inoculations against such "ordinary" childhood diseases as measles or whooping cough.

Importance of the Prophylactic Regime

It is of primary importance to ascertain the adequacy and currency of the prophylactic regime before a child is admitted to group programming, and the sequential inoculations that may be indicated in the course of the months or years the child continues in the program need to be meticulously monitored. Yet, many centers give no more than cursory (if any) attention to prophylactic care. In some instances, inauguration of the preventive inoculations may have been delayed because an infant may have experienced severe or frequent seizures at a particular point in time; or the series may have been interrupted for some medical or other reason. In the absence of regular medical surveillance thereafter, the child may remain partially or completely unprotected. Infants with a history of seizures seem to be particularly at risk in the absence of such protection.

The following cases illustrate the untoward consequences of prophylactic neglect. In the first, a moderately disabled infant of normal or somewhat better than normal intelligence developed whooping cough 3 months after admission to nursery school. Complicated by pneumonia, the child experienced several episodes of severe respiratory distress. He survived, but sustained severe and multiple physical disabilities in addition to becoming profoundly retarded. The second case was that of a child who contracted measles. Although the upper respiratory symptoms at the onset of the disease did not cause much difficulty, he later developed a high temperature over a prolonged period and died following the onset of the additional complication of meningitis. It cannot be too strongly recommended that attention to the prophylactic regime be given high priority by all agencies providing developmental services for atypical infants.

Oral Hygiene

Problems in achieving mouth closure and in coping with drooling may persist beyond infancy. Along with therapeutic approaches to help the child achieve mouth closure, as well as adequate and coordinated suck–swallow action, several health-related factors in attaining oral hygiene merit consideration. The atypical infant has trouble enough in achieving warm personal and social relationships; a fetid mouth odor should not be permitted to constitute yet another barrier. Consultation with a physician or dentist is obviously in order. In general, however, a normal saline solution—made by dissolving half a teaspoonful of salt in 8 ounces of water—is a good cleansing agent. A finger wrapped in a gauze square and dampened in the saline solution can be used to cleanse the mouth. Care should be taken to ensure that the gauze does not slip down the child's throat. The gauze must be tightly wrapped and securely held. Where volunteer help is enlisted in dealing with large groups of such children and where staff surveillance may be minimal, it is advisable to have the volunteer attach a stout string securely to one corner of the gauze square and a strong safety pin to the other end of the string. The string should be pinned to the child's clothing *before* the gauze is used to cleanse the mouth, thereby avoiding any danger of the gauze slipping down the child's throat. Cotton swabs are useful too, but here again caution is mandatory. Unless tightly wrapped, the cotton tip can become detached from the stick and choke the child.

Since the gums of some children tend to become spongy and bleed easily, the use of firmly attached cotton swabs, rather than a toothbrush, may be indicated for routine dental care. Hyperplasia (overgrowth) of the gums may also occur among some children, particularly those who require prolonged use of some of the anticonvulsant medications. While this condition may not always be entirely preventable, regular and firm gum massage does help to retard the overgrowth. A dentist or dental hygienist can teach family members and staff how to do gum massage, which takes only a few minutes to carry out in a routine way during tooth-brushing time.

Among children who have trouble with mouth closure and breathing through the nose, the saliva may be quite a bit more viscous (thicker) than normal. This condition is troublesome. If the child aspirates saliva, it is harder to cough up. For this reason, the supine position is not usually the most suitable. Also, children who maintain the head to one side in supine, due to a persistent asymmetrical tonic neck reflex, may tend to drool into the orifice of the ear. While normal saliva tends to be slightly antiseptic, contamination can occur with some speed and ear infection is a frequent complication. Until this excess salivation is controlled, prone positioning is suggested for sleep or for play, with due regard for the infant's ability to turn the head and great care that bottom sheets are tight enough not to gather up and impede respiration of the child in prone. The use of a bolster or wedge for play periods is also helpful for children who are disabled to the extent that they cannot sit up, stand, or move about. For naps or sleep, the health professional may suggest the side-lying position, with absorbent material placed under the mouth area.

Excess salivation also tends to cause irritation of the skin around the mouth–chin area, also to the neck and chest if children are without vinyl-backed bibs, bib-front dresses, or coveralls. Frequent but gentle cleansing with soap (the family can usually indicate what brand of soap the child tolerates best), followed by application of a mild, water-repellent cream, will help maintain good skin hygiene.

Skin Care

Children who are delayed in achieving the ability to walk, but are able to crawl, need all the opportunities they can get to explore their environment and move about. But this type of mobility is rough on the skin of the hands, arms, elbows, and most of all the knees. Jeans and long-sleeved shirts provide some protection, particularly if the family uses a rinse in the wash to keep the fabric smooth and soft. Sewing an oblong "pocket" over the knee area of the child's jeans and then inserting a pad of plastic or rubber foam into this pocket will further reduce callous formations on the knees. The foam pad can be removed for laundering. Applying cream to the "wear" areas of the skin helps reduce the tendency toward callous formation.

After the child has moved about in exploration of the environment, it is of considerable importance that the hands be freshly cleansed before a snack or a meal. Such washing is a simple health measure, easy to incorporate into the daily routine by all who deal with the child. As soon as it is feasible, being taught and learning to carry out health measures is just as important as any other aspect of the curriculum provided for a developing child. Even if it should not prove possible for a severely disabled person to achieve self-help skills along these lines, it is part of the developing self-advocacy role of the disabled to know about health measures and mobilize such assistance as may be needed to see that caregivers carry out the health regime on his or her behalf.

Children with moderate to severe athetosis tend to perspire quite profusely. When there are associated suck–swallow problems, dehydration can occur. Among other problems, dehydration causes scanty, concentrated, dark-colored urine, which is quite irritating to the skin and may cause distress to the child when urinating. Again, prevention is the approach of choice. Naturally, alert staff and family members will not permit dehydration to occur in an infant or child who is not yet able to fetch a drink or clearly indicate thirst. However, if skin irritation has occurred, frequent cleansing and changing to dry clothes, plus the application of a soothing baby cream (or a special cream prescribed by the physician) will bring comfort and foster healing. The stool of a dehydrated child can also be hard, dry, and irritating to the anal region. (Chapter 3 includes dietary suggestions for maintaining hydration and controlling constipation.)

It is suggested that infants and children with excoriated skin not be kept in waterproof pants for significant periods of time. If "security" is mandatory at those times when the child is being cuddled or rocked on the lap of the caregiver—or some other member of the child's circle—then this warm nurturance is probably worth much more than a dry bottom. At other times, however, it is helpful if the infant or small child is given only light covering between diaper changes. If the skin is not actually cracked open and subject to secondary infection, removing the diapers or training pants completely for periods of time during play and at nap time will help to promote healing.

Excess perspiration poses special problems in both hot and cold climates. The difference in temperature between a heated playroom and the icy outdoors in northern states during the winter can be quite dramatic. Therefore, thermal underwear can make the baby too hot indoors. Lacking sufficient porosity, the child's skin can become very wet. Multiple thin layers of lightweight, porous shirts, vests, and sweaters are a better choice. The child who both perspires heavily and drools excessively faces multiple problems of being wet over the chest and other areas of the body. The caregiver needs to check carefully to make sure that the child's clothing is dry before he or she is subjected to chilly temperatures. Being constantly wet is also apt to cause skin irritation.

Children in warm climates are not much better off, since they may come in from a period of play in the warm sun to a blast of cool air conditioning. Certainly, it is viruses rather than temperature changes that cause colds, but the state of being wet and cold lowers the body's resistance to such viral infections and renders the child much more susceptible to them.

Finnie's *Handling the Young Cerebral Palsied Child at Home* (1975) contains a wealth of simple, practical, health-related measures worthy of study. All personnel dealing with infants whose disabilities are of organic origin will find it useful in coping with the host of everyday circumstances that arise with predictable frequency and challenge our abilities to meet the needs of such children.

Toilet Training

Although an abundance of toilet-training aids and guides are generally available, even those supposedly geared to the needs of atypical infants usually overlook such problems as the positioning of children with abnormal tone. A child who has excessive extensor tone needs positioning that will enhance relaxation of the abdominal musculature and, in addition, provide arm or foot support to facilitate downward expulsion of the stool. (Chapter 5 contains specific information on the positioning of atypical infants which is applicable to toilet training; Chapter 3 is also relevant, from the dietary point of view.)

Texts and manuals on the shaping and modification of behavior related to toilet training rarely address those aspects of the matter that are of greatest importance to the child whose dysfunctions are of organic origin. For instance, in addition to the basics common to all children, there are health and physical factors that determine whether toilet training is an appropriate goal for a particular child at a given stage of development. There are also other components of the child's disability, as well as the circumstances and life style of the family, that need to be taken into account. Some of the questions to be considered are: Is there impaired sensation related to bladder and/or bowel control? Does the child have an immature bladder? Is a generalized hypotonia also reflected in peristalsis and/or in sphincter control? Is there evidence of hypertonia affecting bladder or bowel function? Does it affect the sphincters? Do medications taken by the child have a side effect on elimination?

In addition to the input of health professionals, which is desirable, the Finnie book is again recommended for guidance on toilet procedures and particularly for suggestions on the various kinds of available equipment (e.g., potty chairs, toilet seat adaptations). (Specifications for making a box type floor potty are found in Appendix A.)

Accidents and Other Emergencies

Wherever young children are gathered together, as in nursery schools or day care centers, the adults responsible for their care should be prepared to cope with emergencies. For sooner or later emergencies will occur.

Those involved in accrediting or validating an infant development or early childhood education program for the disabled should determine the level of the staff's knowledge and skills not only in providing routine developmental programming but also in coping with possible emergencies. A key factor is the staff's knowing the name and address of each child's primary physician and how to reach him/her in an emergency. There should also be an established "backup" system, approved by the child's physician and family, in the event that either or both are unavailable at the time of an emergency.

Some calculated risks have to be taken if a motor-disabled young child is ever to learn and be motivated to move in space and explore the environment, rather than spend his life wrapped in lambswool. Nevertheless, measures to prevent accidents need to be built into the program, as well as measures to cope with an emergency, should it occur.

Regular inspection of the premises for accident hazards by

a health professional or safety engineer is essential. For staff and volunteers there should be regular discussion of, as well as a posted list of, potential accident hazards. Among the preventable hazards to be sought out and guarded against are nails protruding from woodwork as a result of a dry spell having caused the wood to shrink, tall play equipment such as a socio-bowl on a hard floor without encircling padded mats, and swings that have hard or sharp-cornered seats.

Hemorrhage

Of immediate importance in the case of hemorrhage, whether internal or external, is staff knowledge of first-aid measures that can be instituted until professional medical help can be obtained. Staff and family members can learn and practice the simple and clear instructions contained in the *Red Cross First Aid Manual,* as part of an ongoing in-service program of health education.

Some individuals with severe and multiple disabilities of central origin are susceptible to internal hemorrhage, one symptom of which is the vomiting of dark red (old) or bright red (new) blood.

Statistics suggest a very low probability that the staff of a nursery school or other group program for children will ever be faced with a case of internal hemorrhage, even when those children are severely handicapped. However, the staff should be trained to recognize and be able to deal with such cases if they do occur.

In a case of internal hemorrhage and vomiting, the child should be placed on his side with the head tipped slightly forward to keep the air passage free. Rapid body movement should be avoided and the child should be wrapped in a blanket and kept warm while he is quickly transported to the nearest hospital. A quiet calm approach should be combined with maximum speed in obtaining medical assistance.

How to identify external bleeding as arterial or venous and what measures to institute for control in each case are matters also clearly spelled out in the *Red Cross First Aid Manual.* Staff should be taught and be given the opportunity to practice these measures under supervision. In the case of external bleeding, loss of blood fluid may be compensated to a degree as long as the child is able to swallow liquids; a normal saline solution (half a teaspoonful of salt in 8 ounces of water) can be given orally. In contrast, a child with internal bleeding who is vomiting blood must *not* be given fluids by mouth. This child requires prompt medical attention since severe blood loss can occur very rapidly.

The points made here are intentionally brief—intended only to suggest that it is not enough for an agency providing services for atypical infants and young children to post "emergency information" on a wall or to assume that an ambulance or other transportation will be immediately available to take a child to the hospital in the event of an emergency. A child's blood supply can be very rapidly depleted and his life can rapidly become endangered if an important artery has been severed and there is no one present who knows how to stem the bleeding and what additional first-aid measures to employ until medical help can be obtained.

Important Life-Saving Procedures

Two important life-saving procedures should be learned by every staff member who is in contact with the children. The first is the Heimlich maneuver, which is used when a piece of food is lodged in the trachea. The maneuver consists of putting pressure on the diaphragm, thereby forcing some of the residual air in the lungs upward and outward, which pushes the lodged food out of the trachea.

The other life-saving procedure consists of two techniques that should be used concurrently for cardiopulmonary resuscitation: Mouth-to-mouth respiration should be started and continued (the child's jaw should be brought forward so that the tongue is not obstructing the airway) and at the same time closed cardiac massage should be employed by another person.

The above measures have now become part of the Red Cross first aid teaching program and would, therefore, be included in any such program. Persons who received their training some years ago should sign up with the Red Cross to learn and practice these more recently instituted procedures.

Signs of Child Abuse

It is sad to face the fact that any child may be subjected to battering and that atypical infants are no exception. The presence of multiple bruises or of an unusual swelling or other sudden change in the contour of a limb warrants the attention of the physician or nurse who is responsible for health matters at the center. It is important, however, for staff to be discreet and not jump to unwarranted conclusions or accusations. For instance, a child who was noted one morning to have multiple black and blue spots on the trunk and extremities certainly needed medical attention. However, it would have been a serious matter to accuse the caregivers of battering this child. As it turned out, she had developed a problem with the clotting factor in her blood and the black and blue spots were unavoidable, even with the utmost care in handling, until the blood condition was corrected.

Symptoms of Illness

Infants who have incurred central nervous system damage have sometimes also incurred an impairment in the body's ability to monitor body temperature. As a consequence, such infants and children may suddenly evidence a very high fever. Often this occurs in the presence of stress, but it may also occur for no apparent reason. Observant parents will soon be aware of this manifestation and may be able to predict with some accuracy when it is likely to occur. Such infants may also become chilled rather more easily than others, suggesting that alert staff should unobtrusively monitor the color of the child's lips and his general demeanor and skin temperature—when, for example, the child is playing in the wading pool or has been undressed for an evaluation or therapy session—and quietly remedy the situation without calling undue attention to it.

Very few illnesses manifest themselves with great rapidity; however, there is no doubt that babies can change from an apparent state of health to being very sick rather quickly and dramatically —for instance, when they are experiencing an allergic response to a food or other substance, or are "coming down" with an illness of some type. A rapid elevation of temperature, a sudden episode of respiratory distress, the quick extension of a small patch of redness to a rash covering the whole body, the onset of convulsions which continue in rapid sequence—these are among the symptoms that may occur in certain circumstances. The point to be made in this context is that the health professionals at the development center need to see that there are clearly defined policies and instructions which ensure that staff will function appropriately in such circumstances. Staff members who are experienced in the care of infants during the first months of life are usually sensitive to the subtle, as well as the more obvious, signs that appear when infants are unwell. However, it may be wise to assess staff competence in this regard. In-service programs or other avenues for staff education can then be planned at a level that will be of interest and appropriate to staff learning needs. Also worthy of mention is the need for staff to be able to describe the changed behavior or symptoms accurately and objectively, and for them to be apprised of the agency's policy concerning communications relating to health matters. Staff members can then be prompt in using these channels so that the child receives attention appropriate to the circumstances.

Poisons

The news media and professional literature regularly feature information about the dangers of poisons in and around the house. However, in dealing with children who learn about their environment by putting things into their mouths, some special responsibilities have to be assumed. Attention needs to be given, for example, to the contents of the area under the nursery kitchen sink and to the sprays used by the part-time gardener in the yard where the children play—as well as to where those sprays are stored.

An important poison hazard is paint containing lead. In many of the renovated buildings housing atypical infant and toddler programs, it is necessary to look beyond the bright and spotless new decor to check the lead content of the paint *under* the freshly applied coat as well as the lead level of the plaster underneath. Enthusiastic but ataxic and otherwise wobbly children who are learning to push a weighted go-cart, ride a bike, or throw a block can easily chip paint and plaster. Many of the children tend to taste and swallow these chips.

The local health department can help in checking lead levels. A sad and urgent reminder of the importance of such checks is to be found in some of the children who are enrolled in these programs—who have, in fact, incurred brain damage *because* of having ingested paint or plaster with a high lead content. Pica, a craving for unnatural food, is what has caused some of these children—many of whom live in old, neglected housing, especially in inner-city areas—to become disabled in the first place.

Meeting the regulations and standards of the local health and fire departments is usually a prerequisite to being licensed to render services to children in any community. However, it is worth reemphasizing that these standards are sometimes rather minimal. Without turning a nursery or other program setting into a sterile, unattractive environment, many additional preventive measures—most of them quite simple—need to be adopted in order to guard against those accidents and health hazards that can be foreseen and prevented.

Convulsive Disorders

It is misleading to equate seizures in general with epilepsy, for the variety of convulsive phenomena is vast and complex. A convulsive disorder can be defined as a paroxysmal alteration of brain function that begins and ends spontaneously and has a tendency to recur (Van den Berg & Yerushalmy, 1969). Behavior may be noted among the children served in a program for infants and toddlers that cannot be termed a fit or a convulsion but is nevertheless due to the paroxysmal alteration of brain function. Thus, it is of the greatest importance to ensure that the possible presence of convulsive disorders has been evaluated medically.

In designing behavior modification programs, staff and family need especially to take into consideration the possible organic origin of the behavior to be shaped. They also need to be alert to the seizure-triggering effects of such everyday occurrences as looking at a flickering television screen or riding at some speed past trees or telephone poles.

Convulsive disorders can be expected to occur with some frequency among infants with neuromotor impairments. Reporting on the children whom they studied, Aird and Cohen (1950), for example, reported seizures in 34 percent of the children with athetosis and in 66 percent of the children with spastic disorders. The comparative findings of Perlstein, Gibbs, and Gibbs (1947) were 71 percent and 86 percent respectively. In certain cases, metabolic abnormality, such as low blood sugar, low blood cal-cium, or low blood magnesium, may be a contributing factor in seizure disorders. Special dietary procedures may need to be fol-lowed should the physician identify such conditions.

Also to be looked for, in particular, are infantile myoclonic seizures, which may be evidenced by a sudden contraction of the flexor muscles of the trunk and may be accompanied by abrupt flexion of the arms to the chest and of the thighs to the trunk. At other times, the forearms may be retracted and the hands pulled to either side of the head, so that the seizure resembles the Moro reflex. Since a sharp cry may precede or accompany the seizure, these behaviors may be thought due to colic. The baby's face may assume a momentary blank or shocklike expression. Such attacks may be precipitated by sudden noise, by some manipulation of the infant, or by feeding; or they may occur just before the onset of true sleep or immediately upon waking.

Petit mal, minor motor, psychomotor, and grand mal seizures may all occur during infancy, but the minor motor type is most common. Baird (1963) has called attention to the occurrence of abdominal epilepsy in infants and young children. This is a pos-sibility worthy of special consideration by the public health nurse or others assigned to follow infants who are not under regular and consistent medical surveillance. Unobtrusive but effective surveillance is indicated for children who experience unusually persistent or severe episodes of so-called colic.

The personnel in infant day care or Head Start programs need to be alert to the possible presence of seizures. They should be trained to detect the symptoms and to report their observa-tions, so that program design and implementation can be modified accordingly. In one instance, an "acting-out" child who had not been identified as having a history of seizures was confined to a small, closetlike though well-lighted space—a generally accepted means of behavior modification—whereupon he sustained multiple bruises and abrasions. His so-called "acting-out" behaviors were in fact involuntary psychomotor manifestations of seizure activity. The use of blanket swinging for vestibular stimulation is a pop-ular and frequently used component of curricular activities for disabled infants and children. However, personnel alert to the possibility of a history of seizures, and to symptoms suggestive of them, will seek specific medical guidance before instituting such activities, lest they exacerbate the incidence of seizures.

A considerable array of medications is available for use by the physician in the treatment of seizures. These include barbiturates such as Luminal (phenobarbital), Mysoline, Gemoniel; hydantoins such as Dilantin; oxazolidinediones like Tridione; and others such as Valium and Zarontin. Usually the physician initiates treatment with a single drug, which is slowly increased to the required level. Additional medications, if required, are added in a careful, systematic way.

Nurses on the staff have a multiple role to play, particularly in supporting and facilitating the continuous cooperation of the family in maintaining medical surveillance of the child who is subject to seizures. Such surveillance is essential as atypical babies go through the various required diagnostic and treatment procedures, including electroencephalograms almost universally employed in the initial evaluation and sometimes repeated at the neurologist's discretion, plus periodic blood and urine tests. Additionally, some physicians now monitor blood levels to assist them in adjusting drug dosages. Nurses need to alert relevant others to the possible side effects of some drugs which may affect kidney function or blood composition. Of singular importance is astute observation of the child's behavior, conducted in a discreet and unobtrusive way and reported objectively. The health professional can be particularly helpful in enhancing the skills in this regard of parents and teachers, who are usually with the child on a continuous basis and for long periods of time. Their observations can be of great assistance to the physician.

The nurse also acts as an essential liaison with other members of the staff. It is of great assistance to a teacher, for example, to be quietly alerted by the nurse that a child may be somewhat drowsy and lethargic on a particular day as a result of medication prescribed by the physician; or that the phenobarbital administered to the child with cerebral palsy may make him more irritable and excitable, rather than having a sedative effect as is more usually the case. Medication for control of seizures frequently affects the child's attentiveness and other behaviors relevant to learning or testing situations. When duly informed, the teacher can be alert to the possible need to adjust the program accordingly.

Medication

Other than for control of seizures, few drugs have been found effective in the management of cerebral palsy and related disorders. Some reports of investigations on diazepam (Valium) suggest it may be of some help in relieving excessive movement and tension in children with athetosis. Perlstein, who conducted in-depth investigations of new drugs for cerebral palsy, felt that alcohol, especially wine, was the most effective drug (Perlstein, 1947).

In 1974, the Federal Drug Administration approved the use of dantrolene sodium, under the trade name Dantrium. Reports presented at the 1974 and 1975 meetings of the American Academy for Cerebral Palsy indicated that some benefits might accrue to selected persons with cerebral palsy. However, some of the studies indicated few if any beneficial or long-lasting effects. Other drugs that are being used experimentally are L-Dopa and gamma-hydroxy-butyric acid (GHB), but it is too early to tell what beneficial effects these drugs might have.

Since medications are usually prescribed on a specific time schedule, they may be required by a child during the time he is attending a center-based program. The agency is responsible for developing and enforcing clear policies in this regard. A professional committee of physicians, nurses, and pharmacists should be activated to formulate guidelines, instruct staff members, and monitor implementation of the medication policies. Determining where the drugs are to be kept, who is authorized to have access to them, and who has the responsibility for administering them and for reporting on their effects are all factors to be considered in program management. Some agencies avoid responsibility by requiring the child's mother to come to the center and administer whatever medication is required; or admission is denied to any child who requires medication. Neither is the approach of choice. Safeguards are important, but they can be built into the agency's policies, rather than the whole issue being sidestepped.

Surgery

Orthopedic surgery may make little difference in the presence of athetosis, except to improve the appearance of the walking gait or perhaps to attain a more functional walking pattern. However, in the presence of spasticity, surgery may play a role in relieving the stretch reflex and muscle contracture by lengthening or weakening the muscle. Muscles are usually lengthened by means of surgery on their tendons or weakened by cutting a portion of their nerve supply. In these cases, physical and occupational therapy in one-to-one or group-treatment sessions may be required. Family and staff will also need instruction regarding the functional integration of therapeutic goals into the child's daily routine.

Surgery may also be done during the early years to prevent bone deformity. For example, release of the spastic hip flexor muscles (iliopsoas) and hip adductor muscles has proved to be a successful long-term preventive method of counteracting partial or complete dislocation of the hip. Orthopedic surgeons are constantly upgrading their methods of preoperative analysis so as to employ surgical approaches only when truly warranted.

Surgical treatment for functional and cosmetic improvement of the walking pattern is approached with considerable caution. For instance, in the spastic knee-flexion gait pattern (crouched walking), excessive lengthening of the tendons behind the knee (the hamstrings) can result in overstraightening (hyperextension) of the knees and severe swayback (lumbar lordosis). However, there is no doubt that orthopedic surgery and prescribed treatment by a qualified physical therapist before and after such surgery have a prominent place in the presence of spastic cerebral palsy.

From time to time, reports appear in the lay press about impressive results attained in the control of excess movement of various types through new approaches to brain surgery. Parents and affected individuals are understandably eager to learn about the possibility that such surgery can alleviate or remedy the abnormal movements with which they must contend. Caution is in order, however, until further studies have been conducted to determine who is likely to benefit from these procedures and under what conditions. Brain surgery is obviously not without hazard. Center staff members have a responsibility to keep up with new findings. Recognizing the false hopes that may be engendered among individuals with lifelong disabilities, and their families, it is always prudent to refer such inquiries to medical specialists for precise and detailed explanation of all the information available, including the results of reasonably long-term follow-up studies.

Family Health

The birth of a disabled infant can cause physical as well as emotional stress within a family. Before the home-based aspects of a program are designed, center staff need to be aware of the basic health status of the family and the energy level of the parents, particularly the baby's mother.

Often the parents and other family members are eager to help the baby to achieve his or her optimal potential. However, some families are so overburdened by other concerns that the needs of this new infant are just too much to face. There may not be the will or the energy to cope. Overwhelming such families with the multiple home "follow-through" recommendations tends to destroy, rather than enhance, their ability to cope. Considerable discretion is required in order to enhance the measure of coping skills the family has been able to mobilize. Sensitivity to the situation of the total family is basic in program planning, and the astute guidance of the social worker, psychologist, and public health nurse can be invaluable in planning the optimal approach to family involvement to be used in each case.

Great variety is evident in the way and the extent to which grief and mourning affect parents and other family members. Periods of grief and mourning can be so prolonged and severe that the physical health of the family is compromised. But, even where the problem is less acute, staff members need to be aware of the developmental stages of grief as described by Kubler-Ross (1969) in relation to death and dying, and that grief may come in waves. They need to try to match this ebb and flow, adjusting the services offered or the amount of involvement required on the basis of a careful regard for the members of the individual family.

In most circumstances, placing too much pressure on a family that is already unstable will decrease their management abilities; it may even lead to ill-treatment of the child. One need not be a personal witness to the status of an already disabled baby who was subjected to battering to remain alert to such a possibility. In retrospect, someone might have foreseen the possibility and prevented it. However, evidence is emerging that some families initially overwhelmed are later able, by means of a variety of resources that can be mobilized, to achieve excellent nurturing and coping skills in spite of an earlier traumatic episode.

Staff members need to be hesitant in declaring a family "noncooperative" or "unhealthy," since information may be incomplete or based upon an erroneous interpretation of early behavior. Therapists, for instance, are not the only ones able to promote the habilitation of a physically handicapped child; nor are teachers the only ones who can teach. As staff members develop the ability to mobilize, encourage, and support families, they will note how superbly parents can function as teachers and how skillfully they are able to integrate therapeutic goals while maintaining their primary nurturing role. Experience with agencies where the staff have confidence in the parents suggests that many families are both able and willing to mobilize their strengths, often previously untapped, on behalf of their atypical infant, and that they are able to do so without impairing their own preferred life styles.

Design of the family-centered and home aspects of the program should build in some prophylactic approaches. For instance, some atypical infants are apt to be quite delayed in achieving ambulation; a child may need to be lifted and carried for several years. Therapists, together with other staff members, need to think about the possible long-term effects of this situation on the family. Family members can be taught, while the child is still young, to lift and carry in the way that is both best for their health and promotive to the child's development. When one learns early how to bend the knees and lift with a straight back, such procedures become routine. Patterns established during the early months can possibly prevent those responsible for the child's care from developing painful back problems as the baby becomes older and heavier.

Knowing the correct way to lift heavy, bulky, awkwardly shaped items (including people) is a very useful and practical skill. Many industries include research and training in "lift-and-carry" techniques as part of their in-service programs, so as to minimize the back injuries of workers. Education programs for the parents and family members of children who may be at special risk of delayed ambulation or of possible lifelong inability to walk should routinely include training programs in lifting and carrying.

Families and their health-related concerns change, just as the infants do, as time goes on. Therefore, a profile of family-centered health factors should be an ongoing matter, not limited to the single survey or study conducted at the time the infant is admitted to service and provided with an initial evaluation. Monitoring the changing health needs of the families as well as of the children requires concerted and continuing staff attention.

The physician and nurse who serve a particular family should be encouraged to share their knowledge of the family and its needs with other members of the center staff. This should be a consistent practice, built into the center's program, rather than a disjointed series of isolated contacts.

The staff social worker and health professional assigned by the center to serve a family have the responsibility to be available to encourage, guide, and assist family members in tapping community health care resources—helping them, for example, to locate a family physician, join a group health program, or attend a health clinic. The center's nutritionist can also be of assistance to families in need of guidance related to foods and feeding. Utilization of such services will depend upon the ability of the staff to alert and interest the family in securing such information and assistance.

In summary, since the infant attends the infant service program for only a few hours of his daily life, those responsible for his care at home, whether parents or parent surrogates, are inevitably the primary teachers and caregivers. Just as the health of the infants is regarded as important to all aspects of the agency's services, so does the physical, mental, and emotional health of their families warrant attention in all programs organized to serve atypical infants.

PART TWO

THE DEVELOPMENTAL PROGRAM

CHAPTER 5

MOVEMENT

W<small>HILE</small> the normal newborn infant is not simply a mass of reflexes, there is more evidence of reflexive behavior at this point of development than in later months. The higher centers of the brain are not mature in the neonate and have not yet imposed full control over the reactions of the lower centers. Therefore, the motor responses integrated at the lower centers express themselves more fully than they will at a later date (Fiorentino, 1972; McGraw, 1963). For some animals, such primitive movements are all that they need to satisfy life demands. For example, a frog requires a simple flexion and extension (bending in and straightening out) of the limbs to permit it to progress through water, a process that requires minimal ability to move and balance against gravity.

Normal Motor Development

However, the requirements of the human organism are infinitely more complex, resulting in a developmental process that continues for a long period of time. The greater part of motor development is not complete until the child is at least 5 to 6 years of age, although many of the important components have been introduced by the end of the first year. This long process of development culminates in an organism that has the capacity to

The major contributors to this chapter are Maureen Keenan Abell, Lois L. Bly, Donna Hanson, Nancy Kinney, Billie Levine, Sharon McDermott, Barbara Šálek, Jerry Staller, and G. Gordon Williamson.

raise itself against gravity, maintain a stable posture against gravity, and move against gravity without losing the stability of posture (balance). The mode by which this is accomplished is the gradually increasing influence of higher centers of the central nervous system, which assert themselves by imposing control over the reactions of the lower centers. This control takes the form both of inhibiting the lower responses and of modifying them into new motor responses.

The baby learns from the sensations of movement, which are gained mainly from active, rather than passive, movement. In this dynamic process, the ability of the higher centers to mature are partially dependent upon sensory information brought to them. Sensory information (such as tactile, proprioceptive, visual, or auditory) is transmitted through the nervous system and integrated at appropriate levels of the brain and spinal cord. In turn, responses are then sent out in the form of motor acts. As messages are integrated at higher and higher levels of the nervous system, the motor responses change accordingly. With new forms of motor expression, new sensations are fed back into the system. These experiences are reflected in the cortex by the elaboration of interconnecting links between brain cells in a complex system of pathways. This process permits the higher cortical centers to assert an ever-increasing influence over the lower centers.

Since the sensory and the motor systems are so intimately related, it would seem appropriate to refer to this dynamic process not as normal motor development but as normal sensorimotor development. The two cannot be considered separately. According to Gesell (1970), McGraw (1963), and O'Donnell (1969), normal sensorimotor development can be seen to follow these five principles:

1. Development is sequential. It occurs in a definite sequence over time, with each new acquisition based on those that went before. The baby uses those components of movement that he has already achieved and combines them in new forms, which then become the new motor act. No functional motor act is possible unless this foundation has been laid. For example, at 6 or 7 months, most babies are capable of sitting independently in a normal manner after having been placed in that position. However this act would not be possible if the baby had not

spent the previous 6 months practicing and achieving such skills as head control against gravity and extension of the spine. These skills were probably practiced by the baby in the prone position, but they relate directly to success in the sitting position. Although the rate at which normal children progress varies, the sequence of development remains fairly constant.

2. The sequences are overlapping. In other words, it would not be correct to describe a baby as being exclusively in a particular stage at a particular time. While the baby is mastering a certain motor act, he is already experimenting with components of various succeeding stages.

3. Increasing sensorimotor maturity is characterized by dissociation, that is, the breaking up of gross movement patterns, which involve the total body, into finer, more selective patterns, which permit parts of the body to move independently of other parts. An example is dissociation of the head from the shoulders, in which the child learns to turn his head in all directions without affecting the body as a whole.

4. Development proceeds cephalocaudally (from the head downward). Skills generally are coordinated first in the upper regions of the body and proceed to the lower regions later. For example, head control is achieved before control of the legs.

5. Development proceeds in a proximal to distal direction. The areas of the body closer to the midline are controlled before the areas toward the periphery. For example, control of shoulder movements occurs before control of finger movements.

The righting reactions and the equilibrium reactions are two means by which the five principles are achieved. To "right" means to bring or restore to an upright or normal position. The righting reactions are stimulated by the various sensory modalities mentioned earlier. They permit the baby to maintain the position of his head in space and also give him the ability to restore the correct alignment of head with trunk and trunk with limbs when alignment has been disturbed. They provide the infant with the new component of rotation within the body axis (twisting of the trunk) as a means of accomplishing this alignment. It is an illustration of the gradual breaking up of the total body responses that characterize the younger infant. If one considers the example of the 6- to 7-month-old baby who has developed independent sitting, it can be seen that the baby has achieved one level of "break up," that is, the ability to break up the total pattern of extension of the back that he has been practicing for 6 months in the prone position. At about 6 months of age, he is then able to flex at the hips while being able to maintain extension in his spine at the same time. Earlier he could not do this. However, it will take several more months of practicing rotation between shoulders and pelvis until the righting reactions are mature enough to permit him to rotate from the prone-lying into the sitting position independently. The righting reactions are usually fully integrated at about 9 months of age.

The equilibrium reactions are balance responses that use the more primitive righting reactions and modify them still further. They take the form of either invisible changes in muscle tone or fully visible countermovements of neck, trunk, and limbs when the center of gravity is displaced. These tonus changes and countermovements occur in such a way that they tend to pull the center of gravity back to where it belongs to restore balance. These patterns of coordination are very similar in each individual. It is possible for the equilibrium reactions to be developed throughout life, as in the case of athletes, who can train their bodily responses well past the limits usually considered to be full maturity.

Normal sensorimotor development can be considered an important basis for all other forms of development. In fact it is artificial to consider the normal development of cognition, self-concept, language, and speech separately from motor development, although for organizational purposes it is frequently presented that way. The infant's first sounds are produced in association with movement, and it is these sounds which the infant may later use to achieve verbal communication. Especially in the very young baby, adaptive behavior is dependent upon motor acts. In fact at this stage motor and perceptual acts are the vehicles through which cognition is developed and expressed.

The rest of this section is devoted to a detailed description of the actual achievements of the baby at significant points in his life. It should be remembered that the times of acquisition of the skills are approximate, since each baby's rate of development differs somewhat from that of others; however, the normal baby's acquisition of motor skills falls generally within the time frames presented here. During the first 4 months (birth to 4 months), the baby learns to control his head and orient it in space. In the following 2 months (4 to 6 months), the baby learns to sit. In the next 2 months (6 to 8 months), the baby usually learns to creep. The last part of his first year (8 to 12 months) he devotes to developing motor components that will allow him to raise himself to a standing position. Around the end of his first and beginning of his second year (12 to 18 months), he starts to walk but will still need to use his arms to keep his balance. The latter half of his second year (18 to 24 months), his arms and hands are freed for manipulative tasks while walking. Finally, well into his third year (24 to 30 months), the child can combine fine motor skills to demonstrate his understanding of concepts such as size, form, and position in space (Egan, Illingworth, & MacKeith, 1969; Gesell, Halverson, Thompson, Ilg, Costner, Ames, & Amatruda, 1940; Illingworth, 1970).

The reader is advised to analyze each skill that the baby has acquired according to the following:

1. What components of movement are necessary in order for the baby to have mastered that skill?
2. For what future skills can this one be considered an important component?
3. What areas of developing cognitive ability are likely to be facilitated by this motor act?

Birth to 4 Months

One of the most noticeable behaviors of very young infants is their motor activity. Research indicates that the unborn fetus may have several movement patterns. Many women report the sensation of "kicking" in the womb, and there is a change in fetal position during pregnancy. It has been suggested that fetal movement resulting from several primitive responses may assist in the birth process. It would seem that movement experience is a part of the prenatal environment of the fetus. It is no wonder that the neonate has a complex repertoire of motor activity, including flexion and extension of the arms and legs, slight head turning, and an occasional hand-to-mouth pattern resulting in finger sucking (Brazelton, 1962, 1974; Paine, 1966).

Historically, many theorists felt that early motor development depended more on physiological growth (maturation) than on environmental stimulation (learning). Current research tends to support both physiological maturation and environmental learning as essential to normal growth and developmnet. Children in deprived sensorimotor environments are delayed in reaching certain motor developmental milestones. In many studies, institutionalized infants who were normal and healthy but had not experienced certain types of environmental stimulation—for example, children who had never been placed on their abdomens or in supported sitting positions—demonstrated considerable developmental lag in the acquisition of such gross motor behaviors as head control and sitting (Dennis, 1960; Rutter, 1972; White, 1967).

During the first several months of life, there are many changes occurring in the infant's development as he addresses himself to his new environment. Internal bodily processes—breathing, heartbeat, and digestion—are stabilized, while external movements—of the arms, legs, head, and trunk—are experienced. In the following months, as primitive reactions are integrated into the central nervous system, the infant increases his repertoire of voluntary motor skills.

Regardless of the newborn's position, flexor tone predominates in the normal full-term baby. It is noticeable in the gross random movements of the infant's arms and legs, which are generally somewhat flexed, never completely extended. The baby's limbs tend to be held close to the body and resist straightening. Although flexor tone is more marked in the prone position, even in the supine position the baby never assumes full extension at this stage. The predominance of flexor tone is also demonstrated by the infant's inability to hold his head up in the prone position (Ingram, 1959; Prechtl & Beintema, 1964).

In the next several months, extension is gradually developed in all positions. As primitive reflexive reactions are integrated into the central nervous system, the baby develops head control skills, which allow him to lift his head and turn it in the direction of sounds or to move his head from side to side as his eyes follow objects moving in the environment. As this process continues in a cephalocaudal direction and as he develops more shoulder control, he is able to hold his head up in the prone position while

FIGURE 5.1 *Extension proceeds in a cephalocaudal direction, initiated by head righting in the prone position.*

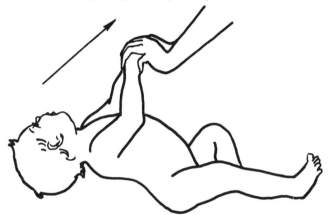

FIGURE 5.2 *Head lag when pulled to sitting from the supine position.*

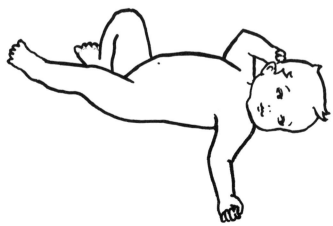

FIGURE 5.3 *Asymmetrical tonic neck reflex in the supine position.*

supporting himself on his forearms (see Figure 5.1). Thus he begins to develop upper back extension, a greater sensory awareness of his arms and shoulders, and an ability to view his hands while in the prone position. However, if an attempt is made at this stage to pull the baby up from the supine to a sitting position, there will be a noticeable head lag (see Figure 5.2).

When lying on his back, the baby initially lacks the control to maintain his head in the midline, and it is therefore usually held to one side or the other. One may then notice the classic asymmetrical tonic neck attitude. The arm and the leg on the infant's face side are relatively extended, while the arm and leg on the skull side are relatively flexed (see Figure 5.3). This "fencing" position may not be easily discernible; but differences in tonal quality between the sides may be felt. This position seems to assist the normal child in developing reaching skills (unilateral swiping). At this point the infant's hands are predominantly fisted. In the following months, as his eyes begin to focus he may watch his hand as it moves on the sheet. Initially, placement in the supine position tends to encourage a unilateral effect on the limbs, whereas placement in prone stimulates more symmetrical behavior. During this stage of development the infant seems better able to watch people or objects that are presented to his side rather than toward his midline. Head movements tend to accompany eye movements. The infant's oculomotor system is not adequately sophisticated to allow for independent eye movements in all directions (Van Blankenstein, Welbergen, & de Haas, 1962).

If the infant's head is strongly turned to the extreme side, his body may rotate as a whole in the same direction as the head, due to the neck-righting reaction. Thus if the infant's head is strongly turned to the left when he is lying on his back, he may roll to a side-lying position on his left side or completely roll over onto his abdomen. In this stage of primitive rolling, there is a lack of the segmental rotation of the body parts that generally accompanies mature rolling.

4 to 6 Months

At the age of 4 to 6 months, many activities requiring the ability to extend against gravity are being incorporated into the baby's repertoire. As the baby's central nervous system matures with the development of inhibitory control from the higher centers, many primitive reactions are modified. The baby now automatically utilizes varied movement patterns in the acquisition of functional motor skills. The infant's head control continues to increase in all positions. He is also able to bring his hands together at the midline—as when playing with his undershirt, bringing objects to his mouth, or exploring his clasped hands. Around 5 to 6 months, the primitive clutching becomes a palmar grasp in which the ulnar fingers (those nearest the little finger) are the most active.

As extension develops in the prone position, the infant occasionally assumes a posture known as "swimming"—while supporting most of his body weight on his abdomen, his arms and legs are stretched out and off the mattress—a further acquisition of extension against gravity.

The infant also practices movements and subtle weight-shifting activities while supporting himself on his forearms. Equilibrium develops in the "prone-on-elbows" position which will give the baby the ability to lift one arm and reach out while supporting himself on his other forearm. This is the beginning development of the rotary component in the trunk that enables the baby to combine flexion and extension into more directed and controlled activities.

In the supine position, the baby is now able to maintain his head in the midline for longer periods of time. If interested in a toy or excited by the appearance of a face as it comes toward him, he may demonstrate a two-handed (bilateral) approach in reaching toward midline for the object.

The relative independence of the head from the limbs (called dissociation) frees the limbs from complete domination of the head's position. This newfound ability to maintain his head in the midline allows the infant to explore his body. Thus the baby of 4 to 6 months exhibits the following motor capability:

1. Bilateral arm and leg movement is present, in contrast to the unilateral movement seen earlier. Most movements of the arms and legs are characterized by total movement patterns (the limb moves as a whole) and follow the principle of proximal to distal development. The most proximal joints—shoulder and hip—seem to direct the gross reaching or kicking movements.

2. As the infant explores and differentiates leg movements, he adopts a "pedaling" action—with his hips bilaterally flexed, he extends one leg, then the other, and then returns both legs to the starting position of bilateral hip flexion. Part of this movement resembles reciprocal kicking. However in reciprocal kicking both legs are not simultaneously returned to the same starting position (flexion or extension) but continue to perform the reciprocal alternating movements. At times the infant may rest one foot on the mattress and push. This results in a pelvic twist that may roll him over onto his side.

3. The baby's hips may be bilaterally flexed and externally rotated so that his knees point outward to the sides rather than toward the ceiling. In this froglike position the baby often elevates his bottom from the mattress, which raises his legs and eventually brings his feet into his visual field. He is now able to play with his feet and put them into his mouth (see Figure 5.4). This "bottom-lifting" activity is seldom seen until the end of the 4- to 6-month period.

When the infant is placed in a supported sitting position, he is able to hold his head up fairly straight, although it is still wobbly. The upper region of the back is extended, the lower part rounded. He still lacks the lower trunk control needed to maintain an independent sitting position. The development of head control in the supported sitting position (antigravity posture) is very important to the child's visual understanding of his environment; it enables him to view the world from an upright orientation. Increased mobility of the head allows him to monitor visually a much larger portion of his surroundings. His eyes now follow moving objects through a wider arc in front of and around him.

6 to 8 Months

By this age, the baby has developed good mobility in the prone position. He has learned to prone pivot in a circle, with his hips completely extended and abducted (spread wide apart) (see Figure 5.5). The task requires symmetrical use of the limbs as opposed to the asymmetrical activity in the newborn. Weight-shifting and reaching activities, begun earlier, have developed so

FIGURE 5.4 *"Bottom Lifting" and exploration of the feet.*

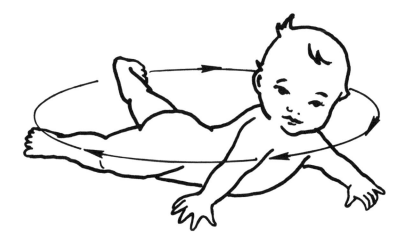

FIGURE 5.5 *Prone pivoting in a circle: Arms and legs both move into abduction and extension.*

that now the baby performs them on fully extended arms when in the prone position. Trunk extension and rotation are required to perform the reach (see Figure 5.6).

The baby will often push himself backward along the floor, apparently by accident at first. When pushing himself backward, he may lift his abdomen off the mattress and end up sitting between his feet. Pushing back and forth in this manner will reinforce the use of the arms for protection when falling forward.

During this period the baby has developed sufficient extension so that his back is quite straight in sitting, not rounded as it was in previous months. At first he does not have true balance in this position and must rely on the use of his arms extended in front of him for support. Later he is able to remove his hands from the floor and even to turn his head and shoulders to one side or the other without losing his balance. With improved trunk control the arms and hands are freed for more sophisticated play activities (see Figure 5.7).

Up to this time, rolling from supine to prone was generally accomplished through the neck-righting reaction. This pattern appears to become modified or inhibited during the age of 6 to 8 months, so that head turning no longer results in the baby's entire body rolling over as a single unit. At this time, rolling becomes more refined and segmental as, with the emergence of the body-righting reaction, the baby differentiates movements of his shoulders, trunk, and pelvis (Rushworth, 1961). When the infant turns his head, his shoulders follow, then his trunk, and finally his pelvis in the accomplishment of segmental rolling. The acquisition of this trunk rotation is essential for the development of the movement patterns that will enable the infant to rise up further against gravity (e.g., to a sitting position, to the quadripedal position, and, later, up to standing). The baby has been practicing rotation through different means for quite a while: In prone there have been the weight-shifting and reaching activities, and, in supine, weight-shifting in the lower part of the body through "bottom-wiggling" activities as well as pushing with one foot on the mattress to achieve pelvic twisting and, sometimes, rolling onto the abdomen.

Segmental rolling can now be initiated by either the upper or the lower portion of the body. Lying on his back, the infant may reach across his body for an interesting toy and, as he reaches, roll over. Or, with strong leg movements, he may use the lower portion of his body to initiate body rolling.

By 6 months of age, the infant has progressed to a more active physical manipulation of objects that includes banging and shaking them. His body awareness has developed to the point that he can now reach directly for an object even when his hand is not in view. Sensory cues tell him where his arm is in relation to his body and in relation to the object, and he is less dependent on visual cues in performing gross reaching activities.

Although he lacks full elbow extension, arm movements are

FIGURE 5.6 *Weight-shifting and reaching action on fully extended arms in prone, furthering upper trunk extension and rotation.*

FIGURE 5.7 *Erect sitting without arm support and enough balance to rotate upper trunk freely.*

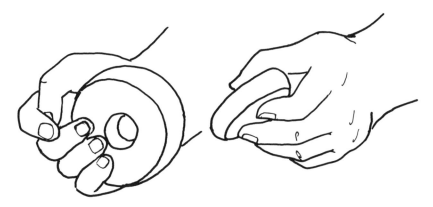

FIGURE 5.8 *Palmar grasps: a) ulnar b) radial.*

continuously maturing as the baby reaches for objects with his arm in a neutral position—a position halfway between the previous reaching pattern of pronation (the palm of the hand facing down away from the infant's eyes) and the future reaching pattern of supination (palm turned up). In this neutral position the infant's thumb is in his full view. These three forearm positions—pronation, neutral, and supination—will be utilized throughout adult life as dictated by the demands of the activity (e.g., throwing a ball underhand, using a supinated posture, as compared with throwing overhand, in which the arm is pronated). It must be remembered that these three positions are initially controlled by the position of the shoulder because at this stage the arm is still functioning as a whole (proximal to distal development). These positions are generally associated with reaching patterns and should not be confused with grasping patterns, which involve movements of the fingers.

Although the baby does not initially use his thumb in grasping, he uses it at this stage as a post or stabilizer of objects, by flexing his fingers toward the palm of his hand in a kind of scratching or raking movement. Since the radial fingers (the ones nearer the thumb) are now more active than in the previous pattern of ulnar grasping, this is referred to as a radial grasp (Figure 5.8 illustrates ulnar and radial grasps). In the neutral arm position, the infant is able to monitor visually the movements of his thumb and fingers as he grasps a toy; whereas in pronation, it is somewhat harder for him to see the thumb and he must rely more on tactile cues for feedback about its position in relation to the other fingers and the object. Visual monitoring of the hand in play seems to assist the child in producing coordinated grasping patterns utilizing the thumb.

Greater wrist mobility assists the baby in banging a held object in an up-and-down vertical pattern or shaking it in a side-to-side pattern. The infant also explores objects in a bilateral fashion—playing with a toy held in one hand, then transferring it to the other hand where it is again actively manipulated, or holding an object in each hand simultaneously.

8 to 12 Months

With increased trunk rotation, the body moves less as a whole and more in segments: The arm is freer to move across the body, instead of in line with the body; the shoulders achieve better external rotation (turning the total arm from palm down to neutral to palm up); and the arm and hand positions mentioned in the previous section are achieved. However, for the rolling movement to be completed so that the baby turns completely from his back onto his abdomen, head and neck extension must accompany trunk rotation.

In the prone position, the baby has already experimented with the posture of extreme extension by swimming movements of his arms and legs. As he develops more control of back extension, his arms and legs are more relaxed and his hands and feet are in closer contact with the surface on which he is lying, with more purposeful knee and elbow extension. This leads to increased weight bearing by the arms, with the chest off the floor. Occasionally the baby may push up with his hips elevated, so that he is on his hands and feet.

He may use this increased weight-bearing ability of his arms to propel himself backward resulting in what is usually the first type of straight-line locomotion achieved by the baby. As control of his upper back and shoulders increases, he may start using his arms to pull himself forward, with accompanying random flexion and extension movements of his legs. These random leg movements may result in his accidentally pushing his legs into extension with the toes, resulting in more dramatic movement forward. With this new sensory stimulation and awareness, the baby may then attempt to incorporate leg movements for forward propulsion. This activity is called belly crawling.

Purposeful straight-line movement requires reciprocal movements of the shoulders and pelvis (i.e., opposite arm and leg advancing forward). This reciprocal movement is also very subtly occurring in the baby's back, resulting in the increased stability necessary for further antigravity positions. As back extension and stability progress, the baby, in one of his backward-pushing actions, may flex both hips and knees and end up in the all-fours position. (Initially this position is often passed through to achieve sitting on or between the feet, as mentioned in the previous section.)

As the baby experiments with this quadripedal position, rocking back and forth by resting his weight alternately on arms and legs and aided by his new capacity for active hip extension and flexion (dissociation of pelvis from trunk), he experiences a new orientation in space in a less supported posture and further develops the equilibrium and balance that he will need to attain the upright position. Eventually, he will attempt to move in the all-fours position by reaching with one arm, maintaining his weight on the other three limbs, and then moving the opposite leg (reciprocal movement). With increased trunk stability, he is able to move an arm and opposite leg simultaneously, maintaining his weight on only two extremities. This results in the form of location called creeping, which usually emerges toward the end of the first year. Creeping is often the major form of independent locomotion for a number of months, and the child may later revert to it at times of stress or instability.

Prior to achieving the reciprocal movements of arms and legs involved in creeping, the baby most often rotates in only one direction at a time—either with the shoulder or with the hip, as in the segmental rolling pattern. The reciprocal movements of arms and legs involved in creeping require a new element, that of counterrotation—the shoulder rotating in one direction and the hip in the other—which is a very important component of the erect forward progression that develops later.

At this time, improved trunk rotation is used to achieve a more stable sitting position. Independent sitting was initially achieved by rolling from supine to prone, pushing backward to sit between the legs, and then bringing the legs out to the front in a circular movement—a symmetrical, straight-trunk activity.

Now, from supine, the baby makes only a half turn, so that he is virtually in a side-lying position; with his body weight supported by the arm and leg closest to the floor and his other arm and leg crossed over his body to the floor, he comes to sitting by twisting the unsupported side of his pelvis backward toward the floor while pushing himself up and back with both arms. This movement sequence is completed by twisting both arms toward the front and thereby putting weight on both buttocks.

Once in a stable sitting posture, the child spends a lot of time experimenting with trunk mobility by rocking back and forth (which aids dissociation of trunk from pelvis). Equilibrium reactions and protective responses of the arms enable him to regain his balance when in danger of falling forward or sideways (see Figure 5.9); but protective extension responses of the arms to prevent himself from falling backward are usually not achieved until somewhat later.

When playing in the all-fours position, the baby may reach out to the furniture or crib rail and surprise himself by pulling into a kneeling position, keeping his balance with his hands rather than bearing weight through his hips. And from here he may soon find himself standing. The transition from all fours through kneeling to standing is initially a rapid-flow movement, as the baby is not yet capable of controlling the interim posture. Only long after he is able to move about on his feet will he acquire the balance and control to kneel-stand or to hesitate on one knee with the other foot placed forward (half-kneeling position). At this early stage of "standing," he may rest most of his body weight on his abdomen, by leaning against the support, so that his hands are free for play.

Assuming full body weight in a standing position, the baby stands with his legs spread apart, which provides a solid base of support. The wider apart the baby's legs, the easier it is for him to maintain his balance. The knees vary between flexion and extension, and the toes vary between pressing down against the floor ("clawing") and extending ("fanning")—equilibrium reactions of the feet are essential to normal walking and standing (see Figure 5.10). Since his legs are spread apart, he appears to be standing on the medial (inside) aspect of his feet.

As an erect being, a new world of movement is available to the baby. While holding on to some support, he may bounce himself up and down—by alternately flexing and extending his knees. However, if he lowers his body too far, he may not be able to return to standing but will sit down rather abruptly—he has little control for coordinating the movements essential to a proper standing posture at this stage. Or he may play a stomping game, alternately lifting one foot and then the other.

Most babies learn to cruise sideways before they are able to attempt forward walking. Holding on to the crib rail or other support, the child takes a sideways step (abducts), then draws the other leg up close to the first one, then takes another sideways step, and so on—an example of symmetrical movement of the extremities. Side cruising may continue for a considerable time before forward walking is attempted.

At this age, thumb-and-index-finger grasping patterns are just emerging, as are conscious, or voluntary, release skills. Previously, when the child wanted to release an object, he did so with a total arm movement that often resulted in flinging the toy away from himself. Now, his hands have acquired the grasp and release movements of flexion and extension that enable him to squeeze purposefully a soft, pliable rubber toy. Movement of the fingers is becoming individualized, so that, for example, he is able to point with an extended index finger.

Play patterns have grown considerably. Now the child can slide or push objects around on a flat surface—for example, his cereal bowl around the high chair tray. He is also quite adept at using his hands to crumple paper or crumble cookies. His attempts to tear paper are efforts to organize the bilateral coordination that is characteristic of more advanced play skills, such as pulling popbeads apart. His vertical banging behaviors have become the basis for mastering new emptying activities, such as removing objects from containers by lifting the container up and tilting it toward himself, and activities characterized by take-apart features, as in removing rings from a ringstack or pegs from a pegboard.

During these games, the child typically uses one hand at a time, but he continues to alternate his hand usage. The baby is beginning to grasp with his palm facing upward in supination. As he visually monitors the movements of his hands in grasping, he increasingly separates the use of the thumb and index finger from the other fingers of the hand. When picking up objects, the

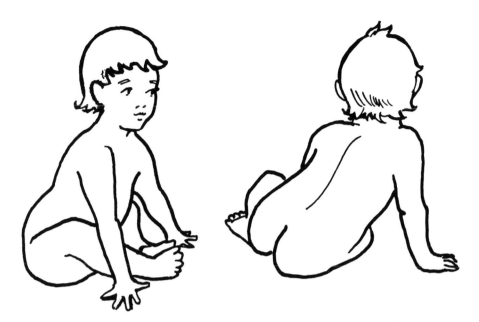

FIGURE 5.9 *When losing balance in a sitting position, the baby protects himself with protective extension forward and sideways.*

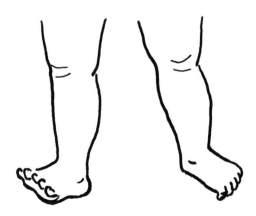

FIGURE 5.10 *Baby learns balance in standing by delicate movements of the feet—"fanning" and "clawing."*

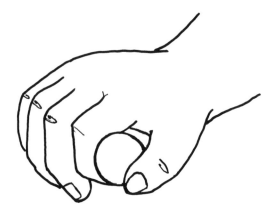

FIGURE 5.11 *Inferior pincer grasp, or lateral prehension.*

infant frequently uses an inferior pincer grasp, in which the thumb is moved toward the lateral, distal aspect of the index finger (see Figure 5.11). Around 12 months, thumb opposition develops, which enables the thumb to move to the tip of the index finger for pad-to-pad touch. This prehension pattern is discussed in the next section.

12 to 18 Months

At the beginning of this period, most children are creeping well. Even if they have begun to cruise, they are likely to use creeping as their major means of locomotion. The creeping patterns may vary somewhat. Some babies, for example, prefer to creep on hands and feet instead of on hands and knees. However in either case the major components needed for successful creeping are the same: (*a*) extension of head, neck, back, and arms; (*b*) counterrotation between trunk and shoulder, and trunk and pelvis; and (*c*) dissociation of shoulders and arms from trunk, and of legs from pelvis.

It is important to remember that most of the components used during this stage have already been experienced by the baby during his first year of life. From now on development takes the form of refining these components to produce smoother, more coordinated movements, and of combining them into new forms.

In the erect position the baby continues side cruising for a time. At some point he may let go with one hand, but he cannot yet rotate his trunk in this posture so as to look or reach back. Later he will be able to twist around and may practice moving one leg forward and back from the hip while looking backward or reaching back with the same-side arm (see Figure 5.12), thus practicing a form of counterrotation while still supporting himself.

At first when the baby attempts forward locomotion, his legs are widely abducted, which helps him maintain balance by keeping the center of gravity low. Since his hips have not achieved full extension, he exhibits a "pot belly" and a hollow (lordotic) lower back (see Figure 5.13). The legs maintain a posture of abduction–external rotation and are moved forward by total flexion; at this stage the baby has minimal active ankle movements and thus replaces his foot on the ground in a full-sole pattern or flatfoot. The distance between the two feet in a step is very short and does not allow him to cover much ground. Thus the child is practicing quick balance on one leg or the other. He spreads his arms far apart in the "high guard" position, which results in strong extension of the upper back to compensate for the lack of good hip extension (Bobath & Bobath, 1962). Thus, initial forward walking is accomplished with upper back stability to enable pelvic, or lower back, mobility.

The baby soon exhibits some rotation in forward walking, but at first in the pelvic area only. As back stability is increased in this position, the arms come closer to the sides. With the arms at the sides and elbows flexed, counterrotation between shoulders and pelvis becomes more obvious through a somewhat irregular arm swing. With greater dissociation of arms from shoulders, regular reciprocal arm movements begin—the right arm swinging forward with the left leg and vice versa.

As trunk stability in the erect position improves, the legs come further under the pelvis and maturing leg movements are seen. For example, the hips and knees have more extension than previously. The foot is also developing plantar flexion, which is utilized in the pushing-off action (called "toe-off") of a more mature gait. Toe-off is then followed by ankle dorsiflexion (turning the foot up) and heel strike. It is the beginning development of a heel–toe gait pattern.

It is interesting to note that the movement pattern of the legs in rolling from supine to prone very closely parallels the weight-bearing gait pattern. For example, in early rolling the leg was held in marked abduction, with external rotation and minimal extension as the baby rolled from back to abdomen. At that time, the legs did not cross the midline as the baby approached the prone position—a pattern similar to the very early standing and walking ones. In later rolling and standing, the legs are closer together and achieve more active hip extension; when the rolling movement is initiated by swinging the leg, the leg more completely crosses the body midline, as is the case with more advanced walking patterns. The distance between the two legs in this position seems to have a direct relationship to the infant's stepping ability when upright.

Note how the baby utilizes components practiced earlier but in a different form. In the prone position he developed extension from the head on down, culminating in full extension with abduction of the limbs. He then broke up this pattern, first by alternating flexion and extension movements (rocking on all fours), later with rotation (reaching), and still later with counterrotation (creeping). This progression enabled him to move smoothly without losing the extension needed for stability. The same sequence was repeated in sitting and in the supported standing position. Extension developed first, then alternate flexion and extension (bouncing), followed by rotation and counterrotation. Now, during the development of unsupported forward locomotion, the sequence is again repeated.

During this period, the child has not yet developed enough balance to pivot around in place on one foot; to turn he must walk around in a half circle. Concurrently he develops the ability to stop his forward progression, bend down to pick up a toy, straighten up, and continue on his way while holding the toy.

By 12 months of age the child has manually explored many activities through a bilateral approach. He has mastered such play skills as pat-a-cake, banging two objects together, and the simultaneous manipulation of an object in each hand. At this stage he demonstrates more unilateral handling. Such activities as building two-block towers, placing large pegs in a pegboard, or nesting two boxes allow the child the opportunity to manipulate materials actively with one hand while the other assists in stabilizing the objects. The infant seems able to use either hand for these activities. As he continues to develop sensory awareness

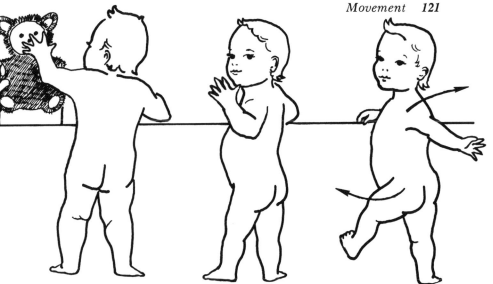

FIGURE 5.12 *Cruising maneuvers: (a) cruising sideways, reaching out; (b) standing, rotating upper trunk backward; (c) standing, reaching out backward, elaborating with swinging movements of the same-side leg, thus producing counterrotation.*

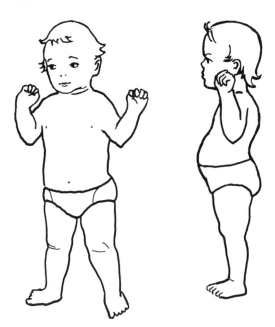

FIGURE 5.13 *Early standing: wide stance, pronated feet, "high guard," "pot belly," and lordotic back.*

FIGURE 5.14 *Superior pincer grasp, or two-point pinch.*

and motor control, he is preparing for the time when he will increasingly use only one hand to complete most manipulative activities. The baby shows greater control in reaching for toys that are nearer to him than those that are further away. He now utilizes supination for such activities as filling containers with objects, turning the pages of a book, and feeding himself with a spoon.

As his fingers continue to develop extension, the baby begins to isolate individual finger movements (e.g., in pressing the keys of a toy piano), a skill that is incorporated into his pattern of prehension. He is now able to pick up small objects between the tips of index finger and thumb, in a superior pincer grasp (see Figure 5.14). Previously, the thumb could not oppose the index or middle finger in a pad-to-pad touch. This fine prehensile pattern is combined with the ability to maintain the wrist in an extended, rather than flexed position, which assists the child in performing such coordinated tasks as stacking two 1-inch blocks and holding his cup for drinking.

18 to 24 Months

From either a prone or supine position, the toddler is now fully able to assume an erect standing position without using furniture for support. In assuming erect standing the toddler utilizes many previously integrated skills, such as rolling over, sitting independently, and assuming a hands–feet position. Generally, if the child is lying on his back he rolls over to his stomach and lifts his chest off the floor. As he lifts his chest up, he places one foot on the floor and then places the other foot to achieve a hands–feet position. Initially he maintains this extended, abducted, wide-base stance as he raises his trunk to attain an upright posture. Later he learns to flex his knees toward the ground as he lifts his trunk upward. At an even later date he will eliminate the prone component of this activity entirely and will stand from a side-sitting position.

The baby continues to explore combinations of movements. He may crawl up and down the stairs using a hands–knees posture or a hands–feet posture; or, coming down the stairs, he may lie on his abdomen with legs extended pushing off the stairway with his arms. Some children prefer to descend stairs by sitting on their buttocks and bumping down from step to step.

During this period the toddler's repertoire of walking behaviors has become quite refined. This is noticeable not only in the posture of his body (a narrower walking base with arms held down to the side) but also in such newly demonstrated activities as walking sideways without support, walking backward, and attempts at running. As the toddler decreases the width of his stepping base, he relies increasingly on equilibrium reactions, rather than a wide-base stance, for maintaining his balance. As body awareness and control skills continue to develop, he modifies the length, speed, and direction of his step to achieve a longer, more uniform stride. He no longer lifts his knees quite so high in the air. Although he occasionally trips and falls over objects in his path because his eye–foot coordination is not fully developed, there is a noticeable decrease in the incidence of falling, which seems related to improved equilibrium reactions and the ability to monitor visually and kinesthetically his trunk, legs, and feet. As he walks reciprocally, increased trunk mobility and the relaxed position of the arms at his side indicate more controlled movements. Thus he is able to combine patterns of forward walking, walking while pulling a toy, and backward walking unsupported.

Although he is capable of changing the linear direction of his walking pattern, he still does not have enough balance to pivot on the ball of his foot. Although he has begun to practice running (fast walking), he demonstrates a stiff, wobbly gait, due to an inability to isolate quick reciprocal knee and ankle movements. Attempts at kicking a large ball are largely unsuccessful, since he often walks into the ball or steps on it. Holding on to an adult's hand, he is able to walk up the stairs in a nonreciprocal gait. That is, he lifts and places one foot on the step, then lifts and places the other foot on the same step, in marking-time fashion. Within the next several months he will begin to utilize this marking-time procedure for descending stairs. While engaged in play, the toddler may explore many different levels: He may stand up for some activities, kneel for others, crouch for yet others—all of which contributes to the development of body balance as he actively moves his body in space.

The child continues to employ an alternating, unilateral manipulation of objects. However, rather than one hand being actively involved in exploration while the other hand passively assists for stabilization, the assisting hand is more actively involved in such bilateral tasks as pulling popbeads apart, holding a cup with two hands, or attempts at stringing beads. The supination movement of the forearm is employed in successful attempts at turning doorknobs or pouring objects from containers. This pouring activity is not to be confused with the directed pouring of liquids—a skill that emerges at a later stage of development. The pouring behaviors are those that a child utilizes to empty containers, for example, turning crayons out of their box or dumping sand out of a cup. However, the supination that the child now exhibits is true supination of the forearm and should not be confused with the palm-up pattern described earlier, which was controlled by external rotation at the shoulder.

Since the child has been actively using his thumb in prehensile patterns, he continues to develop the radial aspect of his hand musculature. This allows him to pick up and grasp simultaneously two small objects, such as 1-inch cubes, with the same hand. This accomplishment is remarkable, considering the comparatively small size of the child's hand, and it indicates increasing sensory awareness as well as muscular control. He has spent the last several months learning to release objects from his hand so that he is able to deposit an item where he desires. As he coordinates the movements of extending his fingers while abducting his thumb, he is able to perform such release activities as building towers of three and four cubes. In such tasks he uses one hand to stabilize the base of the tower while with the other hand he places the blocks one on top of another and in so doing learns the precise timing required in releasing the cube from his hand.

When holding a crayon, the child reverts to the more immature pattern of the palmar grasp. The arm is in either a neutral or a pronated position, while the crayon is held tightly in the palm of the hand with the thumb and fingers flexed around it. In his spontaneous scribbling, the child expresses his understanding of the relationship between writing tools and paper; but he is also beginning to refine gross vertical scribblings into visually monitored writing. That is, when someone demonstrates drawing a vertical line down the page, the child begins to imitate by drawing a vertical approximation. This task is an example of translating visual perceptual information into a motor output.

24 to 36 Months

A continuing example of cephalocaudal development is the further differentiation of knee and ankle movements, enabling the 2-year-old child to master the mature heel–toe gait in walking. With this gait pattern he can utilize a very narrow stepping base. As a result of the reduced size of the stepping base and the increased mobility of the trunk, the child begins to use a fairly consistent pattern of reciprocal walking and arm swinging. He still may have difficulty in making short turns around the corners of his environment—which requires a quick postural adjustment, since the body weight is unevenly distributed to different aspects of the soles of the feet.

His ability to ascend and descend stairs with little or no support using a nonalternating pattern (marking time) seems to indicate the degree of stability he can demonstrate while shifting body weight from one leg to the other. He now can support himself on one extremity for a short period of time. Improved balancing on one leg is noted in attempts to kick a large ball. The fact that the child no longer needs a visual demonstration to show him how to plan the execution of kicking seems to indicate an increased awareness of his body. This ability to weight shift with stability also enables the child to step over a low object lying on the floor. He has become quite adept at running, which is a skill requiring greater flexibility and balance than does walking. At this time the child is still unable to jump down a step in a coordinated bilateral manner, in which both legs are doing the same thing at the same time. Instead, he jumps, while holding on to the railing, by kicking one foot out at a time in a "step jump."

The child displays his understanding of such concepts as size, form, and position in space as he matches geometric shapes, copies coloring strokes, and puts popbeads back together. Not only is he able to construct vertical towers of six or seven blocks, but he is now able to generalize these perceptual motor skills to perform horizontal block construction, that is, placing blocks side by side, rather than stacking them one on top of another. This skill increases his ability to express spatial relationships among objects, as he attempts to copy adult models of trains and houses through vertical and horizontal block building.

When shown how to make a vertical fold in a sheet of paper, the child attempts to mimic this finely coordinated bilateral activity. While the outcome will be far from a perfect copy, in making some type of fold in the paper he has demonstrated an ability to translate into a motor output his visual understanding of the process observed. At this stage the child is quite adept at working with small materials. Thus he can readily turn single pages of a book and drop pennies or poker chips into a toy bank. If the bank is rotated to provide a different spatial orientation of the slit, the child is able to change his hand position as required for direct placement of the penny. This keen body awareness is also demonstrated in a pegboard game as the child holds the peg in a vertical position in his hand prior to placing it in the board.

He no longer holds the crayon in a palmar grasp but achieves greater control by increased utilization of his finger tips in grasping the crayon. Soon his grasping pattern will be identical to an adult's prehension of writing devices. This differentiated grasp allows for more mature "writing" movements, as the wrist is freer and can move more independently of the rest of the arm. A more circular scribble replaces the earlier gross vertical scribbling, in which the crayon was used as an extension of the arm, and he is able to imitate the drawing of horizontal as well as vertical lines.

Around 2½ years of age, the child adapts his locomotor skills to new situations requiring advanced body awareness and control. He learns to adjust his speed, force, and direction when walking on tiptoe or stepping over two obstacles at a time. If a line of tape is placed on the floor, he is initially able to follow only its general direction. But he gradually learns to follow it with minimal stepping off the line, using an approximate alternating heel–toe gait. If two straight lines are taped to the floor about 8 inches apart, the child is able to maneuver along this pathway without stepping outside it. He is becoming quite skillful in walking a board resting on the ground by setting one foot on the board and the other on the floor. Attempts to stand on one foot are less successful. Although he continues to descend the stairs in a marking-time pattern, he has begun to use a reciprocal gait for ascending stairs while holding the rail for support.

At this stage of development, the child has greater wrist control, as indicated in the bilateral, opposing movements of paper tearing. That is, while one hand is pulling the paper toward the body, the other hand is pulling the paper away from the body. This performance can be compared with the more immature pattern in which the child attempted to tear the paper by pulling it away from the midline of his body toward the sides; both arms were then essentially engaged in the same bilateral movements. As with tearing paper, the ability to attach clothespins indicates an improved strength of the hand musculature. In the latter activity the thumb and index finger must maintain a static pinch on the clothespin long enough for the child to clip it to a can or box. Initially the child may have difficulty in visually discriminating which end of the clothespin requires the active manipulation.

When attempting to cut paper with a pair of scissors, the child usually needs assistance in positioning his fingers in the holes. Once the fingers are in the appropriate position, he begins to differentiate the movements that will open and close the scissors. Although he may still have difficulty in managing the paper so that it is in correct alignment with the scissors, the child soon comes to understand the relationship between the two that is required for cutting.

Toward the end of the third year, the child acquires the reciprocal arm and leg patterns characteristic of mature walking. He is now also quite adept in other reciprocal activities, such as climbing a jungle gym or ladder and pedaling a small tricycle. He can start and stop locomotion as dictated by the demands of his environment. For instance, he is quite controlled in dodging obstacles in his path and in executing sharp turns around corners while running. Postural control skills allow him to maintain his equilibrium easily while standing with his heels together or while standing on his toes in a stationary position. Bilateral integration of the two sides of the body is also evident in his ability to stand independently on one foot at a time for several seconds. In mounting stairs the child now utilizes a reciprocal gait, placing alternate feet on each stair, and he accomplishes this active shift of balance without the support of the railing. However, when descending stairs without support, he still utilizes the marking-time pattern.

In the play of a 3-year-old child a pattern of hand preference generally emerges. He tends to initiate most activities with the preferred hand, electing to use the other hand consistently for stabilizing materials. Employing a mature grasp of the crayon (held between the thumb and the index finger and resting on the side of the middle finger), the child is better able to localize his strokes. However, when coloring, he aims his strokes at the total picture and does not differentiate his coloring movements to fit the design. Having internalized the motor-planning aspect of these tasks, he can now copy vertical, horizontal, and circular lines in place of imitating the movements characteristic of these strokes.

The child shows adeptness at working with small materials as he strings tiny beads, builds towers of ten or more blocks, manages zippers on clothing, and begins to attempt unbuttoning, lacing and unlacing, and tying a bow. With the exception of these fine motor activities, the child can independently dress and undress himself. He demonstrates awareness of size concepts in sorting big and little objects, matching objects of the same size when he has three different sizes from which to choose, and sequencing the rings in the appropriate order on the ringstack. He is able to match identical pictures of objects and is beginning to match simple, black line drawings of objects, which indicates an understanding of a more stylized representation.

Motor Development in Atypical Children

In the introduction to the section on normal motor development it was stated that the sequential acquisition of skill depends upon the higher centers of the brain gradually imposing inhibitory control over responses from the lower centers. However, if something occurs that interferes with this dynamic process, the course of development will proceed along very different lines.

Damage to the brain before birth or in earliest childhood may prevent sensory messages from reaching or becoming fully integrated at the higher levels of the central nervous system. Instead, these messages are "short-circuited" to lower portions of the nervous system, and the responses that emerge are appropriate to responses from those lower levels. Since the lesion has occurred in an immature brain, before development has been completed, the highest centers of the brain may never get a chance to evolve full control over the lower centers. The movement responses that are deprived of higher-level control are manifested as motor patterns that are stereotyped, atypical, and usually associated with an abnormal quality of muscle tone (Bobath, 1966). The muscle tone may be too high (hypertonus), as in the spastic child; too low (hypotonus), as in the floppy child; or fluctuating between high and low, as in the athetotic child.

All very young infants show evidence of reflexive motor behavior. The child with brain damage may display these motor responses in an exaggerated form (Paine, 1964; Paine & Brazelton, 1964). The asymmetrical tonic neck reflex is an example. While the normal baby will occasionally assume the "fencing" position, he will be able to move out of that posture with relative ease. The brain-damaged child may be "locked" into that posture every time his head turns toward one side or the other, preventing him from putting the toy he is observing into his mouth or exploring it with both hands, and greatly limiting his visual field. Such a child may, therefore, never develop the ability to integrate fully his visual, tactile, kinesthetic, and auditory modalities.

In addition to the exaggerated quality of lower central nervous system responses, these reflexive behaviors also tend to persist for a longer time than in the normal infant. They can be elicited by the position of the baby's head in space or by the position of the head in relation to other parts of the body. When the reflex is stimulated, the baby's whole body may be involved and more selective movements may be impossible. For example, a baby who is under the influence of the tonic labyrinthine reflex may assume complete extension whenever he is lying on his back or whenever his head falls backward of a 90° angle to the horizontal. Since the reflex dominates his entire body, he is unable to initiate isolated head or arm movements. In general, the developing motor patterns of the normal baby assist him to attain antigravity activities, whereas when the patterns and tone are abnormal they tend to pull the baby into gravity. They therefore interfere with subsequent development.

The baby may not perceive the irregular muscle tone and motor patterns as abnormal, since they are the only sensations of movement that he has experienced. In overutilizing the aberrant movements in his early explorations, he may be limited to basing subsequent motor achievements on a foundation of abnormality. Thus a situation evolves where the baby may develop along a course that becomes increasingly abnormal, resulting in the habituation of undesirable movements. The severely involved spastic child may have minimal, if any, free movement; he remains in pathological static postures that reinforce his motor handicap. As a result of the continued use of aberrant patterns of movement with abnormal tone, the child's physical disability may become more severe as he grows older, and such secondary disabilities as contractures and deformities may subsequently develop (Crothers & Paine, 1959; Holt, 1966; Milani-Comparetti & Gidoni, 1967).

In curriculum planning, it is important to assess the infant in all developmental areas and determine the manner in which his physical handicap may be limiting his overall learning. Activities and methods of handling should be chosen that will minimize his physical difficulties and free him to enjoy more normal cognitive–sensorimotor experiences. Special positioning adapted to the child's unique needs can facilitate motor development, reduce the likelihood of contractures and deformities, and at the same time enhance social, language, and cognitive skills.

Since the motor behavior of different handicapped infants is very dissimilar, it has been necessary to divide the remainder of this chapter into sections based on diagnostic categories. Consequently, the sections are delineated according to children with spastic diplegia or quadriplegia, hemiplegia, athetosis, ataxia, and hypotonia. The medical diagnoses are based on the physical and motor parameters of these atypical infants, with the type of intervention highly dependent on the quality of muscle tone and the degree of involvement. But it is recognized that the "labeling" of children is not necessarily desirable and that these categories are somewhat arbitrary; also, that many infants have a "mixed" type of involvement that cuts across categorical lines. Although specific attention is not assigned to children with such handicapping conditions as spina bifida, developmental delay, childhood amputation, or congenital anomalies, the chapter contains much information of direct relevance to these populations. Each section discusses the nature of the motor difficulty, its effect on development, principles of intervention, and samples of their application.

Children with Spastic Diplegia or Spastic Quadriplegia

The spastic child manifests greater muscle tone than one might expect to see or feel in the normal child. All newborns exhibit rather high flexor tone in every position, especially in the prone position. As development proceeds, this high tone diminishes gradually to permit increased extensor activity against gravity. In contrast, the exaggerated hypertonus of the spastic child does not diminish over time—rather it tends to increase. It usually displays itself in somewhat predictable patterns of movement and of posture, and is dependent to some extent on the infant's position or the type of movement he attempts.

The child with spastic quadriplegia has generalized involvement that includes the trunk and all four limbs. The involvement of the diplegic child is primarily in the lower trunk and legs, with much less involvement in the upper trunk and arms. These two clinical diagnoses are usually discussed separately; but for the purposes of this presentation, where concern is focused on those influences in spastic children that are interfering with the normal sequences of sensorimotor development, it seems appropriate to discuss them together.

Subtle signs of spasticity may be noticed quite early in some babies. The head, neck, and trunk may show hypertonicity before it is apparent in the limbs. One early sign is an inability to tolerate the prone position. It may be related to a pull into gravity, caused by increased muscle tone, which prevents the baby from lifting his head and turning it from side to side. Consequently the infant prefers lying supine. In this position more extension may be present than is usually expected. (It will be recalled that the normal young baby does not go into full extension even when on his back.) In the spastic baby, the increased extension is often due to exaggeration of the tonic labyrinthine reflex, which under regular conditions exerts only fleeting influences.

Instead of the head merely lagging backward as the baby is pulled into sitting from supine, one may feel an actual pulling backward into gravity. The downward pull may be noticed also in the arms and shoulders as they retract backward toward the mattress. In addition the baby may not exhibit the wide variety of random movements that are expected of normal infants, such as wiggling the wrists, fingers, ankles, and toes. These signs may be so subtle that they are not readily observable and can only be felt by handling the child. They demonstrate the importance of what is subjectively felt as well as of what is objectively seen in the total assessment of an infant.

In the case of severe involvement, the child may assume a characteristic flexed posture in the prone position: the head is pulled down, the arms are pulled in under the body, and the hips, knees, and ankles tend to flex. In the supine position exaggerated extensor spasticity may dominate: the neck and shoulders press backward, the spine arches, the legs scissor, and the toes claw. Usually the influence of the asymmetrical tonic neck reflex is strongest when the child lies on his back.

In the mildly involved child, the motor signs may be seen or felt to a lesser degree or they may not be apparent until the baby is about 8 months old. Parents frequently become concerned at this time when the baby fails to be able to sit. However the informed observer might have been able to detect signs of impairment earlier. For example, while the mildly involved spastic baby may develop the ability to push up with extended arms while in the prone position, it may be noticed that the legs are not abducted as widely as one might expect. There may be abduction at the hips, but only when associated with flexion and never with extension at the hips. This tendency for the legs to pull together when the hips are in extension would indicate that the baby was under the influence of a total extensor pattern and had not been able to inhibit or "break up" the pattern. (The total extensor pattern of the legs consists of extension combined with adduction and internal rotation—straight legs, pulled together, and turned inward.) By contrast, the normal 6-month-old baby is able to combine hip extension with abduction and external rotation of the limbs and he is also able to combine extension of the back with flexion of the hips, enabling him to sit with a straight back.

The influence of the total extensor pattern can account for the baby's inability to maintain the sitting position. Extensor spasticity tends to force him backward, with insufficient hip flexion causing him to sit on his lower spine instead of on his buttocks, his legs pulling together instead of remaining apart (see Figure 5.15). The baby may compensate by rounding the upper portion of his back and leaning his head and shoulders forward (Bobath & Bobath, 1975).

In some instances the diplegic infant is so mildly affected that it is initially believed that the involvement is limited to the legs. However, stressful activity, such as maintaining an unstable sitting position, can lead to the development of an abnormal flexor pattern of the arms (shoulder depression and adduction, elbow flexion, forearm pronation, and wrist flexion). In this way the involvement of the arms and even of the trunk may become apparent. Excessive effort or overstimulation can produce a phenomenon known as associated reactions, in which movement in one part causes an increase of muscle tone into abnormal patterns of movement or posture in other parts of the body.

Complete development of the righting reactions does not

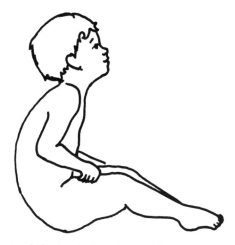

FIGURE 5.15 *Spastic child in sitting: insufficient hip flexion, rigidly extended and scissored legs, rounded spine, and hyperextended neck.*

occur. Full rotation between shoulder and pelvis cannot develop when spasticity is present. Restricted trunk rotation due to spasticity is the reason that many children are unable to assume the sitting position by rotating from the prone position to the side-sitting position and from there to long sitting; or it may prevent the child from assuming the all-fours position (see Normal Motor Development: 8 to 12 months). Although the more mildly involved child may initially have minimal spasticity of the trunk, overuse of the arms to compensate for the reduced ability to rotate within the body axis can increase the spasticity in the legs and cause the trunk and arms to become increasingly spastic as well. In the process, the development of whatever rotation was potentially present may be limited. This increase in spasticity may cause the child to lose some of the fine motor skills that he had previously developed.

In attempting to accomplish the tasks common to other children of his age such as sitting and creeping, the infant may be forced to compensate for his insufficient rotation, usually by lateral flexion of the trunk. This compensation does not lead to perfection of the righting reactions. The incomplete development of the righting reactions in turn precludes the acquisition of the equilibrium reactions that are necessary for true independent sitting balance and the more sophisticated motor skills.

Since many spastic children are not able to come to a sitting position in the normal way, they frequently attempt the task with great effort by tightening at the abdomen in order to pull the head and trunk straight up from the mattress. This method seldom succeeds, since the exertion needed increases the overall tone, which results in rigidity and possible scissoring of the limbs through associated reactions.

The spastic child may discover that from the prone position he can achieve sitting by pushing the body backward over passively flexed legs, using stiffly extended arms with the neck and head held in a hyperextended position (asymmetrical tonic neck reflex). Although this "W" sitting position (resting on the buttocks between the heels of the feet) is a temporarily functional position for the child, it should be emphasized that use of this reflexive behavior impedes further motor development and can increase the spasticity already present.

Some children eventually learn to propel themselves on the

it helps to reduce the abnormal tone. (A spastic limb should not be pulled or quickly stretched, since stretching only increases the spasticity. Inhibit the high tone first and then encourage the limb to move freely.)

The beachball is particularly useful since it is a movable surface and accentuates the motion of the child. The movement of the pelvis on the spine "breaks up" the spasticity of the trunk. Slow pacing is required to give the infant time to adapt. The adult continues the rocking motion until relaxation is noted in the hips and the trunk is mobile. The same procedure can be employed for the upper trunk by placing one hand on each side of the upper spine. By pushing down and toward alternate sides, the upper spine can be gently rocked in relation to the pelvis. This handling technique particularly helps to decrease spasticity around the shoulders.

Once spastic tone has been reduced, innumerable activities can be performed on the beachball to enhance cognitive–perceptual–motor development. If engagement in a task causes spasticity to begin to increase, the ball can be gently rocked until the infant's body tone returns to a more normal level and thus allows more optimal movement patterns. For example, a child in the described position can be asked to reach for an overhead mobile, which requires him to extend his arm and rotate his trunk upward. The reaching facilitates extension and rotation of the trunk with extended, abducted, and externally rotated legs (see Figure 5.16). Reaching with rotation helps the child to experience the motions permitted by the basic integration of the righting reactions. It also helps to "break up" the abnormal spastic patterns. Rotation with extension is a prerequisite skill required for proper standing and walking.

■ From the position described above, the infant can be slowly lowered until his feet rest naturally on the floor. He can then be maintained in supported standing with legs in extension, external rotation, and abduction, and with the arms reaching upward onto the ball for support. This activity should be attempted only if the child has been relieved of spasticity first. It is one way of having the child experience a more normal standing posture.

■ Another option for reducing generalized tightness is to place the child on his abdomen across the lap of an adult who is sitting on the floor or on a chair. The adult's legs are spread apart to avoid pressure on the abdominal muscles of the child. One of the adult's legs prevents the infant's outstretched arms from pulling down into a flexed position; the other leg helps to extend the hips (see Figure 5.17). The adult gently rocks the buttocks from side to side to relax the spastic tone of the hips and trunk, at the same time keeping the child's legs apart. Focus can be placed on developing head control, back extension, reaching with the arms, or hand activities. If the baby begins to tighten with spasticity (i.e., the hips start to bend and the arms to pull down and back), the adult resumes slow rocking of the buttocks. As the tone declines, the infant's torso should not be allowed to sag in the middle so that he is "sway-back." The adult's legs can be brought closer together to prevent this.

■ In this activity, the desired goal is to develop good sitting balance while the infant is in an optimal position with normalized tone. The child sits astride a firm bolster, which provides a good sitting surface since the circumference of the roll maintains the legs spread apart (see Figure 5.18). If a bolster is not available, the child can straddle the thigh of an adult seated on the floor. The child's knees are externally rotated and not allowed to press inward against the roll. The feet rest securely on the floor with the ankles at a 90° angle. The infant should sit solidly on both buttocks with his trunk erect or brought slightly forward, so that he does not sit in a slouched position on the lower spine. Since the hips are adequately flexed, he does not curve his spine to keep from falling backward. Initially the infant may need to place his hands forward on the roll for additional support. The arms should be straight and rotated out, and the hands open so that he is bearing weight on the palms. Although the elbows are extended, they should be mobile and not locked. This pattern of the arms counteracts the tendency to pull back abnormally at the shoulders, flex at the elbows, and fist the hands. In this position a mirror covered with a diaper or tissue paper can be placed in front of the young child. He may enjoy reaching forward with one hand to pull the covering away, thus revealing the reflection

FIGURE 5.16 *Reaching activity with muscle tone "normalized" and body in proper alignment.*

FIGURE 5.17 *The adult's right arm can simultaneously rock the buttocks and guide the child's legs apart.*

FIGURE 5.18 *Sitting astride a bolster and doing reaching activities to encourage extension with rotation of the upper trunk and shoulder girdle.*

of his face and body. The caregiver may then say his name and may point to different parts of the body. This social experience enhances self-awareness and body image.

The infant should not be allowed to become physically tight when seated on the bolster. Spasticity is noted when the trunk and/or arms pull down into flexion. If this happens, the bolster can be gently rocked from side to side in order to decrease the tone of the trunk and limbs. The slow rolling of the bolster is continued until tightness is sufficiently reduced so that the child can again sit with an erect spine and his arms can reach forward with straight elbows.

■ With the child seated astride a bolster, sawhorse chair, or adult's leg, trunk rotation and balancing reactions can be elicited by having him reach across his body with one hand to grasp objects such as popbeads or clothespins to put into a container. By having him reach far to the opposite side and upward, he will achieve maximal twisting of his trunk with an extended back. The infant should not be permitted to shift his weight onto one buttock and merely tilt his trunk laterally to the side. If this lateral bending of the torso is substituting for the desired trunk rotation, place the object farther forward. Then he will reach in a forward–sideward–upward direction and achieve trunk rotation with a straight spine.

■ Another means for achieving rotation of the trunk when seated astride a bolster or adult's leg is to have the young child reach down with both hands to pick up large objects from the floor. Reaching bilaterally helps to assure trunk rotation instead of lateral bending of the trunk (which is easier). Language can be stimulated by having the child pick up three-dimensional objects (and later pictures with a hard cardboard backing), identify the item, and then place it on the floor to the other side, so that he is rotating his trunk first to one side and then to the other.

■ If the child has started to "bunny hop" or "commando crawl," an alternative means of locomotion should be offered. It could take the form of a scooter board (see Appendix A), which holds the child's hips in extension, abduction, and external rotation while the trunk is angled upward to promote extension of back and arms.

■ The following position can be used for a wide variety of everyday activities which are necessary and enjoyable for the young child. The adult sits in a crosslegged (tailor) position, forming a "valley" in the lap. The infant's buttocks fit into this valley as he faces away from the adult. His body weight needs to be on his buttocks and not on his lower spine in order to inhibit the typical spastic pattern of the legs. Thus the child's hips and knees can be maintained in a position of relative flexion over the adult's crossed legs. The caregiver's own body can be used to support the child's back if necessary or can be withdrawn if support is not needed. This position facilitates dressing the spastic child, since the adult's hands are free and inhibition of spastic patterns is accomplished through the positioning. The activity can be done in front of a mirror if it is considered important for the caregiver and child to be able to view each other's faces.

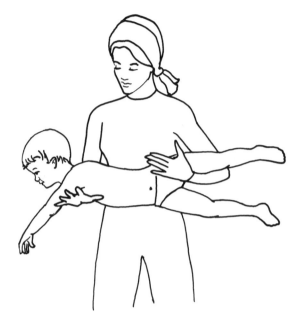

FIGURE 5.19 *Carrying the spastic child in prone.*

■   *Carrying Positions.* Depending on the child's physical capabilities, there are a number of carrying positions from which to choose. A common position is to have the infant straddle the caregiver's hip with his legs externally rotated and abducted (the opposite of the abnormal extensor pattern). The infant's trunk is rotated so that he faces away from the adult to view the surroundings; this twisting of the torso helps to keep it loose and flexible. The adult's arm supports the infant's buttocks and thigh. Thus support is kept to a minimum to encourage independent trunk control.

Another possible position useful in the case of the infant with flexor spasticity is to carry him in prone (see Figure 5.19). One of the adult's forearms is placed under the infant's shoulders to keep his arms forward. The other forearm is placed between the thighs, to keep one hip straight. As the other leg hangs loosely, the infant's pelvis is twisted to achieve rotation of the lower trunk. Thus the abnormal pull into flexion is inhibited, the trunk has more mobility due to the rotation, and the infant develops extension as he lifts his head.

■ *Sleeping Positions.* The normal infant moves frequently during sleep and assumes a variety of positions. However the spastic infant is often inactive and maintains a static, abnormal posture that reinforces his aberrant motor behavior. It is therefore important to introduce alternative sleeping positions that provide better body alignment. The desired positions may be initially introduced for short periods of time during the day or at nap time, until he becomes accustomed to the new posture.

In the prone position the young baby can practice lifting his head and possibly pushing up on his elbows before and after sleep as well as during periodic waking moments. This practice develops head and trunk extension, which will be required later to assume antigravity positions such as sitting. However a prerequisite for sleeping in prone is the ability to turn the head from side to side to allow for unimpaired breathing. This precaution is particularly relevant for a spastic infant who presses his head and shoulders down into the mattress when lying on his abdomen. Due to this spastic flexor pull, he may be unable to move his head to avoid possible suffocation.

An intervention for adapting the prone position to make it safe and therapeutically sound is to place a pillow or small roll under the arms and upper trunk of the infant. This keeps the arms elevated overhead and thus inhibits tight flexor pull of the head, shoulders, and arms. With the tightness reduced, the infant may prefer the prone position, since he is able to lift and turn his head to both sides more freely. Care should be taken that the pillow or bolster is not so large as to cause a marked curvature of the lower spine (lordosis or "sway-back"). A foam wedge with a vinyl or cloth covering may be used as an alternative to the bolster. The wedge supports the thighs and abdomen (thus preventing lordosis) and its gradual incline extends the upper trunk. (If used in a crib, the wedge should be cut to the crib's full width, to prevent the child from rolling off the wedge and being caught between it and the crib side.) The arms can be raised overhead in this position in order to further inhibit flexor spasticity. An overhead mobile stimulates desired head raising and arm reaching as well as visual exploration.

For the moderately to severely involved infant with marked

flexor spasticity, a side-lying position may be indicated since it inhibits the tonic labyrinthine reflex. In side lying, the infant sleeps with his head slightly flexed or in alignment with his spine, his arms forward, hips straight, and knees bent. The straight back and hips should help prevent further development of spastic flexion of the trunk and hips, which frequently becomes stronger with age. Bolsters or firm pillows can be used to maintain the spine and hips extended and the arms forward (thus preventing abnormal pulling down of the shoulders with elbow flexion). During waking periods the side-lying position encourages independent play (see side-lyer in Appendix A).

For the spastic child who tends to throw himself back into stiff extension, the prone positions described earlier are often desirable. They inhibit the tendency to press back with head and shoulders by keeping the arms forward. However, many infants with strong extensor tone cannot tolerate prone lying and will arch the body in an attempt to flip over onto their backs. They are most comfortable in supine because it reinforces the abnormal patterns to which they are accustomed: retraction of the head and shoulders, arching of the spine, extension of the hips, and possibly "scissored" legs. Sleeping in supine should therefore be avoided. If the infant cannot accept sleeping on his abdomen, the side-lying position is an alternative.

For the infant who is able to sleep only on his back, a hammock may be used. It can be hung inside a crib or even temporarily in a doorway very close to the floor. The child is placed in the hammock with his head flexed, shoulders and arms forward, and hips bent. The curvature of the canvas helps to maintain this posture, which is the opposite of his abnormal pattern of stiff extension. Occasional gentle swinging of the hammock will help to reduce muscle tightness. The hammock is also indicated for athetotic infants who throw themselves back into stiff extension.

Another adaptation of the supine position is to have a firm pillow under the head and upper trunk as well as a pillow under the knees. Thus the total extension pattern is inhibited by flexion of the upper torso and legs.

While assistive equipment (bolster, hammock, wedge) helps to maintain good positioning, the infant should have some flexible movement of his head, arms, and legs. He should not be locked into a static posture. The aids are used only as an interim step until the child has more independent control of desired movement. As he learns in his daily play to assume a variety of acceptable positions that can be utilized for sleeping, the adaptive equipment should be gradually eliminated.

■ *Standing Position.* A useful intervention for the child who is walking independently but poorly, in the spastic pattern described earlier, is the following procedure. First, spasticity is reduced, possibly employing the suggested interventions using a large beachball. Once the child has assumed the supported standing position from the ball (feet flat, hips in extension and external rotation, arms up on the ball), he can practice shifting his weight from one foot to the other. The adult assists by placing his hands on the child's hips and encouraging the side to side motion. Then the child is asked to place one foot on a low stool. With the adult's hands still stabilizing at the hips, the child is asked to roll the ball from side to side. Thus the child experiences weight shift together with good extension and rotation of trunk and arms. Care should be taken that the child does not pull downward with his arms.

Children with Hemiplegia

The hemiplegic syndrome in young children does not differ in principle from the quadriplegic or diplegic conditions. But it does pose very particular clinical problems, since the child with hemiplegia has one half of his body relatively intact. The hemiplegic child is capable of many so-called normal activities, although the one-sidedness in performing such motor skills is never normal in the true sense of the word. The sensorimotor integration of the two sides of the body, so important for normal neurodevelopment, seldom takes place in these children. Their development of bilaterality and later reciprocality tends to be incomplete. This limitation impedes perceptual development in general and the development of a normal body percept in particular (International Study Group, 1961).

Although the difficulties in movement experienced by the infant with hemiplegia may be most noticeable in the involved arm and leg, the trunk and neck are also affected. In addition, some hemiplegic children have facial and/or oral neuromuscular involvement and impaired vision in one or both eyes; speech and hearing problems may also be present. All symptoms are clinical manifestations of a brain lesion that the child acquired either *in utero* or in early infancy. However, children who experience accidents or other trauma resulting in hemiplegia at a later age present a picture very similar to that described here.

It should be kept in mind that it is the impaired function of the child's brain that is directly responsible for the local phenomena his musculature displays. Thus treatment and handling must take into consideration not only a particular local muscle but the child's entire body musculature. One must regard his total body in posture, movement, and balance, and pay great attention to his visual, auditory, and general sensory deficits. Intervention aiming simply at physical gains will give poor results if the child does not receive sensory preparation. For instance, tolerance and appreciation of touch and contact precede the ability to tolerate weight bearing. While formerly this sensory preparation was thought to be separate from gross motor intervention, the two are now considered interrelated and should be treated at the same time (Ayres, 1972).

There are two kinds of abnormal muscle tone found in the hemiplegic child: the spastic and the athetoid types. The former is by far the most common, and the discussion that follows pertains mainly to hemiplegia with spasticity. However, general principles can well be applied to the hemiplegic child with athetosis.

The patterns of spasticity in the child with hemiplegia are not unlike those found in an adult who has had a stroke (Bobath, 1970). The involved side may show spasticity within the trunk and thereby some increased degree of lateral trunk flexion. The shoulder may be pulled down (shoulder depression), and the pelvis may appear to approximate the rib cage. Very often this latter phenomenon is interpreted as a leg-length discrepancy and is treated as such. While true differences in leg length sometimes do exist, the spastic shortening of one side of the trunk is a far more common reason for the leg appearing to be shorter. It is not unusual for the hemiplegic child to keep his whole involved side somewhat behind the sound one during locomotion and other activities. This asymmetry seems related to the impaired sensory awareness of that side and the one-sided extensor spasticity of the trunk, which may tend to retract the shoulder and hip and cause the rib cage on that side to rotate backward. Thus the trunk of the hemiplegic child shows a combination of lateral flexion and backward rotation. As part of the spine, the neck will similarly show increased flexion toward the involved side. However the face is usually turned away from that side, probably due to the constant visual orientation away from the affected side. Depending on involvement of the child's vision, the opposite may sometimes occur. Typically, the hemiplegic arm shows dominance of overall flexor spasticity, while the hemiplegic leg shows dominance of extensor spasticity.

In the very young infant this asymmetry is less obvious. If the child has not yet begun to move much, the spasticity or athetosis may be only potentially there, ready to emerge as the child becomes more mobile. In the place of a more obvious asymmetry, he may display some primitiveness of the involved side while the sound body half shows steady development toward maturity. For instance, the involved leg may retain the froglike pattern of flexion–abduction–external rotation at a time when more extension is to be expected. It may also move in total patterns of flexion and extension when the other leg is beginning to exhibit independent knee and ankle movements. Similarly, if the infant uses his involved arm and hand at all (which he may very well do at this stage), primitive reach and grasp may never become modified into more mature patterns of movement.

The sensorimotor behavior of the more severely involved hemiplegic child is quite characteristic. The child will seldom tolerate touch, let alone pressure and weight bearing, on his involved side. There is an early and strong reluctance to use the impaired arm and leg. In fact the infant will appear to be tactually defensive on that side. Any attempt to bring the involved body half into the sphere of interest will usually result in resistive or defensive withdrawal. If the hemiplegic side is left alone because of this behavior, the child will probably neglect that half of his body completely and become adept in solving all locomotor, balancing, and manipulative tasks using only the sound body half. In the meantime, the few movements of the involved side that the child had originally mastered may deteriorate due to associated reactions. The involved side contracts reflexively, moving the limb into the spastic pattern. Consequently, orientation toward and exclusive use of the sound side is detrimental to a symmetrical development.

It is important to realize that even if the original lesion is not progressive, the child's exclusive use of only his sound side may arrest, or even cause deterioration in, the function of the involved side. Moreover, if the child is left to learn balancing and manipulative tasks with his sound side only, he may soon have to resort to greatly exaggerated movements of that side in order to manage. That is why many hemiplegic children show abnormal movements even of the nonaffected side. Prevention of this occurrence becomes a very important aspect of intervention.

The hemiplegic infant often skips important developmental milestones. For instance, he may not put his hands together in midline or bring the involved hand to the mouth. The development of eye–hand coordination becomes one-sided, as does the young baby's whole visual–motor exploration of his body. The hemiplegic infant fails to develop midline orientation and frequently perceives the center of his body as shifted toward his sound side. His posture becomes asymmetrical since he most often places his center of gravity (body weight) onto the nonaffected side. This pattern of weight distribution persists whether he is lying, sitting, kneeling, or standing, and it may lead to a disturbed sense of spatial relationships. For example, the child may bump into furniture with his involved side when moving about. The hemiplegic baby may also develop head and body righting reactions against gravity in an asymmetrical fashion. He will usually prefer to accomplish in only one set manner such motor tasks as rolling or coming up to sitting. His development of balance reactions will consequently also become asymmetrical.

The child's earliest mode of locomotion is often a kind of belly crawling (commando crawling) in which he drags along the floor with the help of his arms. It is very common to see the hemiplegic arm get tighter and tighter as a result of this repeated pulling into the flexion pattern. If excessive fisting of the hand has not yet occurred, it will usually become pronounced at this time. The affected leg may still be capable of primitive crawling movements and the child uses it to give himself the contralateral pattern necessary for forward propulsion. The leg on the sound side remains rather inactive in this belly crawling, which may confuse the observer. When the child starts to develop some sitting balance and arm support (which he usually does somewhat later than would normally be expected), he discovers a new form of locomotion: the typical one-sided hitching motion in sitting. Bearing his weight on the sound hip only, he pushes with his sound arm and pulls with his sound leg to propel himself forward. He tends to favor this mode of locomotion rather than normal creeping on all fours, which is a developmental task that he may skip altogether.

When the child is learning to get up to standing via kneeling and half-kneeling, he will do so by putting the involved leg forward. But instead of transferring his body weight over that foot, he will usually transfer it backward onto the sound leg (see Figure 5.20).

By this time he is already so accustomed to bearing weight on the noninvolved leg that he has a total one-leg stance, with the hemiplegic leg used merely as a prop. Since up to this point the involved arm may have been totally neglected and under the influence of associated reactions, it is now showing marked and increasing flexion. Although the hemiplegic leg shows an overall pattern of spastic extension in standing, with plantar flexion of the foot, it sometimes appears to be externally rotated at the hip. This external rotation is deceptive and usually depends upon the backward rotation of the pelvis. If the pelvis is brought forward

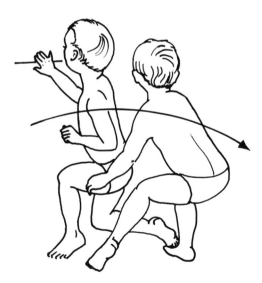

FIGURE 5.20 *Hemiplegic child transferring to standing via half-kneeling.*

into a neutral position, the typical internal rotation that goes with the whole spastic extension pattern will usually become obvious.

It could also be argued that in very young children the spastic extension is just beginning to impose itself upon the primitive froglike pattern of flexion–abduction–external rotation that has prevailed until now, and that this is the reason why the leg appears to be in flexion while in fact it is extensor spastic. With the child's increased ability to ambulate, this primitiveness is likely to disappear very quickly. With every step he takes there is an added influence of the extensor thrust elicited by the very touch of his forefoot to the ground. In the course of a few weeks this abnormal form of ambulation will usually cause pronounced extensor spasticity to develop in the child's entire leg. Despite this tendency toward greater extensor tonus, the hip remains in some degree of flexion. This hip flexion may be related to the fact that the child has never developed normal extension against gravity and as a result the trunk is now incapable of remaining erect in relation to the supporting leg. Thus in long-term cases the combined effect of a lack of normal antigravity action at the hip and the pull of the adductor muscles in the spastic extensor pattern may lead to permanent flexor deformities at the hip (Mathews, Jones, & Speiling, 1953). The adductor muscles pull the legs together and have a slight flexing effect on the hip joint. The inability to extend fully at the hip in a normal way will also necessitate hyperextension at the knee, particularly if the foot is stiff in plantar flexion. Sometimes the child with these patterns of movement is encouraged to put his heel down in walking. He can do so only by further hyperextending his knee and flexing the trunk toward the thigh, thus further accentuating his abnormal posture and movements.

The hemiplegic gait is usually a very fast one, more of a half-run than a walk. This may convey an impression of hyperactivity, and hemiplegic children are sometimes labeled as such. Although hyperkinesis may be present in some hemiplegic children, the youngster is not usually hyperactive in the true sense but simply has a problem keeping his balance in walking. Since he does not transfer his body weight over to his involved leg, the brief moment during which he does prop onto his involved leg is insufficient for the sound leg to take an adequate step forward. He therefore gives the impression of half-running or hopping as he tries to walk forward. Hemiplegic children who are not too severely involved will run much better than they walk. In running there is little necessity for transferring weight, since the body is kept more in midline while the legs are moving.

Another characteristic feature of the hemiplegic gait is the child's inability to bring the involved leg forward in a relaxed stepping manner. He lacks the dissociation of the pelvis from the trunk that normally enables one to drop the pelvis, relax the knee and swing the leg forward in a heel-strike step. Instead, the trunk is tight with spasticity, preventing pelvic relaxation. The leg is brought forward merely with the help of trunk spasticity as the child lifts and at best circumducts the total pelvis–leg into a forward propping position. The heel-strike never occurs, since it represents the ultimate in dissociated movement—a combination of pelvic relaxation, slight hip flexion, knee extension, and dorsiflexion of the foot.

When the hemiplegic child has to change direction, he will walk around in a circle instead of pivoting on one foot. He invariably turns toward his involved side, for the same reason that he will tend to roll in only one direction: the retraction of the shoulder and hip on his involved side makes it difficult for him to initiate turning around over the sound side. To take a step backward with the involved leg is quite difficult as well, because it requires independent extension at the hip in combination with knee flexion. It may be difficult to take a backward step with the sound leg also, but for a different reason. This maneuver requires bearing weight on the involved leg in combination with a relative forward rotation of the pelvis on that side. Since the overall inability to step backward makes it difficult for the child to keep his balance (backward stepping is a common automatic balance reaction), he falls frequently, especially toward his hemiplegic side. The arm and leg on the affected side do not assist in the weight bearing that is necessary for counteracting balance reactions to take place on the opposite side. The child may also fall toward his sound side, since he is incapable of automatically adjusting with countermovements of the involved side.

The involved arm of the ambulating hemiplegic child seems to increase in tightness through associated reactions and from the fear of falling, which generally makes the child tighter. So, an arm that originally may have been fairly functional and capable of some support and primitive grasping is at this stage very limited. Obviously the child does not develop a natural arm swing in his gait pattern, since the arm movements seen in a normal gait are secondary to counterrotatory movements between shoulder and pelvis. The counterrotation never develops because one side of the trunk is stiff with spasticity.

Intervention

The basic philosophy of intervention is to strive toward normalcy in the child's functioning where possible. Intervention should take into account every aspect of the child's sensorimotor deficits and strengths. Methods of therapeutic handling are basically designed to

1. Normalize tactile, proprioceptive, and kinesthetic input
2. Emphasize symmetry of body postures and movements, and encourage midline-oriented activities
3. Inhibit the deteriorating influence of associated reactions
4. Avoid the development of abnormal compensatory movements on the sound side
5. Prevent contractures and other deformities from developing, particularly in flexion of the involved arm and extension of the involved leg.

It is often possible to detect infantile hemiplegia at a very early date. Sometimes the earliest signs are manifested in the oral region as, for instance, consistent asymmetry of the tongue and lips in crying and smiling, or early feeding problems. It is true that there are other childhood syndromes that resemble hemiplegia, but from an intervention point of view there is little sense in waiting for a full-blown clinical picture to emerge before acting. The hemiplegic infant often displays symptoms that are primitive but not yet abnormal. Very early intervention may minimize and sometimes eliminate some of the problems that are likely to evolve if the child is allowed to continue his orientation toward the sound side (Bobath, 1967).

Much of this early intervention is naturally carried out by the parents of the infant. They can be taught to handle him during such daily activities as feeding, carrying, dressing, bathing, and playing in ways that will limit the effects of sensory disturbance and abnormal muscle tone (Finnie, 1975). To increase the infant's sensory awareness of the involved side, it is sometimes a good idea to tie a ribbon and bell around the wrist or ankle or both. In this way, every movement will give both auditory and visual feedback to the child. The baby can also be encouraged to bring both his hands and both his feet to the mouth and together in the midline. Both of his hands should be helped to touch various parts of his own body such as his abdomen and legs. In this way, parents may foster the development of a more normal body percept in their baby. To feel various textures and pressures in the open palm of the hand and on the sole of the foot will prepare the baby for future tolerance of weight bearing and locomotion. Visual and auditory tracking tasks that emphasize crossing the midline of the body in both directions are indicated. The hemiplegic infant will usually have difficulty in tracking the object past midline when the object is moved from his sound side toward his involved one. The child should be evaluated for the presence of a homonymous hemianopsia, a visual field defect on the involved side. In such a case he can be taught to compensate for the deficit by head turning.

Feeding time is a great opportunity for the caregiver to emphasize symmetrical postures in the baby. Feeding him in a face-to-face position facilitates eye contact between caregiver and infant—always important, and particularly so for the infant who has visual involvement—as well as midline orientation. If the baby needs some assistance with jaw, lip, and tongue control during feeding, it can also be well accomplished in the face-to-face position (see Chapter 6).

If the baby is bottle fed, his hands should be gently guided to hold the bottle. It is a very natural way to have both hands engage in the midline. It is also an activity that is repeated several times a day, which makes its therapeutic value inestimable. When the baby is ready to feed himself a cookie, he should consistently be given one in each hand. When he starts to drink from a cup, it is advisable to have one with two handles and let the baby hold it with both hands.

Dressing and undressing are natural activities that can easily be made therapeutic. The caregiver can name and have the baby look at his various body parts while dressing and undressing.

Dressing of the young infant should preferably be done in a supported position such as the one described for the infant with diplegia or quadriplegia, that is, with the adult in a crosslegged position and the baby seated in the valley of the lap. Both can be facing a mirror. The adult leans slightly forward so as to counteract the baby's tendency to thrust backward—which all children are likely to do at times when they are being dressed. While in a normal baby this does not adversely affect his overall motor development, it will be recalled that in a baby who displays spasticity the thrusting will perpetuate overall extensor spasticity and should be counteracted.

A good way for the child to learn to put on a shirt or a jacket in this position is to place the garment frontside down before him. The adult lifts the garment from the bottom and makes the armholes visible to the child, who is encouraged to put his arms through them. He is then told to raise both arms while the adult pulls the garment down over his head. Even when the child is later ready to put a jacket on by himself, this procedure is useful. It has two therapeutic components: the bilateral reach forward and the active raising of the hemiplegic arm overhead, which counteracts overall flexor spasticity.

Diapering may have to be done while the baby rests on his back. But if he tends to push his head back or push his body backward with his feet, it may be a good idea to diaper the baby in the prone position. The diapers can also be taped or pinned in an appropriate way to counter the tendency of the baby's legs to be either too close together or too far apart.

In bathing, it is important to create a comfortable and safe position for the baby in the tub and still allow him to enjoy water play. Sometimes a special bathtub seat on suction cups and with a seat belt is the solution to the problem. Or the baby can sit inside an ordinary inflated "doughnut" tube of correct size. When washing the child, strong rubbing of the hemiplegic side with the washcloth helps to foster sensory awareness. To encourage the infant to use both hands, numerous water games can be employed, such as simple splashing and playing with bubbles.

Generally speaking, the toys given to a hemiplegic child should encourage the use of both hands. From the beginning, rather large toys such as balls and cuddle animals can be employed to encourage bilateral reach and grasp, a developmental stage that the hemiplegic infant tends to skip entirely. It should be recalled that young babies reach and grasp with both feet also and this can easily be encouraged in the baby who is playing in the supine position. All "hold-on" toys, such as play cars with steering wheels, rocking horses with reins or handles, and tricycles with handlebars, are useful for the hemiplegic child. In his case, it may be a good idea to introduce the tricycle even earlier than one would with another child, in order to discourage early walking (for reasons that are discussed later in this section). As a substitute for walking, a tricycle can sometimes satisfy the child's need for mobility. It also encourages reciprocal use of the legs, which may prove helpful in future ambulation.

It is common to find that, to the extent that the child is capable of grasping with the involved hand, this is accomplished only with a total flexion pattern of the arm. An early goal of intervention is to have the child sustain a grasp regardless of the position of the rest of the arm. One way to accomplish this is to provide yarn or string or chains for the young baby to play with. As he holds on to one end, the adult pulls and tugs at the other, encouraging the baby to sustain his grasp all the while—thus providing mobility in the arm and shoulder. When he is older, such bilateral activities as hanging from a bar, climbing a ladder, or the like are to be encouraged. Producing musical sounds is always fun. Musical instruments that require bilateral use of the hands—such as cymbals, drums (with or without drum sticks), and triangles—are ideal for the hemiplegic child.

When the child has learned to walk, or while he is learning to do so, he can push a carriage with both hands—either a doll carriage or a sibling's actual carriage. There are also other push toys, such as a toy lawnmower, that may be appropriate for the child at this time. The important point is to have the child hold with both hands while pushing the toy.

Correct management of the hemiplegic child in terms of feeding, dressing, carrying, and the other aspects of general care are of great importance in his overall neurodevelopment. If the child is handled throughout his day in ways that consistently counteract his spastic tendencies, spasticity may have little opportunity to establish itself and such secondary deformities as contractures, scoliosis (curvature of the spine), or dislocation of joints can thus be avoided. As the child gains function of the involved side and learns to use it for practical purposes, these normal movements themselves help to ensure a more normal tonus (relative absence of spasticity).

In addition to special handling in the activities of daily living, gross motor development in a hemiplegic youngster can be further facilitated by the following suggestions. The reader is advised to refer to the section on normal motor development in considering their application.

1. When the infant starts to roll from supine to prone, he may tend to avoid rolling that is initiated with the involved side. He should be encouraged to roll in both directions.

2. When the infant begins to reach for objects, he should be encouraged to do so with both hands simultaneously (bilateral reach). This is equally important in the supine and supported sitting positions.

3. When the infant is supporting himself on elbows or extended arms in the prone position, he should be encouraged to reach out and grasp with the sound hand. This approach will develop his tolerance for weight transferring onto the involved side. He should also learn to pivot on his abdomen in both directions.

4. When the infant has learned to master the rolling patterns to the point where he can interrupt the movement and remain in a side-lying position supported on one elbow, he should be helped to do this on his involved as well as his uninvolved side.

5. Independent sitting should not be encouraged when it is accompanied by more pronounced retraction of the involved arm, greater than normal extension of the involved leg, and a rounded spine that does not show normal, straight antigravity extension. Prolonged sitting in this fashion will not lead to a correct sitting posture but will perpetuate overall spasticity. The baby needs to spend more time in the prone position to develop stronger symmetrical righting against gravity.

6. Activities in the prone and sitting positions should be encouraged to prepare the hemiplegic infant for creeping— a skill he may tend to skip entirely. The motor components

necessary for getting into an all-fours creeping position are developed in prone and sitting activities. The pushing up on extended arms and the spinal extension against gravity in the prone position are elements that will be utilized as the baby learns to assume the creeping position. Furthermore, the "breaking up" of the total extension pattern, which must occur before the baby can achieve normal sitting (spine extended, hips flexed), is also a necessary prerequisite for assuming the creeping position.

7. When the child has developed the ability to go from prone lying through side lying to a sitting position by pushing up with the sound hand, he should be encouraged to experience the same rotation into sitting using his involved side. This will be easier if the baby (a) has spent sufficient time on his abdomen transferring weight to the involved side by reaching out with the sound hand, (b) has practiced pushing up on extended arms in the prone position, and (c) has mastered normal rolling patterns in both directions.

8. When the child is learning to pull himself up to a standing position, his caregivers should intervene in such a way as to promote movements that are as normal as possible in terms of both their quality and their timing, bearing in mind all the components of this motor sequence. The baby should not be permitted to give undue preference to one side or the other in assuming the half-kneeling position that is a transitional component toward full standing. He should also be encouraged to hold on with both hands as he stands up.

9. At the stage where the baby has learned to cruise sideways, he should be encouraged to travel in both directions. Since he is using the same motor components as are required for pivoting in a circle in the prone-lying position, successful cruising will be related to the degree of success he has achieved in the pivoting pattern. Extensive experience in walking sideways is a critical factor in the development of leg extension with abduction and will help to prevent a later tendency to walk with the involved leg turned inward.

10. As the child begins to show signs of wanting to walk, it is of the utmost importance that he develop good standing balance

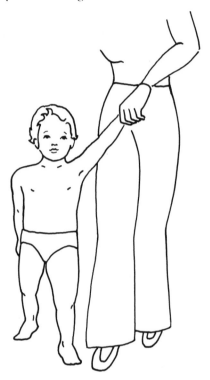

FIGURE 5.21 *To assist in achieving a correct walking pattern, the hemi-plegic arm is elevated overhead.*

before he starts to advance forward. It is worthwhile to dis-courage forward walking until the child has mastered good balance (a) in standing with his legs slightly apart, (b) in standing with his feet in the step position (one foot in front of the other) , and (c) in standing on one leg at a time. Again, his success in achieving normal walking will depend on a number of factors directly related to the overall gross motor development that has preceded the walking stage.

11. When the infant has developed forward walking, it is helpful to make a habit of slowing down his walk so that he has time to transfer weight properly. Holding his involved arm elevated overhead with the palm turned up aids a good walking pat-tern, since it facilitates weight shifting toward the hemiplegic side and inhibits flexor spasticity of the trunk and arm (see Figure 5.21) .

Since hemiplegic children tend to walk at a somewhat later date than their peers, it is common practice for a short leg brace to be employed to speed up the development of independent walking. Initially the brace may enable the child to stand and walk better. However after a short time the braced leg might starts to exhibit increased spasticity. A common feature of spasticity is that it increases when resisted in this confining manner. Therefore the child who wears a brace frequently shows not only exaggerated extensor spasticity but also some degree of flexor spasticity (spastic cocontraction). As a result, neurological overflow to the trunk and arm due to associated reactions may occur and overall function may deteriorate.

Since it is the *quality* of walking that is the major concern, bracing should be avoided—or at least delayed until therapeutic handling has improved the component requirements for a normal gait pattern. A tricycle with some simple adaptations may satisfy to some extent the child's need for mobility (see Appendix A). The child should be taught to hold the handlebars with both hands and pedal reciprocally.

Lengthening of the Achilles tendon, a common surgical procedure in hemiplegic children, may sometimes be necessary despite good physical management. For a child receiving therapeutic services, the timing of such surgery is crucial. The long-term results of a heelcord lengthening seem to depend on the degree of normal hip and knee control the child has acquired prior to surgery. It would therefore seem wise to wait until the child has developed normal antigravity action in the whole leg before surgery is performed. The Achilles lengthening introduces a flexion component; if the child is unable to combine this with extension at the hip and knee, he may tend to sink into flexion with the whole involved side. If therapy is successful in developing normal antigravity reactions and dissociated movements of the hemiplegic side, the child will be capable of combining dorsiflexion of the foot with extension at hip and knee, and surgery may be unnecessary. There are a number of other surgical procedures that may have to be considered later as the child grows, for either functional or cosmetic reasons, but they are beyond the scope of this present discussion.

The following samples of therapeutic and educational activities should be seen only as an adjunct to the preceding guide-lines for general handling. They are of little or no value in isolation. Moreover, they serve merely as *principles* of interven-tion; their application should be carefully geared to the particular situation and to the needs of the individual child.

Sample Activities and Interventions

■ To increase the infant's tolerance for bearing weight on the involved arm, he can be placed on his elbows in prone with his legs apart. In this position his weight is distributed equally on all limbs. As the child reaches out with the sound hand to grasp a ringing bell and then proceeds to explore its properties, his weight transfers over to the involved side. This activity overcomes the child's tendency to rest his body weight exclusively on the sound side, with the involved arm pressed inward against the chest, forearm pronated, and hand fisted. With the inclusion of such descriptive statements as "The bell is ringing" or "You are ringing the bell," the infant is given the appropriate language for reinforcing the cognitive concepts. This language technique is sometimes referred to as parallel speech.

■ The hemiplegic baby tends to sit asymmetrically, with his body weight on the sound hip and the involved leg held out straight and stiff. To promote increased tolerance of weight bear-ing on his involved hip, the child can be placed in a side-sitting position (see Figure 5.22). The hemiplegic arm can be gently guided up and turned so that the palm faces the ceiling. This position will eliminate the tendency of the hemiplegic side to pull down into flexion. After a while, attempts can be made to guide that arm down to the floor to a supporting position, maintaining an open palm.

■ To help the child achieve tolerance for bearing weight on the involved leg, his caregiver should have him kneel-sit with both hands resting on a supporting surface in front of him and gently assist him to kneel-stand while he transfers weight onto the affected leg. The hemiplegic arm should not be permitted to withdraw. As the child gains stability, "crazy foam" or shaving cream can be placed on a cookie sheet, and the child can practice making unilateral or bilateral arm movements across the slippery surface.

FIGURE 5.22 *Encouraging side sitting on the hemiplegic hip.*

FIGURE 5.23 *Standing up from straddle sitting with symmetrical weight bearing on hands and feet.*

■ The hemiplegic infant often gets to standing by shifting his weight onto the uninvolved leg only. This habit results in a pulling away of the impaired arm, and rotation of that whole side backward. One goal of the following intervention is to achieve simultaneous weight bearing on the arms and legs while the body is in proper alignment. The child sits straddling a roll or bench, with his hands in front of him on the roll, palms open, fingers spread. Maneuvering him from behind, the adult should have him stand up while he bears his weight on feet and hands equally, with heels well down and palms open (see Figure 5.23). A language goal can be incorporated into the motor activity by the adult singing a song like "Pop Goes the Weasel," stressing the concepts "up" and "down" as the child is moving up and down.

■ To elicit normal equilibrium reactions, the infant sits on a rather tall stool with his feet dangling. By cautiously lifting his uninvolved leg up, the adult causes the infant's weight to shift over to the involved side. The child should keep his balance by righting himself and not falling over to the affected side. This task necessitates desired compensatory movements of the head, arms, and trunk.

■ Balancing reactions in standing may be incorporated into block play or ring stacking by having the child stand at a table with his feet apart, legs turned out, and hands engaged in midline in front of him at shoulder level. While the infant experiments independently with the toys, the adult should cause him to stand and balance on his involved leg by gently lifting the other one up. By controlling at the raised leg one can facilitate small rotary movements of his body over the standing foot. Take care that the toes do not claw, and that the knee is mobile and not stiffly extended.

■ Often the hemiplegic infant does not use his involved arm for propping or for protection when falling over. To encourage him to do so, the child can be placed in the prone position lengthwise over a roll, while held from behind by the legs. Gentle tilting of the body weight over to the involved side may elicit a protective extension of the involved arm. The child is also likely to right his head and trunk away from the tilt.

Children with Athetosis

There is marked variability in the motor behavior of athetotic children. Indeed, Phelps and his associates describe a dozen types of athetosis (Phelps, Hopkins, & Cousins, 1958). Bobath (1966) has classified these children into four groups based on the quality of muscle tone:

1. The athetoid with spasticity is the individual whose muscle tone fluctuates between normal and hypertonus. Moderate spasticity is often present proximally, with athetosis at the distal joints.

2. The athetoid with tonic spasms has tonal changes from low to high. He is usually hypotonic, with intermittent tonic spasms. Therefore he tends to assume extreme postures of flexion or extension.

3. In the choreo-athetoid group, the muscle tone may fluctuate between low and normal or between low and spastic. Movements are large, involuntary, and disorganized.

4. In the rare condition of the pure athetoid, postural tone varies between hypotonic and normal. Particularly in the distal limbs, movements are characterized by involuntary, slow writhing.

Many children diagnosed as athetotic show overlapping between these four major categories.

Although the effect of fluctuating tone may be most obvious in the arms and legs, influences are also noted in the mouth, face, neck, and trunk. Intermittent extensor hypertonus, which affects the rest of the infant's body, may cause tongue thrusting and a marked open mouth. Therefore feeding, respiration, and speech are frequently affected. Due to involuntary movement and a lack of head control, the athetotic infant may have difficulty in visually attending to and focusing on his environment. Some children may be unable to isolate eye movement from head movement, causing them to lose postural control and fall when tracking an object across the visual field. Usually the arms are more physically involved than the legs. When the child tries to grasp an object, the fingers may hyperextend, rather than flex around it. This withdrawal reaction may result in an inability to hold onto objects.

Related to the abnormal fluctuation of tone is the poor coordination of antagonistic muscle groups. There is not the fine grading of contractions in opposing muscles that is necessary for smooth, fluid movement. Consequently, resulting movement is random, irregular, and jerky (Polani, 1959). The inability to coordinate movement causes extremes in motion, with midrange activities most difficult. For example, the child may find it easier to play with a toy that is at the extreme end of his extended reach or very close to his body rather than in any position in between. (This tendency is often related to an abnormal retention of the asymmetrical tonic neck reflex.) In spite of the effort required on his part, he will try to move, but he does so in a disorganized manner. An illustration of this would be the athetotic child who tries to color a simple shape centrally located on a piece of paper. The activity results in a "windshield wiper" type of movement, with scribbling over the whole paper. The degree of effort may also be apparent in random movements in other parts of the body (associated reactions) and possibly drooling.

Many young athetotic infants have low tone, with infrequent intermittent extensor spasms. There is an absence of normal right-ing reactions, even the most primitive neck-righting reaction. In the prone position, head movement is limited to minimal turning for survival breathing. The child's inability to extend his head while lying in prone may be due in part to the pull into flexion exerted by the tonic labyrinthine reflex. This reflex may also in-crease extensor tone in the supine position, causing the head to pull back into the mattress. The head is rarely maintained in mid-line. As it falls from side to side, the presence of an asymmetrical tonic neck reflex may be seen or perhaps just felt. These tonic reflexes, and the related failure to achieve head control, seem to have a dominating impact on the infant's motor development. The low tone and poverty of head movement thwart further devel-opment of trunk extension; thus there is no sustained postural control or proximal stability as a stable foundation from which to move.

The child with "mixed" athetosis and spasticity, whose tone varies from near normal to hypertonic levels, shows a different clinical picture. Very early in infancy there is a suspect degree of extensor tone. In the prone position there tends to be a greater ability to extend the head and trunk than one would normally expect in an infant of comparable age. If abnormal in tone, this extension will cause associated changes throughout the body. Extension of the trunk does not follow a sequential, segmental development down the back; rather, the whole spine extends as one unit; the mouth tends to be pulled open and extension in the limbs is accompanied by internal rotation and adduction. The amount of involvement will affect the degree of these tonal changes. Usually spasticity increases as the infant grows older. Initially it may only be detected as resistance to passive movement of the limbs in flexion, external rotation, and abduction.

As a result of fluctuating tone, incoordination, tonic reflexes, and associated problems, the athetotic child fails to develop control of a wide variety of selective movement patterns. Instead, he learns to utilize abnormal total patterns of flexion or extension to accomplish tasks. For example, he may hyperextend his head and trunk to roll as a single unit (log rolling) from the prone to supine position. Then he forcefully extends his total body to move along the floor. By abnormal arching backward of his head and upper trunk and thrusting his legs into extension, he propels backward. This motor behavior is contraindicated, since it reinforces abnormal extension patterns and prevents the child from acquiring the sensorimotor experience necessary to achieve and maintain a sitting position independently.

Another example of how a child may use total movement patterns for functional skill is overreliance on the asymmetrical tonic neck reflex. Without the acquisition of true trunk extension, there is little opportunity to develop proximal shoulder stability that enables the child to swing at or reach for a toy. He learns that, by turning his head toward an object, he can elicit consistent extension of his arm. The problem is that once there, neither the hand nor the elbow can function to bring the toy any closer. The only alternative is to turn the head to the opposite side and not look at the toy. Frustration is high, and involuntary associated reactions throughout his body increase. The effects of the asymmetrical tonic neck reflex on the face, neck, trunk, and legs cannot be ignored. The reflex is usually stronger toward one side than the other, which accentuates the child's asymmetry. There is great danger of such deformities as scoliosis (curvature of the spine) and hip dislocations at a future date if this activity is allowed to persist. Note that a physically intact baby may initially use this reflexive attitude for unilateral swiping. However, he is never limited to the stereotyped pattern, and its influence is inhibited around 4 months of age (Bobath, 1971).

Forward locomotion is usually accomplished by means of the "bunny hop." This position, similar to that assumed by the spastic child, is used primarily for the stability that it affords. The athetotic child supports himself on extended arms locked at the elbows. While "fixed" or postured in this manner, he can reinforce his head control by propping the head between the shoulders. The trunk is required to do very little stabilization in this position. The flexed and internally rotated legs provide a broad base of support. He progresses by springing forward on his locked arms and drawing his knees under him. Often the child sits by allowing himself to drop back onto the floor between his legs, in the "W" position (see earlier section on children with spastic diplegia).

As mentioned earlier, "W" sitting and "bunny hopping" are detrimental, since they discourage the development of extension, abduction, and external rotation, which are important components of a normal gait pattern. Bearing weight on locked arms and flexed hands reinforces the tendency toward fisting—which interferes with coordinated use of the hands. The posture is often maintainēd by the undesirable use of the asymmetrical tonic neck reflex. A preferable mode of locomotion is knee walking, since it encourages the development of hip extension and the isolation (dissociation) of hip from knee movements.

Mildly involved children may develop adequate stability and control to pull to standing and walk before 3 years of age. Usually they cruise walk using any surface that provides support and weight bearing for the arms. Random, involuntary movements can cause the child to lose his balance and fall. Or he may "lock" or "fix" in a characteristic stance (see Figure 5.24). There is a tendency to maintain the hips in extension by locating the center of gravity behind the hip joint and hyperextending the knees. There is an accompanying placement of the shoulders backward (the arms may be in a symmetrical or asymmetrical position). The head and neck frequently thrust forward in a "swan-neck" posture. The child usually has a "prancing" gait, marked by walking on the toes (equinus), scissoring the legs (adduction and internal rotation), and hyperextending the knees (recurvatum). As in other activities, grading and control of movements in the midrange

Figure 5.24 *Typical standing posture of the athetotic child.*

are extremely demanding. It is more difficult for the child to stand still than it is for him to keep moving.

Balance and equilibrium reactions may be present and fairly mature at all levels of development, but the physical response is usually exaggerated and disorganized. In an effort to maintain his balance, the child overreacts in his movements. As he grows older, he learns to hold himself in rigid patterns, to prevent extraneous motions while he is attempting tasks. Reliance on these abnormal, stereotyped, "tensing" postures, which become increasingly evident around 5 or 6 years of age, is to be avoided.

Intervention

A primary aim of intervention with the athetotic child is to prevent or keep to a minimum his involuntary movements. They are a major obstacle to his gaining functional control, and there is always the danger of these movements being incorporated into his habitual movement patterns. Therefore, controlling the amount and type of stimuli presented to the child is important. Tasks that require the manipulation of objects should be presented only when the child is well supported or when he has developed enough head and trunk control to be stable while using his hands. Extreme effort increases the athetotic movements. For many of the children, requiring them to maintain proper body alignment against gravity while engaged in a manipulative task is too demanding. If the child is to maintain a desired body posture, stimuli should be presented that require only observation. When manipulative tasks are required postural support should be provided. However, the athetotic child tends to become dependent on any support given to him, and care must be taken to provide the minimum degree of support necessary for his safety. Thus he is protected while still encouraged to function to his maximum ability.

Initially, intervention is focused on increasing head and trunk control (Semans, 1967; Stockmeyer, 1972; Voss, 1972). It is essential that the baby develop proximal stability. He should be placed in positions of weight bearing, such as sitting or kneeling, to encourage holding his body against gravity (stabilization of the proximal joints). When the infant can sustain a posture, he should experience slow, graded weight shifting in that position. For example, on hands and knees he can rock forward and back, side to side, and obliquely at a diagonal. In addition he should slowly raise and lower himself by flexing and extending his elbows. This activity will help to develop (*a*) stability around the shoulders and (*b*) control of arm movement in the midrange. For the child with fluctuating tone, it is generally easier to learn to grade movement patterns while bearing weight. Once the infant has mobility in weight bearing, he is prepared to initiate the movement pattern into space without eliciting extraneous movements.

Another factor relevant to intervention with the athetotic child is to eliminate or reduce use of the asymmetrical tonic neck reflex. Activities and stimuli should be presented in the midline to avoid eliciting the reflex. The child needs a relatively calm atmosphere in which to learn to impose control over his movements. A distracting atmosphere reinforces his motor hyperactivity. Consistent feedback in the form of visual, tactile, and verbal cues are necessary to help him adjust his posture and grade his movements, to make him aware of the desired movement patterns and consciously avoid the abnormal ones. He needs to duplicate a movement repeatedly over time before he can internalize the control.

Goals and strategies for intervention must be individualized for each child and continually reevaluated. Although athetotic infants have in common fluctuation in tone and poor stability against gravity, the nature of their motor pathology varies. The applicability of the following interventions has therefore to be specifically evaluated for each individual.

Sample Activities and Interventions

■ With many athetotic infants, the development of head and trunk control (proximal stability) is better achieved in a sitting than in a prone position. Upright, the child has to work against the greater effects of gravity and there is proprioceptive input of weight bearing down the axis of the body. This often results in greater stability of the head and trunk, with fewer flailing movements.

However, with the severely involved child a side-lying position is useful for independent play. External support, in the form of bolsters, pillows, or a side-lyer (see Appendix A), may be required to maintain the posture and prevent extensor thrusting. The position facilitates bilateral engagement of the hands—bringing them together and to the mouth—and inhibits the asymmetrical tonic neck reflex. Noisy bracelets or toys tied to the arm encourage reaching and swiping skills.

■ A child with developing trunk stability may be placed in a kneeling position before a large sheet of paper taped to the wall. An extended arm with open hand against the wall provides proximal support and, through weight bearing, inhibits extraneous movements. Initially the paint containers may rest on a small table at hip height within easy reach, so that the task requires only mild weight shifting to maintain the position while painting. Care must be taken to ensure good alignment of the head, trunk, and hips. As motor skill increases, the paint cans are placed on the floor. Now the child must grade leg and arm movements within the middle ranges as he lowers his body to reach the containers and then raises it to full kneel-standing to paint. Thus differentiation, or dissociation, of movement is achieved between hip and knee, shoulder and elbow.

■ Dowel adaptations can be employed to foster a good sitting position. The child is seated at a table to which a vertical peg or a horizontal bar on upright supports has been secured at partially extended arm's length. Holding the dowel discourages the tendency to sit with hiking and pulling back of the shoulders. The child can either place both hands on the dowel adaptation, to maintain body symmetry while observing his surroundings, or he can hold with one hand (to prevent shoulder and arm retraction) while engaged in a unilateral activity. The placement of the dowel should be periodically varied to avoid the child's locking into a rigid pattern. The dowel can be secured by suction cups or screwed into the table top (see Appendix A).

■ Placement of the seat belt in the wheelchair, regular chair, or standard stroller is important. As a general rule the seat belt should come up and across the child's hips at a 45° angle and clasp over the groin. The pull of the belt is then down and backward, keeping the buttocks firmly in the seat. In contrast, the seat belt strapped around the waist is usually uncomfortable and ineffectual. Pressed against the soft belly, it pinches and interferes with respiration. Without control at the hips, the child slides forward under the belt; eventually the belt is at chest level and he is "hanging" on it. Since the hips are a key point of control for the body, having the seat belt bisect the hips at a 45° angle is generally indicated, regardless of the child's diagnosis.

■ A vinyl- or cloth-covered, hard foam wedge attached to a chair seat, with the thick end of the wedge facing outward, provides hip flexion which inhibits extensor thrusting in the moderate to severely involved athetotic child. The hips should be placed well back in the chair, with the spine erect. Body weight is supported on externally rotated, abducted legs and the feet rest flat on the floor. The wedge can also be made of wood in a rolled-seat fashion, with a rounded edge at the knees; the surface of the seat is made of wooden strips, to allow for air circulation.

In general, it should be noted that the use of any adaptive equipment should be viewed as only a temporary measure until the child learns to control his movements.

Children with Ataxia

The diagnosis of ataxia in the young infant is complicated by a number of factors. First, ataxic movements usually become more pronounced over time; they may not be noted initially. A movement that is considered ataxic in the adult may be quite appropriate for the normal infant whose neurological organization is immature. Also, the baby who is later identified as ataxic is often floppy in the early months. Moreover, a case of pure ataxia is seldom seen; usually it is accompanied by athetosis, spasticity, or both.

The child whose primary diagnosis is ataxia has poor balance, lacks coordination, and at times exhibits tremorous movements, which are related to the instability of his body against gravity. Usually the infant has low muscle tone, but in some cases muscle tone is normal. He is unable to contract opposing muscle groups appropriately to achieve stability and fluid movement. As a result, the child has difficulty sustaining a posture or shifting postures in a coordinated manner. Righting and equilibrium reactions are often unreliable and develop later than normal. Postural instability may make the child fearful, causing him to lock himself into a few secure positions.

The infant may find it difficult to initiate movement. When movement is begun, it is often jerky and excessive in range. Movements tend to be in primitive patterns of flexion or extension, and the execution of movements that require a blending of the two is demanding (e.g., the combination of shoulder flexion and elbow extension in reaching forward). Stiffness in the trunk often appears between 8 and 10 months of age and limits rotation. For the ataxic infant, rotation of the pelvis while the shoulders are stationary is usually more difficult than the shoulders twisting while the pelvis is stationary. Poor rotation of the generally immobile trunk increases ataxic movements and accentuates unsteadiness in moving from one position to another.

The signs of ataxia may become more obvious as the baby gets older. As he begins to assume more upright postures and the influence of gravity is increased, the stabilization necessary in head, trunk, and limbs to maintain a firm position often proves to be inadequate. In the attempt to steady himself, the child may overtense his muscles. In the older child, purposeful reaching may be characterized by a distal, "wavering" tremor, which increases when he attempts a task requiring effort (Walsh, 1963).

The ataxic child shows a delay in attaining developmental skills and may skip some. Particularly difficult are those motor skills that require a combination of flexion and extension patterns, or rotation of the trunk (such as creeping on all fours and side sitting). If standing is achieved, it is with a broad base and hyperextended knees. Walking occurs late and is usually slow, clumsy, and staggery. There is rarely an arm swing. Since equilibrium reactions are usually overexaggerated and unreliable, the child often stumbles and falls. When walking, he may visually fixate on an object in the environment to help sustain his posture.

The infant with ataxia may have other, associated problems. Nystagmus (rapid, tremorous movements of the eyes) may be present. Speech may be delayed and articulation slurred. The voice quality is frequently "shaky."

Intervention

Therapeutically, the ataxic child needs graded movements into and out of antigravity positions. As noted, many of these children learn to stiffen the trunk abnormally, to increase proximal stability. To avoid this development, they should experience rather speedy weight shifting in these positions: prone on elbows, sitting, all-fours, kneeling, and standing. In addition, it is important to focus on transitions from one position to another, to prevent their becoming limited to a few stereotyped movement patterns and postures. While the child is developing control in moving between positions, he should be temporarily stopped if the movement becomes disorganized.

As the infant progresses motorically, he should spend plenty of time playing in the kneeling position, since it provides weight bearing on flexed knees while developing hip stability. The child should be observed carefully to ensure that he is not subtly flexed at the hips and compensating with a swayed back (lordosis). The acquisition of good trunk, hip, and knee stability and mobility is necessary to avoid the later tendency, in standing, to hyperextend the knees. To prepare for walking, the child should be encouraged to practice shifting his weight from one leg to the other, side to side, and back and forth. This activity can be accompanied by rhythmical music.

Thus, intervention should concentrate on executing body movements while bearing weight on the limbs. Tasks to refine distal control will be futile if proximal control and stability are lacking. Requiring the child to concentrate on fine manipulation may exacerbate his tremors without improving his dexterity, because fine visual–motor coordination is based on adequate head and trunk support. Repetition of movements that gradually progress from gross to fine is required, so that responses become reliable. At all times one must be aware of body tone; activities that increase the ataxic tremors or stiffening should be avoided.

The following sample activities are intended for the educational and therapeutic management of infants with essentially pure ataxia. However, since children with ataxic signs frequently have a mixed involvement (with spasticity and/or athetosis), the great variations in their movement behavior necessitate individual program planning.

Sample Activities and Interventions

■ Having the ataxic infant on a prone board (see Appendix A) serves many purposes. It promotes increased stability in the upright position by encouraging weight bearing on the hips and legs in proper alignment, and the hands are free for activities requiring more finely coordinated movements. For example, self-feeding demands (*a*) good head and trunk alignment (which also facilitates normal swallowing; (*b*) control of the oral musculature, and (*c*) visual–motor coordination of the hands. By assisting in accomplishment of the first requirement, the prone board facilitates better control of oral and hand movements.

■ Lightweight, slippery, and very small toys may increase the incoordination characteristic of the athetotic and especially the ataxic child. Toys of greater weight, such as those made of wood or heavy rubber, are easier for such children to manage. Sand play provides some resistance to movement and is excellent for a multiplicity of therapeutic and educational purposes. Finger painting with pudding or thick, nontoxic paint may be a more realistic expectation than use of a paint brush.

■ Bathing the ataxic child who has poor sitting balance is often an exasperating and fatiguing chore for the caregiver. A commercially available infant bathtub seat may be helpful (see Appendix A). Since it has a low back, it provides some support while still requiring trunk control; suction cups on the base keep the chair from slipping, and there is a seat belt for those infants who need it. In this position, the child can participate in washing, socialize with the caregiver, and play with floating toys. For older children or those requiring more stability, a meshed plastic laundry basket can provide back and lateral support while in the tub.

■   During daily activities, the child can wear a weighted vest to increase postural tone and stability against gravity. Small sandbags or metal weights are sewn onto the garment in symmetrical placement. This intervention is indicated only if the child has developed good body alignment and good mobility in his supporting limbs.

Children with Hypotonia

There are innumerable types and causes of hypotonia in infants. For the purpose of this discussion, children with hypotonicity will include (*a*) the Down's syndrome population and (*b*) the "floppy" infant (who may later develop athetosis and, sometimes, spasticity or ataxia). These children are characterized by a combination of abnormally low muscle tone, hypermobility of the joints, and delayed motor development. The low body tone is usually of symmetrical distribution, involving head, trunk, arms, and legs. These babies are frequently described as looking and feeling "like rag dolls" (Paine, 1963).

Due in part to low tone, hypermobile joints, and diminished proprioceptive sensation, the infant may assume unusual attitudes and show little interest in readjusting his posture for better alignment. The froglike position is frequently encountered and is typically assumed during sleep. In this pattern the chest appears flat; the hips flexed, abducted, and externally rotated; and the arms flexed, with hands fisted. Remaining in a static position for prolonged periods of time may lead to deformities. For instance the froglike posture may encourage hip dislocation (Dubowitz, 1969).

The floppy infant usually experiences an increase in muscle tone with age, consequently his diagnosis may change. When muscle tone begins to develop, it frequently takes the form of intermittent extensor spasticity. This development may be related to the constant tactile input the child receives in prolonged lying in supine. He may learn to propel himself on his back by kicking into extension. An asymmetrical tonic neck reflex often becomes apparent with the emergence of this extensor thrusting.

Many hypotonic infants appear unresponsive to the environment. They show little interest in exploring their bodies by playing with their hands and feet and are generally inactive, dependent, and self-contained. The baby may stare blankly at fingers or past toys to an unfocused point in space. In contrast, some infants with Down's syndrome are active and socially responsive. The hypotonic baby may have shallow breathing and little sustained phonation, even when crying. Feeding can be a problem, due to poor head control and the usually protruding "floppy" tongue.

As discussed earlier in this chapter, two major achievements in normal motor development are (a) the ability to extend and move against gravity; and (b) the ability to maintain positions with stability. The "floppy" or Down's syndrome infant usually develops these abilities at a much slower rate than the normal child, partly because of low muscle tone. He may have difficulty developing the extension and stability of the head, upper trunk, and shoulders that are necessary for the normal prone progression —lifting the head, resting on forearms, and raising the head and chest on straightened arms. When pulled to sitting from supine, there may be a head lag, sometimes accompanied by facial grimacing as he attempts to keep his head up. The infant may have insufficient trunk extension to straighten his back, and, if placed in a sitting position, he may fall forward with head and chest between the legs. Although he may later be capable of maintaining the sitting position, it is likely to be with rounded back and head held forward. Since he does not have the muscle tone and proximal stabilization to function adequately against gravity, the infant seems oppressed by his weight. He may therefore be limited in his ability to investigate his surroundings and interact with his family. He may turn to self-stimulation such as hyperventilating, playing with his tongue, and head banging. These behaviors should be replaced with alternate activities.

When the hypotonic child eventually achieves standing, he utilizes a wide base of support: the legs are turned out, the hips are bent, the lower back is arched. The upper trunk may be rounded, with the arms dangling and rolled in. Due to low tone, the trunk responses may be limited, thus inhibiting effective equilibrium reactions. Standing activities should not be encouraged until the child has the prerequisite skills necessary for proper body alignment and stability.

Since these infants feel limp and fragile, there is a tendency to carry and handle them like very young babies. Parents tend to hold the infant so securely that he is not required to develop head and trunk support. Such babies are often considered to be "good," since they are quiet and have little active movement. This dependency is frequently reinforced unknowingly by the parents. For example, a 2-year-old who is unable to maintain a stable sitting position may habitually be dressed and undressed while lying supine, whereas a normal 2-year-old child is dressed in a sitting position, so that he can observe and assist with dressing. Lying flat on his back, the hypotonic child cannot see what is happening and is less involved in the activity. If he does not make any attempt to slip his arms into the sleeves, his mother may stop coaxing him to try. Thus the auditory and visual stimulation that lead to the emergence of body awareness may be denied unless the caregiver perceives the need to provide continual enrichment throughout all stages of the child's development.

Intervention

A major principle of intervention with the hypotonic child is to provide him with appropriate stimulation, which he may lack as a result of a multiplicity of factors. The choice, variety, and intensity of cognitive–sensorimotor stimulation should be systematically graded to meet the infant's specific developmental needs. The child may have difficulty integrating stimuli if he is being "bombarded" through all the senses. Experiences should be selectively chosen for their educational and therapeutic value, and introduced gradually so as to judge the child's response. An optimal environment supplies sensory input, safety to seek and explore, variety, and repetition. It is through constant interaction within the home that the child develops sophisticated motor and language skills, spatial perception, and social-emotional independence.

With his muscle tone raised to a more normal level through special handling, the child may be able to achieve certain motor behaviors that were previously beyond his ability. Through repetition of these behaviors while assisted by an adult, it is hoped that he may eventually learn to perform the motor skills independently.

Intervention initially focuses on the development of head and trunk control. To stimulate general muscle tone throughout the body, the child can be carefully bounced on the adult's lap or on a beachball or other inflatable equipment. During stimulation in the prone or sitting position, it is important that the child's head, trunk, and limbs be in good, symmetrical alignment. Since he should experience normal extension patterns against gravity, disorganized postures or responses should be avoided. For example, if the child is bounced while straddling an adult's lap (or one leg), his head should be in midline and the back as erect as possible. The bouncing movement will then give the child the feeling of bearing weight on his buttocks and may stimulate a contraction of the trunk muscles—resulting in greater stability with an extended spine. Bouncing will also stimulate his overall activity level.

Firm joint compression in antigravity positions facilitates a contraction of the muscles crossing the joints, thus increasing proximal stability. To achieve the best effect, the joints to be compressed should be as much in extension as possible (Voss, 1972). For instance, to promote kneel-standing with erect body alignment, the adult should hold the child's waist with a hand above each hip (superior portion of the pelvis). By repeated firm pressing downward simultaneously with both hands, extension of the hips is facilitated to achieve postural stability. For the younger infant, extension of the head and upper trunk in the prone position can be encouraged by placing him on a hard foam wedge, with the head and upper trunk overhanging the thick end of the wedge and the elbows resting on the ground. Joint compression from partial weight bearing on the elbows helps to stimulate the shoulder musculature to contract and this increased proximal control makes it easier for the infant to lift his head and extend his upper spine against gravity. Greater joint compression can be provided by applying intermittent sustained pressure on the child's shoulders.

The infant should be continually reassessed regarding the nature and distribution of his muscle tone. The tendency to lie habitually in the supine position, thus acquiring extensor spasticity, should be discouraged. Instead, developmentally appropriate movement patterns and postures should be promoted. Continuous observation is required, since some floppy infants experience marked tonal changes within a period of a few weeks.

The wide continuum of normal motor development makes the achievement of "milestones" of only limited significance. Important are the learning processes or components that must be achieved before a developmental skill can be attained and later generalized to new situations. Information on the quality of performance and the presence of movement components provides a more complete developmental evaluation than does the noting of major milestones. Thus, among the critical questions are the following:

1. Is there variety of movement?
2. Does the infant move each side of the body with equal effectiveness?
3. Is he able to isolate movements and coordinate movement patterns?
4. Is there a motor progression against gravity?
5. Are his arms free to reach out from a stable trunk?
6. Is there physical responsiveness to environmental stimuli, peers, and adults?
7. Must the child be passively taken through the movement activity before he demonstrates the interest or ability to participate in the task?
8. Which sensory modalities (i.e., visual, vestibular, auditory, tactile) seem to assist the child in wanting to perform motor activities?

Listed below are a few examples of special handling that can be incorporated into the everyday care of the hypotonic infant. The activities enable the infant to acquire more normal movement patterns while discovering his environment. These children need consistent, carefully graded stimulation to achieve their developmental potential.

Sample Activities and Interventions

■ There are endless possibilities for general stimulation to foster the infant's awareness of his senses and to stimulate movement. A few examples include rolling on textured surfaces, such as a rug or grass; playing with water, dough, or sand; bouncing on inflatable equipment; playing such musical toys as a drum or xylophone; and negotiating an obstacle course. It is also beneficial to rub the child's body with hand lotion, baby powder, or other materials of varying texture.

■ The hypotonic baby should not be permitted to sleep in the froglike posture. To prevent the deformities that can follow from this positioning, he can be placed on his back in a hammock or on a partially inflated air mattress. This will keep the arms and legs in neutral alignment with slight trunk and head flexion and may stimulate the baby to engage in hand and feet exploration in the midline of his body. If the hammock is mounted in a crib with sides that raise and lower, the head end of the hammock can be raised, changing the baby's spatial orientation to increase his view of the room. Other possibilities to inhibit the frog posture are side lying or sleeping between two long bolsters in the prone or supine position.

■ An "umbrella" stroller—collapsible stroller with a hammock-like vinyl seat (see Appendix A)—provides adequate support for the baby who has little or no trunk and head control. However, as the infant develops, external support should be gradually reduced. He should have only the minimal support required for his safety.

■ When the infant has developed enough extension against gravity in the prone position to push up on extended arms but has insufficient stability to maintain the all-fours position, he can be placed over a small bolster or rolled towel in the quadripedal posture. While the roll provides some chest support, the body gains experience of what the all-fours position feels like. Occasionally an adult can push down on the infant's shoulders and hips with firm, sustained pressure. This will (1) increase proprioceptive awareness of weight bearing and (2) provide greater stability around the proximal joints by increasing muscle tone.

As the child develops control of this position and acquires enough balance to shift his weight backward and forward, and side to side, the roll can be reduced in size or it can be entirely eliminated. In this sample intervention the child's arms are engaged in maintaining his posture. Thus the adult must use his imagination to sustain the child's interest and maximize learning. As an educational experience, a windup toy can be utilized to demonstrate causality. With the infant observing, the toy is activated and placed on the floor in front of the child. When the toy stops, the adult should wait for the infant to indicate that he wants it reactivated. Numerous repetitions of various such activities may be required before the infant can conceptualize the cause–effect relationship.

CHAPTER 6
PRE-SPEECH

$\mathbf{I}$N THIS program guide, the term *pre-speech* refers to the developmental period that precedes the first meaningful word. The skills that emerge during this period form some of the foundations on which oral communication is laid. However, it is necessary to remind the reader that these skills are not the only factors necessary in developing oral communication; therefore a child who achieves the developmental milestones described here may not necessarily develop speech. This is an important concept to impart to parents, so that realistic goals can be established and false hopes avoided in the "pre-speech and feeding therapy" program.

Normal Pre-Speech Development

The skills necessary for the development of speech are begun within the first few minutes of life. The coordination of the infant's oro-facial structures and the respiratory mechanism needed for voice production and articulation are being developed through his oral reflexes and the oral movements of feeding and play (Bosley, 1965).

Oral Development and Feeding

As the normal newborn is being fed, certain reflexive phenomena can be observed. The first is when the child's face is

The major contributor to this chapter is Leslie Davis.

183

touched around the region of his mouth: he turns his head in the direction of the stimulation and opens his mouth. It seems as if the infant knows exactly where the food is being presented. This rooting behavior can be observed any time the infant's face is touched, except immediately after the baby has been fed. It is not until the baby is approximately 3 months old—or later if the child is being breast fed—that the rooting reflex becomes integrated and modified. Now he is able to respond differentially to a touch around the mouth during play or the touch of the nipple during feeding.

Observing the infant closely, one may be able to determine a highly rhythmic pattern to the sucking and swallowing as the baby nurses. It is a reflexive action (the suckle–swallow reflex), which allows the infant to close his lips automatically around the food source, suck repeatedly, and then swallow. As this reflex diminishes, between the ages of 2 and 4 months, the caregiver may notice a change in this rhythmic pattern: the baby has developed a more voluntary sucking action and a more independent feeding pattern.

Parents of infants often report that their child appears to be chewing. They observe a repeated up and down biting action during play or feeding when the lips or gums of the infant are touched. This reflexive behavior (bite reflex) appears at approximately 1 month and disappears at approximately 6 to 8 months, when a more rotary action of the jaws is apparent—usually at the time when the infant has begun putting his fingers or toys in his mouth and thereby adapting to sensation in and around the oral musculature. Although the baby has been able to bring his hands to his mouth since birth (sometimes *in utero*), this activity seems to become more purposeful during the 5- to 7-month period.

The protective gag reflex is present throughout an individual's life. However, since the newborn tends to have a very strong reaction to stimulation, he gags easily. The more the baby continues to explore his world by mouthing, the more he learns to tolerate oral sensation. Oral play helps him to accommodate to a variety of sensations, thus reducing the strength of the gag reflex (Mysak, 1968; Sheppard, 1964). It is important that the infant's play be allowed to include putting harmless objects into his mouth.

This oral exploration gives him an opportunity to experience various textures, temperatures, sizes, and shapes and thereby helps to set the groundwork for language and cognitive learning.

In the early stages of development, babies experience the sensation of movement of the oral structures, and this serves a vital purpose in developing control of oral movements. Between 1 and 3 months the infant begins to play by making noises, the first sounds occurring at random. Later however, he may deliberately attempt to reproduce the movements and sounds that earlier had been produced involuntarily. These playtime activities help to make him aware of how it feels to move his tongue or to press his lips together to create sounds such as "ma-ma." This activity apparently produces a pleasurable sensation, since the child recreates the feelings over and over again (Bosma, 1967). How these playful sounds become meaningful words is discussed in the chapter on language development.

Another important factor in developing independent oral movements is feeding, which serves as a rehearsal for oral movements that may eventually become integrated into sounds. As early as 4 to 6 weeks of age, when the caregiver presents food in a spoon for the first time, the infant closes his lips on the spoon using a lip action that resembles the movements for the sounds of "m," "b," and "p." It is no wonder that mothers often use the expression "uh-mm" to describe what they want baby to do with his dinner. This expression grew out of the pattern the lips form as they eagerly open at the sight of the spoon and then close tightly to remove the food.

When normal sucking and swallowing occur, the baby uses an upward and backward motion of the tongue to work the liquid from the nipple and propel it backward to be swallowed. These movements help to shape the throaty noises one hears while the baby is drinking.

Typically, the infant is breast or bottle fed in a semireclined position, either in the caregiver's arms or in an infant seat. However, supporting the child so that his head is upright may make it easier for his tongue to move in the sucking pattern just described. The upright posture also provides direct face-to-face contact, which is important to a 2- or 3-month-old baby who is beginning to watch carefully the facial movements of those who are relating to him. Direct, upright, face-to-face contact is therefore important to the child's pre-speech and language development.

The introduction of foods of different consistencies may also contribute to the child's oral abilities. The transition to solid food is not a dramatic overnight change. Often, by the time the baby has developed enough head control to be placed in a high chair (approximately 4 to 6 months), his caregiver will have introduced new consistencies of soft foods. At this time, junior baby foods will begin to compose the major part of the diet. Finger foods, such as teething cookies and vegetables, are also important at this point. The texture of more solid food encourages the child to move his tongue from side to side in his mouth for more efficient chewing. Children do not need teeth before they eat textured foods; in fact textured foods often help the baby to teethe more easily.

By the time the baby is 8 months old, it is important for him to experience some coarser table foods. Clinical observation has shown that children who are denied the opportunity to chew between 6 and 9 months of age may develop hypersensitivity to the feeling of solid food in their mouths (Mueller, 1973). Chewing provides the young child with an opportunity to practice coordinating the movements of the tongue, teeth, and cheeks. During chewing, the tongue "learns" to move very rapidly from side to side and from front to back. Since the recommendations of physicians in regard to types and kinds of food vary so greatly, it is advisable to check with the infant's pediatrician before changing the baby's diet.

Between 8 and 10 months, as the child begins to finger feed, his caregiver may notice that he does not wish to be fed with the spoon. The baby is developing a degree of independence (see Chapter 9). During this period, mothers often become anxious that the amount of food the baby self-feeds is not sufficient. To coax the child to eat more food, they may create imaginative games, such as "Here is the car and you are the garage, open wide." It is an important period of language stimulation, fun and growth for the baby, and continuing interaction between parents and child.

When children are beginning to finger feed, cup drinking is generally introduced. As the baby begins to drink from the rim of the cup, he develops lip sucking (a "drawing in" of the liquid) that is not the same as the primitive suckle–swallow reflex described earlier. The child must learn to integrate breathing with the new rhythm of drawing in and swallowing. This coordination is accomplished more easily if he sits erect. Drinking from a cup in a semireclined position is more difficult, as noted by those who attempt to take liquids while lying in bed. During the early stages of cup drinking, the baby will often pull away from the cup to take a breath while his mother is still tilting it to make the liquid available. The child is developing the timing necessary for sipping, swallowing, and breathing.

By the time the baby is a year old, he is ready to achieve independent, consecutive swallowing (one sip after another without stopping). Mothers often introduce cups with spouts to avoid spilling. Although spout cups help to keep the baby clean, they do not foster development of the coordination of lip closure, swallowing, and breathing. The spout is similar to a nipple on a bottle, since the child sucks at the spout as he would at the nipple (with his mouth open and his tongue pressing against the spout), whereas cup drinking offers the child a chance to drink with his lips closing lightly around the rim of the cup.

While the child is mastering cup drinking, his bottle is not necessarily eliminated completely. Some children desire an opportunity to suck on a nipple several times a day. However, most children are bottle-free by 24 to 30 months—the age varies from one baby to another and one culture to another. If children insist on a bottle after they are proficient on a cup, they should be in a completely upright posture when they drink. Use of a nipple straw makes this feasible (see Intervention: Bottle Feeding, later in this chapter). Giving the child a bottle as he is lying ready to go to sleep tends to promote reversion to the primitive sucking pattern. Moreover, the pressure of the nipple on the newly emerging teeth fosters poor dentition, and milk in the mouth overnight may promote tooth decay.

Except for specific likes and dislikes, a 2-year-old is able to handle virtually all consistencies of food that he is given to eat. (However, nuts, raw carrots, and popcorn should not be given to a young child, since these difficult-to-chew foods are often inhaled accidentally and can lodge in the air passage.) By 2 years of age he has also developed the basic oral coordination necessary for speech development. Although this control is a prerequisite for speech, it is not the only factor necessary in learning to talk (see Chapter 7).

Respiration and Phonation

From the moment of the welcome sound of the birth cry, the baby has begun the automatic process of life-sustaining respiration. Throughout the first months of life he will learn to gain some voluntary control over this automatic process and by doing so will develop the energy source for voice production.

Respiratory rates of infants are extremely variable. They change not only as a function of the child's age but also as a function of the child's activity, emotional state, vocalizations, and state of health. During vegetative (at rest) breathing, most respiratory action is observed in the abdominal area (belly breathing). As the child matures, his respiratory rate begins to decrease and thoracic movement becomes visible during the respiratory cycle (Peiper, 1963). A cycle is the length of time it takes to draw a breath in and let it out.

Recent investigations with highly sensitive instrumentation have presented new normative data on neonatal and infant (0–12 months) respiratory rates. The following tabulation* is abstracted from the works of Wilder (1972) and Langlois (1975):

Age Group (in months)	Approximate Breaths per Minute
1	85
4	82
6	60
8	60
10	38
12	40

The normal newborn automatically coordinates respiration and phonation (production of sound). Phonations are limited to rather nasal sounds and usually accompany such movements as

---

*Please note that this is not the complete or precise list of data presented by the two researchers.

kicking or squirming. The newborn to 1-month-old baby exhibits limited vocal intonations during crying or fussing. His mother may not be able to distinguish differences between cries for different needs. At approximately 3 months of age, as the baby develops more independent movements and better head control against gravity, a variety of changes in vocal pitch may occur. Movement helps facilitate the initial phonation of the infant. Therefore, as the repertoire of movement increases, so may the variety of vocalizations. At this point, mothers are able to detect differences in the baby's cries—such as deeper, less nasal tones—and to assign different meanings to the different noises (see Chapter 7). The general tone of the sound is somewhat less nasal, and the child is able to sustain low back sounds (made toward the back of the mouth), such as "ah" or gurgling sounds.

Starting at approximately 6 months, a strange physical phenomenon takes place. As the child develops into a more upright being (sitting and later pulling to standing), the anatomical relationship of the ribs to the spine begins to shift. Gravity exerts a downward pull on the ribs and the angle of the ribs in relation to the spine becomes less than 90°. Structurally, the ribs begin to rotate downward and slightly outward, thus increasing the thoracic cavity, and more thoracic movement is observed during respiration. Longer phonatory patterns begin to occur, in long streams of playful squeals, screams, coos, and babbling. The baby experiments with these vocal changes for the apparent pleasure of controlling his voice. Just as the child has developed more selective movements of his body parts, so does he develop more selective vocal play. Apart from an increase in body size and weight and accompanying increase in vital capacity (the amount of air the lungs hold), which affects the length of utterance possible, the child has developed most of the respiratory control necessary for mature speech production by the time he is approximately 13 to 15 months of age.

Pre-Speech Development in Atypical Children

The pre-speech skills of the physically handicapped child may be impaired due to multiple and interrelated factors (Hixon & Hardy, 1964). The following discussion attempts to delineate these factors. However, it must be kept in mind that the relationship of all the variables is so strong that it is often difficult and sometimes impossible to determine which factor or factors are responsible for the lack of pre-speech development in a particular child (Mysak, 1963).

The physically handicapped child often shows signs of abnormality in oral development from birth. Uncoordinated and/or abnormal oral responses may be early signs of central nervous system damage. These signs are most easily observed in the feeding patterns of the neonate and infant (Köng, 1966).

Observation of the oral reflexes may indicate a possible cause of early feeding difficulties. The rooting reflex (normally present from birth to approximately 3 to 4 months) may be weak or unobservable in some handicapped children. This may be due to the influence of abnormal tonic reflex behaviors, which prevent the child from turning his head in response to facial stimulation. Or the infant may show signs of exaggerated rooting behavior which persists much longer than normal. The prolonged reflex may be related to the lack of self-directed oro-facial stimulation. The infant is locked into abnormal postures (e.g., asymmetrical tonic neck reflex) that prevent him from getting his hands to his mouth.

The weakness or absence of the infant's suckle–swallow reflex is a cause for great concern. Newborns with feeding problems are often fed intravenously or via nasal tube to provide the nourishment they are unable to obtain by breast or bottle feeding. This problem is frequently associated with premature hypertonic or hypotonic babies. If the problem persists, the child is unable to derive the oral sensory stimulation received from normal feeding (breast or bottle), which further exacerbates the sensory deprivation caused by lack of self-directed oro-facial stimulation.

Continuation of the suckle–swallow reflex long after expected extinction also is frequent in the atypical population. The inability of the child to develop nonreflexive sucking can prevent development of the independent tongue movements that are later incorporated into patterns of sound production. Furthermore, examination of the suckle–swallow reflex pattern may show abnormalities. It is common to find an open mouth and protrusion of the tongue during swallowing (tongue thrust). This pattern is the opposite of the normal swallowing pattern, in which the tongue moves backward and the lips close. Tongue thrusting, so common in physically handicapped children, may become stronger with the increase in muscle tone (Mueller, 1972).

Deprivation of oral stimulation may also be a factor in the prolongation and exaggeration of the bite and gag reflexes. Continuation of these responses beyond the normal age makes it difficult to feed the baby or to vary the types and consistencies of food that should be introduced.

Thus, a cycle appears to develop in terms of oral stimulation. First, the child with abnormal reflex patterns and poor muscle tonus is unable to get his hands to his mouth to provide oral stimulation through play. As a result, feeding becomes increasingly difficult, and attempts at variation of diet fail. Oral stimulation through feeding is therefore limited or absent. This in turn prevents the adaptation and normalization of the oral musculature. Early intervention may serve to prevent the development and perpetuation of this undesirable cycle.

The problems of oral tactile sensitivity frequently seen among the atypical population are of two kinds: (1) low tolerance for tactile stimulation in and around the oral area (hypersensitivity) or (2) virtually no reaction to stimuli regardless of placement (hyposensitivity).

Hypersensitivity may be seen in the hemiplegic or spastic child: Increased tone and facial asymmetry may be observed in the oral area during stimulation, and, in some instances, stimulation elicits total patterns of hyperextension throughout the body. Hypersensitivity of the oral area usually leads to feeding difficulties, since the child reacts negatively to each introduction of the spoon or cup or to any new food. In cases of severe hypersensitivity, intense reactions to variations in taste and/or temperature may be noted.

Hyposensitivity is often seen in "floppy" babies or those with Down's syndrome: Even stimulation of the soft palate or back portion of the tongue fails to elicit the reflexive gag reaction that would normally be observable. Safety becomes a prime concern for the caregiver of the child with oral hyposensitivity. In the baby with a reduced gag reaction, large pieces of food or small objects introduced into the mouth can easily result in obstruction of the air passage.

The state of overall muscle tonus in the handicapped child

is frequently reflected in his oral musculature. One may therefore expect fluctuations of low to high tone in the face and mouth of the athetotic child; extreme oro-facial tightness in the child with spasticity; facial asymmetry in the hemiplegic child; and unstable, irregular movements of the mouth in the ataxic child. These abnormal tonus qualities make it increasingly difficult for the child to develop consistent independent oral movements. Abnormal tone may also result in a limited repertoire of sound variations. Some young handicapped children may be able to produce only vowel sounds or sounds that require little or no tongue or lip movement.

Facial expression, an important part of communication in the young infant, may also be inhibited by aberrant tone. For example, the child with low tone may have a "droopy" expression, as if he were constantly sad or unaffected by his surroundings. Care must be taken not to interpret the lack of facial expression as indicating limited interest in or comprehension of the environment. Too frequently the nonverbal child is diagnosed as having poor receptive language skills because he is unable to respond with appropriate facial recognition to test items. A complete evaluation of the child's oro-facial muscle tonus and function will give some indication of the child's physiological ability to demonstrate his inner feelings through facial expression.

Abnormal body movement patterns have an enormous effect on the infant's ability to develop a normal respiratory pattern. Infants who are dominated by increased spastic flexion have their arms pulled tightly into the thoracic region, making it difficult, if not impossible, to develop a deep, regular breathing pattern. Extensor patterns create a tightly retracted abdominal area. The result may be a flared, flattened rib cage, which reduces the child's vital capacity and maintains shallow breathing. The effects of these respiratory patterns are seen not only in the child's inability to sustain and vary his vocal production but also in his inability to resist upper respiratory infections.

The ability to phonate is largely dependent on the establishment of normal respiratory patterns. The physically handicapped infant who has abnormal breathing will evidence sound production that is limited in volume, pitch variability, duration, and initiation. The effects of abnormal tone that may be present in the diaphragm, pharynx, and oral area further limit vocal production. Such problems as (*a*) voicing on inhalation, (*b*) monotonous, "whiny" vocal quality, and (*c*) inconsistency in pitch are often the result of the conditions we have been discussing.

These factors are related to the feeding problems frequently encountered with the handicapped baby. Tongue thrusting, often intensified by the extensor patterns of the head and body, can create a major obstacle. Due to the thrust pattern, the lips and jaws of the infant cannot be maintained in a closed position, and abnormal postural tonus may further prevent closure by causing retraction of the lips. Foods and liquids are therefore constantly being pushed out during swallowing. Apart from resulting feeding problems, prolongation of the constant tongue-pushing pattern, especially where the movement is strong and manifested even when the child is not being fed, may lead to upper jaw and dentition deformities.

A further problem in the feeding of handicapped infants is that normal, coordinated movements of the muscles in the oro-pharyngeal area may not occur during eating. Food may pass to the posterior of the nasal-pharyngeal area and out through the nose.

Immobility of the lips is another difficulty encountered during feeding. In the hypertonic infant this is characterized by a tightly retracted (pulled backward) upper lip; the infant is unable actively to remove food from the spoon as it is being withdrawn from his mouth. To compensate for this problem the mother may tend to scrape the spoon against the child's upper gums or teeth to remove the food as she pulls the spoon out of the baby's mouth. Thus the baby is denied the challenge of trying to remove the food by moving his lips.

Inability to grade the opening and closing of the mouth adds to the difficulties already described. The atypical infant tends to lock the jaws in either an open or a closed position while attempting to eat or drink. In addition to this problem, the athetotic child may display jaw deviation (pulling of the jaw toward one side or the other) during feeding. If there is marked hypotonia throughout the oro-facial areas, continued hyperextension and deviation of the jaw can cause subluxation at the tempero-mandibular joints.

In sum, feeding problems can cause frustration for both the infant and the primary caregiver. Mealtimes, which normally produce feelings of joy and satisfaction between baby and feeder, tend instead to create anxiety and, in some instances disgust, over the "messy," time-consuming chore. Those who feed the infant may therefore have little time or inclination for the games and conversations that might normally occur during this period.

Intervention

It has been shown that the motoric aspects of speech development are greatly influenced by the oral maturation, respiratory development, and feeding patterns of the infant. Therefore, the responsibility of the professional staff begins when abnormal oral patterns are first observed (possibly within the first days of life). Normal patterns of respiration and feeding should be facilitated as soon as possible in an effort to prevent the detrimental effects of abnormal pre-speech development.

Intervention designed to stimulate correction of errors in sound production without considering abnormal body position or tonus, and its effect on the oral and respiratory musculature, may prove to be of little long-term benefit. Attempts by the child to produce sounds or sound patterns (words) while still hindered by abnormal muscle tone are likely to evoke aberrant movement patterns and associated reactions throughout the body. The undesired movements are thus reinforced, making it increasingly difficult for the child to maintain the skills he has struggled to achieve. When creating a therapeutic program for the infant with atypical pre-speech maturation it is therefore necessary to consider the state of development of the child in relation to normal developmental sequences. In addition, a major goal of intervention should be the establishment of neuromuscular patterns and tonus that are as normal as possible, as the foundation for achieving more normal speech development.

Sample Activities and Interventions

■ *Normalizing Oral Tactile Sensitivity.* Mueller (1972, 1973) describes the following considerations in normalizing oral tactile sensitivity. Although the orally hypersensitive child needs to be exposed to oral sensation, it is wise not to give too much stimulation too quickly or for long periods of time (not more than 5 to

10 minutes per day). A baby's sensitivity may be so severe that the individual therapist or caregiver may wish to play games that initially avoid the oro-facial area entirely. For a young baby, the arms and legs can be rhythmically moved up and down and from side to side to the accompaniment of an action song. An older infant can play "dress up" with hats, scarves, or soft necklaces. These activities may be helpful in acquainting the child with new sensations, so that the introduction of facial stimulation is less upsetting.

Specific activities of firmly stroking around the child's shoulders, neck, and face may then be incorporated into play activities. Soft toys, wash cloths, or the baby's hand may be brought to his face for games such as "Here are your eyes, here are your cheeks." In this way the child is introduced to new sensations as well as becoming acquainted with the body parts, which is a necessary part of language growth. It is best to stroke the cheeks toward midline, to help inhibit the possibility of tightness and retraction that may occur during the initial period of stimulation. When the infant has become accustomed to facial stimulation, one may proceed to help him accept oral stimulation. Soft rubber toys, the baby's hand, or the caregiver's clean fingers may be introduced to the baby's mouth. However, since the oral area is significantly more sensitive to stimulation than the rest of the face, this process should be undertaken more slowly, touching only small portions of the mouth during any given session. This gradual pace gives the child an opportunity to adjust to the new stimulation. If the baby exhibits a bite reflex, extreme caution must be taken not to bring the child's hand into his mouth until he has accommodated to stimulation of the gums, thereby reducing the bite reflex.

The section on control of jaw, lips, and tongue, at the end of this chapter, describes the technique used during stimulation to counter the extraneous movements usually seen in the athetotic child, to maintain a midline position of the head, and to inhibit a total rooting response toward the source of stimulation, sucking movements that may accompany the rooting response, and the bite reflex.

■ *Bottle Feeding.* The technique for jaw control is most beneficial in helping the child maintain good closure around the nipple during sucking. Maintaining the child in an upright posture with hip and head flexion tends to break up extensor patterns that contribute to the abnormal tongue thrust.

Fast-flowing liquids are contraindicated; they do not require the child to suck and may encourage abnormal swallowing. To determine if a nipple is too fast for the baby, turn the bottle upside down. If the fluid flows out or drips out rapidly, the child will not have to suck to obtain the food. A slower nipple is indicated.

"Sit-up" straws are readily available in most parts of the country. These snap snugly into the standard bottle nipple (Even-flow, Curity, and Davol seem the most satisfactory) and permit the bottle to be held vertically upright while the baby is being fed in a sitting position. This is helpful in avoiding the tendency to tip the child backward while feeding.

■ *Spoon Feeding.* When introducing foods on a spoon, the caregiver should proceed as follows:

1. Use jaw and lip control technique (described later in this chapter).
2. Introduce small amounts of food on the spoon.
3. Press the spoon firmly onto the top of the midsection of the tongue when the tongue is resting on the floor of the mouth. This pressure helps to encourage spontaneous lip closure and inhibits the tongue thrust and bite reflex.
4. When the lips begin to close automatically, withdraw the spoon straight out of the mouth without scraping the food onto the child's teeth or gums. This will ensure that the child takes an active role in the feeding process.
5. Facilitate jaw and lip closure immediately after the food has been removed from the spoon, in order to prevent the tongue from pushing the food back out.

■ *Solid Foods.* A tongue thrust will prevent lateralization of the bolus of food to the chewing surface. Solid foods should therefore not be placed in the center of the mouth or on the tongue tip, as they will then be mashed against the palate. If the infant is properly positioned and jaw control is adequately administered, placing solid morsels of food on the side of the mouth between the molars, or in that region when there are no teeth, most often will elicit automatic chewing. It is not necessary to wait until the infant has molars before introducing lumpy foods.

The following is a list of some of the foods that may be used as a transition to a diet of solids:

1. Graham crackers
2. Cold cereal (e.g., Cheerios)
3. Pieces of peeled fresh fruit (e.g., apple, pear)
4. Hard cheeses (not processed cheese, which becomes "mushy" and adheres to the hard palate)
5. Cubes of chicken or turkey
6. Cubes (not slices) of bologna, boiled ham, chicken or turkey roll, peeled hot dogs (mild—not highly spiced)
7. Diced cooked vegetables
8. Crusts of firm, hard breads (white bread becomes too sticky in the mouth)

The child needs a well-rounded diet, not only from a nutritional viewpoint but also as an opportunity to experience a variety of tastes, textures, odors, and temperatures. Mealtime or snack time provides an important opportunity for the child to learn the names of various foods, and seasons of the year when certain foods are available. Snack time in the preschool or group setting is a fun time for social and language development.

■ *Cup Drinking.* The technique of jaw control is a major intervention when teaching cup drinking. During the initial learning stages, a pliable plastic cup or heavy duty paper cup can be squeezed to form a spout. The rim is placed on the bottom lip (never between the teeth as that may evoke the bite reflex and inhibit adequate bilabial closure) and gradually tipped until the liquid is available to the child. At first the child will not be able to sip and swallow consecutively. Therefore, until he has developed this skill, only small amounts of the liquid should be offered for swallowing. The caregiver can lower the angle of the cup, to give the baby an opportunity to control the liquid in his mouth, yet leave the rim of the cup on his lip ready for the next sip.

The baby's head should not be tilted backward during drinking, as this enlarges the pharynx, allowing the liquids to funnel into the esophagus (bird style)—a method that does not permit the child to develop the normal front-to-back swallowing pattern or to learn coordination of breathing and swallowing. To prevent the baby's head from tilting backward in his attempt to drain the liquid, a portion of the cup on the nondrinking side may be cut away to make room for the bridge of the child's nose as he is drinking.

The baby may show little or no active movement of the upper lip while drinking. Using the same procedure, give the baby thickened liquids (milk shake consistency) to drink. Liquids of this texture will contact the upper lip and stimulate its movement downward, thus making it become more active in the drinking process.

■ *Straw Drinking.* When cup drinking has been perfected and good lip closure is observed on the cup, the child can be introduced to straw drinking. It is more difficult to seal the lips around a straw than a cup rim, so it is important that the child first learn to perfect cup drinking.

The same procedure is followed as in teaching cup drinking. Do not place the straw on the tongue between the teeth as this will elicit primitive sucking rather than normal straw sipping. A rubber stopper (washer) may be placed on the straw to ensure placement of the straw only between the lips.

■ *Facilitating Normal Respiration.* As a result of the normal breathing pattern being inhibited by the abnormal body position and tonus of the atypical infant, repositioning the child becomes the most important aspect of breathing therapy. A neutral side-lying position helps to prevent both hyperextension and hyper-flexion of the thoracic area. A child can be positioned on his side either directly on the floor or propped on a wedge. The underneath arm should be brought forward with the head resting on the shoulder (see Figure 6.1). This position in and of itself may help to create a more normal, rhythmic breathing pattern. The child should occasionally be changed from one side to the other to provide symmetry and prevent tightness from developing in one static position. The prone position over a wedge is also useful as it inhibits tight retraction of the abdominal area (see Chapter 5: Children with Spastic Diplegia or Spastic Quadriplegia: Sample Activities).

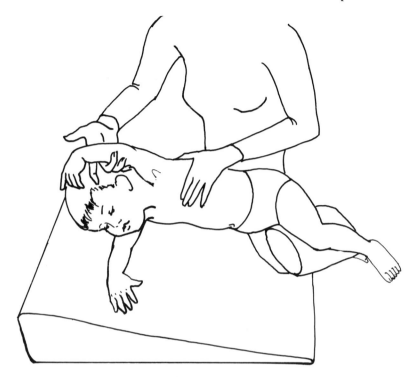

FIGURE 6.1 *In side lying, slight pressure applied to thoracic and ab-dominal area facilitates deeper inspiration.*

The baby's respiratory pattern should be closely observed. If he has a shallow inspiration, a small amount of pressure can be applied, just prior to inspiration, to the abdominal and thoracic area while in side lying (see Figure 6.1) or bilaterally to the side and rear of the rib cage if in prone. This slight pressure helps to increase the amount of air taken in. One might then see increased abdominal and thoracic expansion during the next inspiration. Consistent, gradual pressure should be given during exhalation to help the child learn the feeling of sustained, controlled exhalation, which is contrary to his usual explosive exhalation.

When a child exhibits an arhythmic breathing pattern—one that draws the sternum (breastbone) toward the spinal column during inspiration—apply steady pressure on the sides of the rib cage. This pressure will prevent the lateral expansion of the ribs and promote more abdominal movement during inspiration.

■ *Facilitating Phonation and Speech.*   When improvement has been noted in the areas of feeding and respiration, work can proceed to encourage phonation and sound production. Phonation can be stimulated by vocalizing at the same time that one is working on further improving respiration (using the positions recommended in the preceding intervention). While giving graded inward pressure during exhalation, one should begin to vocalize on a vowel sound such as "oh" or "oo"; gently rocking the baby at the same time may encourage a freely sustained vocalization. As a result of the inhibition of the abnormal tonus and the increase in the period of exhalation, the child may attempt to imitate the sound. He should be praised (through verbal approval, a caress, a responsive smiling face, or a combination of these) whenever he succeeds in producing sound. Once the child is able to sustain a tone for a few seconds without becoming tighter or reverting to previous abnormal respiratory patterns, emphasis can be placed on facilitating specific sounds.

To make it easier for the child (and because consonants rarely appear in isolation), consonant sounds should be stimulated in the medial context, for example, "oomoo." In helping the baby achieve the motor patterns required to produce sounds, jaw control again becomes a major assistive technique. During freely sustained phonation, the caregiver can provide manually the motor pattern for a desired sound. For example, pressing the child's lips together for repeated, brief intervals will produce a babbling pattern of "oomoomoo," much to the child's own delight and reinforced by the caregiver. Eventually the child may imitate this motor pattern on his own. The other bilabial sounds of |b| and |p| may be encouraged in much the same way. Bringing the cheeks forward and holding the lips closed for a slightly longer period of time before facilitating the sounds helps to provide the plosive quality of the |b| and |p| phonemes. Most of the sounds in the English language are not produced with a closed mouth. Therefore not all sounds may be facilitated. However, sound patterns that include the phonemes |l|, |n|, |d|, |t|, |k|, and |g| can be encouraged by moving the child's tongue while he is phonating.

It is important to note that this method cannot result in the child achieving fluent speech patterns while he remains at this level. Therefore, this intervention is most helpful during the initial stages of therapy, by helping the child "feel" some of the motor patterns necessary in speech production (Hawk, 1937, 1942; Young, 1962).

■ *Feeding Positions.* The various feeding positions outlined below will help (*a*) to break up abnormal motor patterns, (*b*) to maintain body symmetry, and (*c*) to maintain head and trunk alignment:

1. *Face to face*: The hypotonic or very young baby who still requires a great deal of trunk support and general overall control can be fed in the following way. The caregiver sits in front of a table with a firm wedge or bed pillow resting partly on the table and partly (the thin edge) in her lap. The baby is placed on the wedge facing the caregiver (see Figure 6.2). If his legs

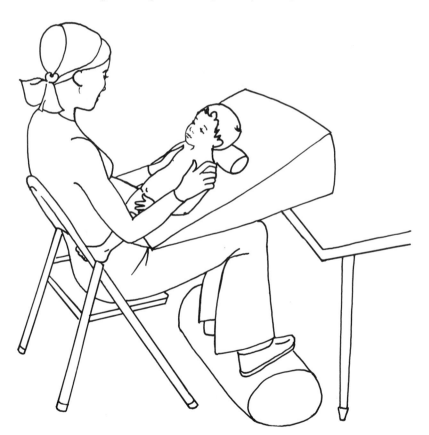

FIGURE 6.2 *The face-to-face feeding position.*

tend to scissor (adduct), they can be spread around the feeder's body to provide abduction and external rotation. If the legs cannot be abducted, they may be flexed, with the feet resting flat on the feeder's abdomen. To provide head and trunk alignment, a small pillow should be placed behind the child's neck. This will supply the necessary neck flexion to prevent head extension and shoulder retraction. Care should be taken to ensure that the pillow is at the nape of the neck and not against the crown of the head. Pressure against the back of the head elicits an extensor thrust in some children. Elevating the caregiver's legs on a small stool or bolster provides extra support to stabilize the wedge. It also improves the caregiver's posture and decreases the likelihood of strain on the back.

The face-to-face position is also feasible with the young baby placed in an infant seat. Again, a small pillow placed behind the child's neck will promote neck flexion and head–trunk alignment.

2. *Held in the arms*: It is most natural to feed a young infant in one's arms. Maintaining the child in an upright posture and providing the baby with sufficient hip flexion to break up patterns of extension will encourage body alignment. The feeding period is an important aspect in the evolution of normal attachments between caregiver and infant. If successful feeding can be accomplished while the caregiver actually holds the baby, the body contact fosters a warm emotional climate.

3. *Seated upright*: The older baby, of 6 to 8 months, needs the opportunity to sit in an upright position. A standard high chair may be altered to provide the baby with increased hip flexion, which will discourage abnormal extensor patterns (legs stiffened out and head pushed back). A foam wedge is placed in the seat of the chair with the thicker side toward the front. The thickness of the wedge is determined by the size of the baby and the degree of hip flexion necessary to prevent him from pushing into extension. A rolled towel may be placed under the baby's knees to accentuate the hip flexion. Pieces of foam or small pillows may be positioned so as to prevent the baby from leaning to one side and losing his midline orientation.

4. *Using a prone board*: The prone board (see Appendix A) aids proper positioning (head and trunk alignment) while feeding. Abnormal extensor patterns can be partially inhibited by providing flexion at the ankles and bringing the child's arms forward onto the tray or table. This position provides the caregiver with the opportunity to help the child touch the food and utensils before him and thus to achieve additional tactile and language stimulation.

■ *Control of Jaw, Lips, and Tongue.* Providing control to the oral area may help the child develop the ability to take an active role in his pre-speech development, including feeding, by enabling him (*a*) to use bilabial (two-lip) closure, (*b*) to inhibit jaw thrusting, (*c*) to reduce tongue thrusting, and (*d*) to maintain midline orientation of the head. The following are suggestions for achieving these goals using two alternate positions:

1. *In the face-to-face position* (see Figure 6.3):

a. Placing a thumb under the baby's bottom lip, on the chin, the caregiver can help to facilitate bilabial closure.

b. Placing an index finger on the baby's cheek, the caregiver can use slight pressure inward and forward on the cheek to decrease the facial tightness if the baby has a tendency toward retracted cheeks (drawn back toward the hair line). Care should be taken to avoid drawing the face into asymmetrical positions.

c. Placing the length of the middle finger under the jaw just in back of the bone, the caregiver can help to inhibit the tongue thrust by exerting pressure upward with the middle part of the finger onto the soft tissue at the base of the tongue. Occasionally the caregiver may have to assist the baby in attaining jaw closure and alignment. At these times slight pressure on the jaw bone may be necessary. However, it is important that the baby not passively have his jaw opened and closed by the caregiver. Rather, the baby should be as active in the feeding or vocalizing process as possible.

d. Keeping the lateral portion of the hand (little finger side) lightly pressed on the baby's breastbone (sternum) during feeding or pre-speech activities will help to maintain proper head and thoracic alignment.

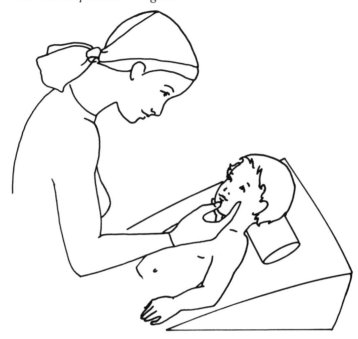

FIGURE 6.3 *Jaw, lip, and tongue control in the face-to-face position.*

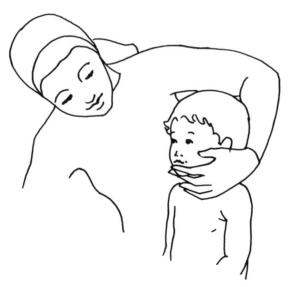

FIGURE 6.4 *Jaw, lip, and tongue control from a side position.*

2. *From the side* (see Figure 6.4) :

a. Bringing the arm around the back of the child's head (to inhibit head hyperextension) but avoiding any pressure on the back of the head, the caregiver places the index finger under the child's bottom lip, to facilitate bilabial closure.

b. The thumb is used to help control the cheek and keep the head in midline. (Avoid bringing the thumb into the child's line of vision.)

c. The middle finger is placed under the baby's chin on the soft tissue. An upward pressure on the soft tissue inhibits a tongue thrust. Occasionally the middle finger may be used to assist jaw closure.

d. Placing the lateral portion of the hand lightly on the child's sternum aids alignment of the head and thorax.

Whatever position is used for jaw control, it is recommended that control of the lips be provided only from under the bottom lip. In this way one can help the child to participate actively in pre-speech and feeding activities, rather than his having the bilabial movements passively provided by the caregiver manipulating the top and bottom lips. The use of jaw control techniques may be gradually modified as the child's feeding skills develop. Less external control of the oral area may be necessary, and proximal control of shoulders and hips may be sufficient to maintain the improved feeding patterns.

It is hoped that the above recommendations will assist in improving oro-pharyngeal function in the atypical infant. However, it must be kept in mind that improvement in feeding patterns does not automatically result in the development of speech. Speech is a dynamic process, and all factors relating to its development must be considered when creating a speech program for any child.

CHAPTER 7
LANGUAGE

THE acquisition and development of communication skills are among the most crucial aspects of the total growth and development of the child between birth and 3 years of age. The ability to communicate underlies social interaction and is critically related to cognitive growth.

Normal Development of Communication

Before discussing normal development of communication, working definitions of *speech* and *language* are necessary. *Speech* is a complex motor act which requires precise coordination of respiratory, phonatory, and articulatory systems and is mediated by the nervous system. The respiratory system provides the power necessary for speech production. During vegetative breathing (quiet breathing), inspiration and expiration are symmetrical. Speech breathing, on the other hand, requires that a short inspiration be followed by sustained expiration. Speech breathing requires more precise coordination than does vegetative breathing, and current data from studies of infant cry indicate that this coordination can already be observed at 7 months of age (Wilder & Baken, 1974–75, Langlois, 1975). Powered by the respiratory system, the phonatory system is responsible for voice production. The vocal folds are set in motion by the expiratory air stream, and voice is further modified by changes in the vocal tract. Finally,

The major contributor to this chapter is Linda Buch assisted by Susan Collins and Sue Gelber.

the speech articulators (movable structures such as the tongue, lips, and soft palate) convert the vocal product into recognizable speech sounds. It should be noted that the respiratory, phonatory, and articulatory systems are closely interrelated and that disturbance in any one of the systems may disturb the functioning of the entire speech mechanism.

Language is a symbolic code used to receive (decode) or transmit (encode) thoughts, ideas, and feelings interpersonally. The child must learn to decode the linguistic messages of the persons in his environment and must use this code to transmit his thoughts to others. Language may be transmitted verbally (speech code), manually (gestural code), or graphically (written code). In addition, verbal language requires that the speaker use the intonation, rhythm, and stress patterns appropriate to his language. Adult speakers have knowledge of word and sentence construction and of the ways in which meaning may be transmitted through the linguistic code. The ways in which children acquire and develop this knowledge is the subject of current research in child language.

The relationship between language acquisition and cognitive development (see Chapter 8) is important and should be clarified before discussing stages of language development.

Slobin (1971), among others, suggests that language is used to express the child's cognition of his social and physical environment. Therefore a child cannot begin to use a given linguistic form meaningfully until he is able to understand what it means. The child codes the knowledge that he has acquired through action upon and interaction with the people and things in his environment. This becomes one important consideration when discussing the language development of the atypical child who, for many possible reasons, may be restricted from interaction with the people and things in his environment.

Traditionally, child language was studied from an adult language framework. That is, the child's language was considered an immature adult form. In recent years, however, language specialists have observed that children have unique patterns which are characteristic of various developmental levels. Descriptions of language performance have led to further understanding of what the child comprehends and what he is able to produce at each level. This line of investigation has been greatly influenced by the generative, or transformational, model of grammar proposed by Chomsky (1957, 1968). A grammar is a description of the rules of a language; it specifies the manner in which all sentences of a language are constructed. Briefly, generative grammar proposes that there are two levels in sentence structure: the deep structure, which relates to the meaning of a sentence, and surface structure, which is the actual utterance heard by the listener. A frequently used example may help to illustrate this point:

> *John is easy to please.*
> *John is eager to please.*

Although the surface structure of these two sentences is the same, the underlying, or deep, structure is quite different. In addition, in order to express different meanings, the child must learn transformational rules. For example, he must learn to transform declarative sentences into questions and negations. These transformational rules are developed throughout the language learning period.

To answer the question, What is normal language development? language behavior will be described in terms of its three major components: phonological development, syntactic development, and semantic development.

Phonological Development

The phonological rules of a language are concerned with phonemic (speech sound) and prosodic (stress and intonation) patterns. Consider, for example, the following sentences:

> *The boy won.*
> *The boy won?*

Although the speech sounds are the same, the intonation patterns convey different meanings. In terms of sound sequencing, certain combinations are not permissible according to the phonological rules of the language and would not be understood by a native listener. In English, such a sequence would be "stpz" or "iqm."

The relationship of babbling (approximately 2 to 6 months) to true speech production has not yet been established. It is possible, however, that during this developmental period the infant is beginning to recognize and produce different speech sound features that may later be applied in combining sounds into words.

At approximately 4 to 6 months of age, the child usually responds to the speech of persons in his environment; this response may take the form of a laugh or some other sign of pleasure. He begins to "communicate" in response to the speech of others. Toward the end of his first year of life, the child may indicate knowledge of gross intonation or stress patterns by responding to changes in the adults "tone of voice."

As the child continues to develop control over the speech mechanism (the respiratory–phonatory–articulatory complex) and is given adequate auditory input and feedback, the variety of speech sounds that he is able to recognize and produce is increased.

Current research is concerned with determining those features of speech sounds (for example, whether a sound is voiced or unvoiced) that are discriminated and produced in infant perception and vocalizations. Results from studies of this type will certainly add to knowledge of the child's acquisition of phonological rules.

To provide the reader with some indication of what speech patterns are usually produced at various age levels, descriptions from a longitudinal study by Berry (1969) may be useful. By 6 months of age, the child may attempt to repeat sound sequences that he hears and may use intonational patterns with jargon. The median age of the first word is 11 months, and by 1 year melodic patterns are copied with greater accuracy. By 18 to 24 months, the child is easily able to repeat syllables or word sequences. Pitch, at this stage, is still uncontrolled. By 24 to 30 months, Berry reports, all vowels as well as labial and labioalveolar consonants may be produced in sequences, but they are not stable.

The child of 30 to 36 months has further developed control of pitch, although there still may be wide variability. At this age, production of speech sounds may not have been firmly established. Menyuk (1971) has observed, however, that the following speech sounds may be mastered by the age of 3 years: |b|, |m|, |n|, |f|, |w|, and |h|.

Syntactic Development

Syntactic development in the normal child begins at approximately 18 months, when the child begins to produce two-word utterances. Although form at this stage is limited, the same form may be used to convey many different meanings. Utterances at this stage in particular must be considered within the extralinguistic framework in which they occur (Dale, 1972).

After the child has begun to use syntactic structures, he applies rules to these structures. As Menyuk (1971) reports, he begins by applying those operations that do not disturb the subject + predicate construction, and gradually incorporates these operations with appropriate structural changes. For example, the negative element "no" may be used in early development to convert *He can eat* to *He no can eat* and later into *He can't eat*. The child demonstrates that he has acquired the rules for syntactic construction. At the end of this stage of development the child is usually producing well-formed declarative, imperative, question, and negative sentences, as well as sentences containing conjunctions and embeddings of two sentences. Simultaneously he expresses incompletely formed types of sentences that are structurally similar to those produced at an earlier stage of development. For example, he produces both *How you do that?* and *How do you do that?*

Semantic Development

In the course of language development, the child must learn not only the meaning of single words, but also the meaning of words in relationship to one another. That is, he must know not only the meaning of the word "ball" but also the meaning of "throw ball," which requires knowledge of the relationship between the two words. Many of the theoretical questions concerning semantic development in the language of children are unresolved, and discussion of them is beyond the scope of this chapter. For example, the relationship between syntactic and semantic development is not yet clear.

The general tendency in the child's acquisition of word meaning is a progression from overgeneralization (for example, calling all four-legged animals "dog") to greater differentiation of that word and its meaning (McNeill, 1970). Longitudinal data from Berry (1969) give some indication of the tremendous growth in semantic development that occurs from birth to 3 years of age: By 9 months, the child displays comprehension of simple words such as "no" and his own name; by the age of 18 to 24 months, the child "understands most linguistic units but does not separate sequences into word units"; and by 30 to 36 months he displays comprehension of such things as sentence structure and can differentiate between such sentences as *The boy pulls the girl* and *The girl pulls the boy.*

Productively, at approximately 2 years of age, the child uses a word very broadly, and he may use that one word to express many different notions. Vocabulary may range from 50 to 75 words. Of these words, 50 percent are nouns. By 24 to 30 months, 272 words have been acquired; and by 3 years of age this number has increased to 446 (these totals represent the mean number of words as estimated by Berry). These data illustrate the rapid growth of the child's semantic abilities as evidenced by his language comprehension and production during the first 3 years.

Development of Communication in Atypical Children

The development of communication skills in atypical children may be delayed or disordered for many reasons. It will be helpful to view these potential problems within the framework that has already been presented. Communication disorders of the atypical child are usually of multiple causation, and we will not attempt to single out specific cause–effect relationships.

A number of handicaps are likely to interfere with normal phonological, syntactic, and semantic development. In cases of cognitive impairment, the developmental sequence in each of these areas is likely to be delayed and possibly disordered. The child's language will be greatly influenced by his level of cognitive development, and any intervention program must take this relationship into account.

Hearing impairment is reported to occur more frequently in the atypical child than in the normal child (Berry & Eisenson, 1956). Because of the critical role that hearing plays in the development of speech and language, an undetected hearing loss or deficit may cause the child to miss critical periods for speech sound development and language learning. He may be deprived of important and meaningful auditory input from his environment. Thus it is very important that caregivers and staff be made aware of (and be able to discriminate between) appropriate and inappropriate auditory responses of the developing child. If the hearing loss or deficit is detected and treated early (through medical treatment or amplification, for example), the atypical child may gain (or regain) the ability to receive maximum auditory stimulation from his environment.

A third general factor that is critical to development in all areas of communication skills is the responsiveness of persons in the child's environment. In many cases, because of severe communication deficits, parents or other caregivers may feel frustration and inadequacy about their ability to stimulate the child. Their response may be to verbalize less to the child, which results in a decrease in communicative opportunities. The atypical child needs increased rather than decreased opportunities, and home programs (planned by team members) may be designed to help the family remedy this situation.

A fourth factor that often contributes to general language problems is the abnormal body position of the child. If the child is locked into abnormal positions, he may be unable to observe the people and things in his environment, unable to associate sound with sound source, and unable to coordinate auditory, visual, and tactile sensory input. In short, he may be deprived of a great deal of the stimulation that his environment has to offer. Occupational and physical therapy team members can make suggestions to the parents and the teacher for appropriate positioning during daily activities (see Chapter 5).

Phonological development may be disturbed for several specific reasons in addition to the general factors mentioned above. The child who has problems in coordinating oral movements will most likely experience difficulty in speech sound development. Retained oral reflexes may interfere with intended speech movements, and the child with these motor problems may be unable to articulate even the earliest developmental speech sounds.

In addition, disturbance in any one of the systems—respiratory, phonatory, or articulatory—is likely to disturb functioning of the entire speech mechanism. For example, disturbance in speech breathing patterns is frequently observed and may be related to abnormal body positions and to lack of coordination of thoracic and abdominal muscles of respiration. (Respiratory patterns are discussed further in Chapter 6.) Disturbances in respiratory–phonatory interaction may also impede the child's ability to employ intonation and stress patterns appropriately.

In relation to syntactic development, the child who is unable to sustain phonation because of disturbance in the respiratory–phonatory mechanism may be restricted in the length of utterance that he is able to produce. In this case, while he may have knowledge of the appropriate rules for syntactic structure he will be unable to generate language because of a disordered speech mechanism. Yet he may be unimpaired in his ability to comprehend the syntactic structures of the speakers in his environment. The atypical child who has damage to an area of the brain that specifically serves language functioning may have more specific language impairment. For example, his speech mechanism may be capable of producing speech sounds, yet he may be unable to order and use these sounds to generate or understand appropriate syntactic structures.

Semantic development may also be disturbed as a result of brain damage (this may be most evident in cases of acquired traumatic injury). The child may be unable to associate sound with meaning on an expressive and/or on a receptive level. This will restrict his ability to comprehend environmental events and to communicate his ideas and thoughts to others.

Finally, because of the child's physical handicap, it may be difficult for the parent to transport him to places outside the home. For this reason, he may have limited exposure to environmental objects and events in the wider world. Word connotations may be very specific and concrete due to limited experience.

In sum, the possibilities for interference with language communication development are numerous for the atypical child. Many of them, however, may be eliminated or ameliorated through early intensive team intervention programs.

Intervention

Therapeutic intervention with the atypical child can be planned and executed most effectively using a transdisciplinary approach that considers the "total child" and his needs. Parent involvement is an essential part of the language communication program. Treatment for communicative disorders must not be confined to the speech and hearing clinic; rather, treatment must be extended into the home and school settings.

Before discussing specific sample activities, a few general guidelines should be noted. Many parents and other caregivers are unaware of the sequence of language and speech development. Moreover, many early language responses may not be recognized as such. It is helpful to discuss the child's language level with the parents and to emphasize the early responses of the baby as positive aspects of his development.

For example, many handicapped babies may be quite capable of the same auditory responses as normal infants. Barring hearing loss or otological abnormality, the auditory system is one of the most highly developed systems with which the newborn interacts with the world. Brazelton (1974) found that many neonates evidence sophisticated orientation to environmental sounds and to the human voice. Because of the importance of auditory input to the child's development, it is necessary that the parents recognize the infant's responses to auditory stimuli and that they respond positively to them.

Throughout the child's development, forward steps in speech and language acquisition and development should be pointed out and demonstrated to the parents. Knowledge of their child's progress may further encourage the parents to take an active role in the intervention program.

The atypical child may need more time than other children to respond in communicative situations. There may be a delay of several seconds before he initiates a response. When trying to communicate gesturally (whether pointing to objects in his environment or signaling for attention), his movements may be slow. Speech may also be slow and dysrhythmic. Parents, teachers, and other caregivers should take this into account when planning intervention.

It is also important that language communication activities be pleasurable and nonstressful. Situations in which the child is required to speak should be avoided, particularly during the early stages of language development. As the atypical child begins to vocalize, he may not have the control to vocalize totally at will (Crickmay, 1970). As this control is developed, confidence in his own abilities will hopefully increase. Only after control and self-confidence is well established should the child be gradually encouraged to vocalize during stress or increased emotion; this development, however, is beyond the age range considered here (Crickmay, 1970).

Speech and language production should be accepted for its content rather than for accuracy of production. The most important point in any program for the communicatively impaired child is that all communicative efforts, whether in the home or center, be immediately and highly rewarded.

Activities to foster language development in a number of areas are discussed. It must be noted that these are samples that may be easily expanded and adapted to the needs of the individual child in a variety of settings. However, team planning for the child is essential for the most effective therapeutic intervention.

During all activities the child should be placed in a normalized body position, as discussed in Chapter 5. It is important that the child be free to watch all activities, that his hands be free to move in front of him, and that he maintain good head and trunk alignment.

Sample Activities and Interventions

■ *General Language Stimulation.* In the home, "parallel talking" (Crickmay, 1970) or verbalizing events and thoughts for the child is an effective activity for phonological development and particularly for syntactic and semantic development. For example, while dressing the child, verbalizations such as "Let's put on a sweater" and "Put your jacket on" (utterances that monitor action) expose the child to appropriate syntactical structure in addition to association of words with actions and objects. This approach can be used during most daily activities.

In addition, if the child has developed speech, his parents may expand his utterances, thus reinforcing his communication efforts and providing an expanded, appropriate language model.

These approaches may also be used effectively in a small group setting. For example, the goal of a group activity at school may be recognition of body parts (as a language activity and to increase body image). As the children respond to the instruction, "Put your hand on your head," the teacher can verbally monitor their actions by repeating, "Bobby put his hand on his head." The teacher may also expand the children's utterances as they address one another in social situations.

■ *Increasing Phonological Development.* The following activity may be utilized to encourage speech sound production. With the child and therapist seated in front of a large mirror (again, be sure to maintain good head and trunk alignment), objects beginning with bilabial speech sounds are presented to the child and he is encouraged to look at and touch the objects. Guided by the staff member utilizing jaw control (see Chapter 6), the child should attempt to produce the initial bilabial sound applicable to the object. All attempts should be encouraged and successive approximations of the sound immediately rewarded. As the child's ability to approximate the target sound increases, tape recordings may be added as further incentive. These also provide the child with important auditory feedback and help him to monitor his progress.

■ *Increasing Syntactic Development.* The child at the two-word or multiple-word utterance stage of language development may need increased opportunities to act on objects in his environment. This opportunity may be easily provided through play. Play situations may be adapted to meet the needs of the physically handicapped child through the use of appropriate play materials and the incorporation of normalized body positioning for optimal movement. For example, the child may be positioned on a prone board (see Appendix A), so that his eyes and hands can effectively function together and so that head and trunk alignment is established. With play materials placed in front of him, he is able in this position to move and act upon those objects. The therapist may then structure the play activity for the child by verbally monitoring his actions. "John rolls the ball" may take on new meaning as the child engages in that action. During these activities, one-word utterances should be expanded and utterances of two or more words should be immediately reinforced. If syntactic structure is inappropriate, the therapist may repeat the activity while supplying the appropriate language structure. Coding events while they are occurring is a strong language experience and is an important part of the language communication program. This approach may be utilized in individual and small group activities at home and at the center.

■ *Increasing Semantic Development.* The primary goal of these activities is to increase the child's ability to relate sounds and words with meaning. A multisensory approach may be the most effective means toward that end. For the child who is learning to name objects in his environment, an object that has been explored visually, auditorily, and tactually has richer meaning than one that has only been seen. The child whose home environment includes a dog should, for example, be encouraged not only to watch the dog as it moves about the room but to pet it (with assistance) and to listen to its barking; in all these ways he will be helped toward the verbal coding of "dog."

CHAPTER 8

COGNITION

Whereas the child's motor or speech development during the infant years is readily observable, cognition is an inner, invisible process. The several theories and suggestions concerning the nature of early cognition are based largely on the inferences drawn by developmental psychologists who have observed infants responding to a variety of stimuli in both natural and controlled settings.

Normal Cognitive Development

Until fairly recently, most psychologists and educators considered the infant generally to be a noncognitive creature. Thinking and language were very often perceived as nearly synonymous. Since infants cannot talk, it seemed fairly obvious that they could not think. The relatively recent disentangling of language and cognition—the recognition that there are forms of thinking and precursors to symbolic functioning that can and do occur in prelinguistic organisms—has helped to focus attention on the development of cognition during the years of infancy.

Several other forces have also been at work to turn the attention of professionals to the study of cognitive development in the infant. By far the most important influence has been the research and theory of Jean Piaget (Piaget, 1972; Piaget & Inhelder, 1969),

The major contributor to this chapter is Helen Bee Douglas assisted by Gloria Boylan, Carol Hosaka, Sharon McDermott, Lillian Shapiro, and G. Gordon Williamson.

who emphasized that the growth of the intellect begins at birth and continues in recognizable progressions throughout childhood (and perhaps throughout life). Piaget's observations of the early steps in cognitive development in infancy have had a profound influence on nearly all other theorists and researchers in the field.

A second force that has added to the upsurge of interest in infant cognition has been a large group of studies on perceptual development in infants, the great majority of such studies being by researchers in the United States (Gibson, 1969; Salapatek & Kessen, 1966; Kessen, Haith, & Salapatek, 1970). The focus of a great deal of the work has been on determining just how early the child has, or develops, a series of basic perceptual skills. How early does the child have depth perception? How early can the child make judgments of size or color? Much of the research on infancy has also focused on the problem of the development of attention in babies. To what do infants pay attention? Do they scan their environment? If so, in what way? How do these strategies of apprehending the world change over time?

The several threads of research on infants—Piaget's and the work of those interested in perceptual processes and attention—have begun to come together. It is now possible to weave together the beginnings of a picture of the cognitive–perceptual skills the child is born with and develops over the earliest months and years of life.

The Sensorimotor Period: Birth to 2 Years

Piaget has proposed that the earliest years of development, which he calls the *sensorimotor period,* can be divided into six stages. During each stage the child accomplishes new understandings and develops new skills with which to respond to and manipulate the environment. In the following discussion, Piaget's substages will be used as the basis for organization, but material from the contemporary work on perception and attention will be introduced as well.

STAGE ONE: BIRTH TO 1 MONTH. Piaget suggests that the starting point of cognitive development is a series of innate reflexes. In Piaget's view, the infant or child always does what he can do, always exercises whatever skills he has. In the newborn, virtually the entire repertoire of available behavior is reflexive. The baby grasps, sucks, looks in the direction of light, makes sounds, and moves his body. However, almost immediately these basic reflexes begin to change, to be modified by experience. Initially the baby will show the rooting reflex for anything that touches him anywhere on the cheek. But over the first weeks of life the motor response gets more specific and becomes more discriminating.

The infant up to 4 weeks of age is considerably more sophisticated perceptually than had been supposed only a decade or two ago. The infant shows some ability to track moving objects at birth, and this skill improves quite rapidly during the first month of life. The newborn is also able to focus both eyes on the same spot, although at birth this skill appears to be limited to objects placed about 8 inches from the baby's eyes. There is limited evidence that newborns have some rudimentary ability to discriminate depth, since they respond differently to a sphere than to a circle (Kessen, Haith, & Salapatek, 1970).

The infant also seems to come equipped with systematic strategies for scanning, examining, or exploring his environment visually. The newborn appears to be attracted by light and by sharp edges and contour (Salapatek & Kessen, 1966). For example, if a triangular figure is placed above the head of a 2- to 3-day-old infant while he is supine, the baby does not scan the entire figure. Instead he looks back and forth over one corner or one edge.

At this same early age there is evidence that the baby shows some ability to habituate to repeated stimuli, although habituation is not as rapid as it will later become. New stimulations—new sounds, new sights, new people—are likely to evoke some kind of response in the baby, but the response depends on the state the infant was in before the stimulation occurred. If the infant was awake and alert but inactive when the stimulation was presented, he becomes more active; if he was awake and active, he generally becomes less active as he responds to the stimulus.

In what way can all these comparatively primitive behaviors be considered the beginnings of cognition? The important point is that the infant from the beginning is responding to the world around him, and doing so in a comparatively systematic way. The infant's understanding of the world around him is extremely primitive. Indeed, there is good reason to suppose that he does not yet understand in any way that there is an "I" and an "other." But, from the beginning, the baby's responses to objects are shaped by his own explorations and manipulations. This experience is the beginning of the slow build-up of concepts about objects, about space, and about people, which make up the child's conceptual framework.

STAGE TWO: 1 TO 4 MONTHS. A number of significant changes in the child's attention and cognition appear to take place between the ages of 1 and 2 months. Piaget calls this the period of "primary circular reactions," by which he means something akin to a primitive habit. If the infant by accident gets his thumb into his mouth, he appears to try to repeat this action, gradually getting more skillful at it, and using a swifter, smoother motor action. But the initial trigger according to Piaget is an accidental occurrence. The infant is not yet at the stage of *intentionally* experimenting with the environment; but given an accidental occurrence of something interesting to do with his body, he will try to repeat it.

During this same period there is the beginning of primitive coordination of the input from the several senses. For example, the baby will look in the direction of a sound or of a touch on his body.

Between 1 and 4 months the baby pays attention to somewhat different things than he did as a newborn. Kagan (1971) suggests that at about 1 month there is a shift from the primitive "rules" of visual attention (contours and movement) to a general preference for things that are moderately complex or moderately novel. Objects or pictures that are familiar to the child, or that are very simple in design, draw less lengthy or intent looking from the baby than do somewhat novel or slightly more complex objects or pictures. Kagan calls this the *discrepancy principle* and argues that it governs the child's deployment of attention and manipulation throughout the first year of life. Of course, as the child progresses, the actual objects or events that are "moderately complex" change and become increasingly complex. So the child progresses gradually, exploring visually, tactually, and through the other senses, familiarizing himself with objects and stimuli and then turning to other stimuli that are more complex or newer to him. Gradually, through this process, the child begins to build up some "schemas" or models of the environment and of the people and objects that constitute it.

This fundamental process—of approaching new things, relating them to earlier experience, exploring them, then modifying existing concepts as the new experience is integrated into the system—continues throughout life and forms the basis of cognitive functioning. And this process can be seen in rudimentary form in the infant's explorations and in his preference for things that are not totally familiar.

During this period the child's perceptual skills continue to improve. He is now able to focus with both eyes on objects somewhat nearer to his face, and he has well-developed depth and size perception (Bower, 1966) and quite well-developed color vision (Chase, 1937). An infant in this stage will respond to an actual bottle but not to a picture of a bottle. This observation tells us that at this age the infant does not recognize a picture as a *representation* of the object; that is a level of symbolic functioning which does not appear clearly until well into the second year of life.

One other item of interest at this stage is that the infant begins to show imitation of others, but only of behaviors already in his repertoire. For example, the baby may imitate a sound the mother has made, but only if it is a sound that he has just made himself; new sounds would not be imitated.

Stage Three: 4 to 10 months. Piaget calls this period the stage of "secondary circular reactions." Again the infant tries to repeat actions that have led to something interesting. The difference is that now the infant goes beyond his own body and responds in the same way to objects. So, where the infant in stage two tried to repeat thumb sucking, now the infant is trying to repeat something he has made happen to an object. For example, suppose there is a mobile or rattle hanging above the infant's crib. By accident one day when he is moving his arms around above his head he hits the rattle. The sound is pleasing, and he appears to try to keep it going. This may lead at first to an increase in total bodily movement, but gradually the body movement is restricted to the movement of the hand. It is not completely clear whether the child's actions at this age are governed by any clearly conscious intention, but there seem at least to be the beginnings or rudiments of intentional behavior.

In the development of attention there are no major changes during this period. The infant continues to show habituation to repeated stimuli or experiences and continues to operate on the basis of the discrepancy principle, preferring moderately novel or moderately complex events or objects.

The more striking development during stage three is the development of the early phases of *object constancy*. The stage two infant does show some very primitive signs that he recognizes that objects have some permanency, some continued existence, when they are out of sight. The fact that he will turn toward a sound, for example, suggests that he has some kind of expectation that there will be a person or object where the sound came from.

But in the third stage there are marked changes toward fuller object constancy. For example, the child begins to anticipate the future positions of objects in motion. One of the tests of this, used in several studies, involves a toy train on an oval track with a screen in the middle of the oval. The baby can see the train appear around one end of the screen, pass in front of the screen, and then turn the corner and go behind the screen again. A stage two baby will continue to look at the point where the train disappeared, but a stage three baby will switch his eyes to the other end of the screen and wait for the train to reappear. So the infant has not only figured out that the train still exists but has also grasped the pattern of movement.

Another proof that the child has some concept of the permanency of objects is that he begins in this stage to search for hidden objects. However, this first awareness of object permanence is usually observed only when the baby has already been involved with the object. The baby will look for something that he has dropped. This searching occurs as an extension of the baby's action. So, if he throws a rattle out of the crib, the search will occur only where the hand has just dropped the rattle. Or if one hides a toy under a napkin, the child will search under the napkin *if* he had already been reaching for the toy when one hid it. The search at this stage is brief and unsystematic.

Other research (Bower, 1966) indicates that the child in stage three develops the concept of object *identity* but not of full object constancy. That is, the child grasps the fact that he has only one mother, that the person now coming through the doorway is the same one that went out a few minutes ago. But he does not yet fully understand that the mother continues to exist somewhere at all times, whether he can see her or not. The beginnings of such constancy are present during this period.

At this point in development the infant also appears to have a beginning awareness of spatial relationships. In his coordination of looking with grasping and sucking, he appears to be learning the relationship of the position of objects in space to his own body movements, as well as the relationship of one object in space to another. To illustrate, an infant may attempt to adjust the movements of his hand to the movements of a rattle swinging over his head.

Another cognitive skill that appears in rudimentary form for the first time during this period is a kind of primitive *classification* (Nelson, 1973a). For example, when the baby is given a new toy, he appears to relate it to other similar toys he has had. He approaches it with a movement or action which he has found successful with that kind of toy in the past. So, if the baby is accustomed to hitting a hanging crib toy to make it jingle, he will respond in a similar manner to another hanging crib toy, even though the new toy may require a pull motion to make it jingle. Eventually, through trial and error the infant may discover the more appropriate approach to the new toy. But the fact that the infant hit at it the first time around suggests that there was some generalization of the learned strategy to something that the child perceives as "the same." And it is this primitive perception of "sameness" that is the very beginning of classification.

Perceptual skills are not greatly changed during this period. The infant sharpens his depth perception skills, gradually using more and more cues for depth perception, and becomes increasingly adept at discriminations of various kinds. A stage three infant can discriminate visually between "mother" and "stranger" and can recognize a number of other individual faces. Also, during this period the infant becomes able to recognize an object on the basis of seeing only a part of it. So, even if only part of an object— such as a toy or a baby bottle—can be seen by the infant, he will still reach for it; thus he demonstrates that he "knows" that the whole object is there and that he is able to recognize it from seeing only a part. Presumably what has happened is that over the early months of life, the child has developed a whole series of expectancies for objects and people. The expectancies are modified by the child's continuing experience and therefore permit him to make better and better discriminations.

STAGE FOUR: 10 TO 12 MONTHS. This period is the first in which there is clear evidence of *intention* on the part of the child. The baby appears to have goals and to organize his actions in the service of those goals. He is not so thoroughly caught in the current moment and can at least begin to plan a series of activities. Such a plan inevitably involves organization of means and ends. The child does X in order to achieve Y. Prior to 10 months (although of course it may occur earlier in individual children who are progressing rapidly), this kind of means–ends relationship is not seen.

As an example, if a pillow is placed between the baby and a desired toy, the child will now push the pillow away in order to get at the toy. In a younger infant, pushing motions and reaching motions were both part of his repertoire, but he was apparently unable to string them together into an effective sequence. It is also important to note that the child has become more flexible in his actions. He uses whatever sort of motion or action will get him to the goal he desires. In the classic experiment involving object constancy, a toy is hidden under a scarf while the infant watches. The younger infant, unless he was already reaching for the toy, did not move the scarf away or search for it; the searching was merely a continuation of the motion that had already begun. But now, in stage four, the child may stop reaching, pause for a minute, reach out to grasp the scarf and move it away, then reach again for the toy. So a sequence of motions has been created that permits the more efficient achievement of the child's goal.

Still more complex is the child's use of other people or objects as means in achieving his goals. The baby may move an adult's hand to a jack-in-the-box toy in an effort to make the toy pop up. This action suggests that he is beginning to see that other persons or things can be causal agents in his environment. So, rudimentary concepts of *causality* are present at this stage.

The infant's expanded understanding of the relationships between objects and events (between actions and ends) is also illustrated by his increased ability to *anticipate* events. Quite young babies show some primitive anticipation when they are picked up. But in the stage four infant, there are quite sophisticated anticipations. For example, the baby may begin to cry at the sight of a food he does not like. It does not take the taste of the food to elicit the crying or rejection. The baby anticipates the unliked taste and begins to fuss merely at the sight of the food.

Also, the object concept becomes more differentiated and more independent of the child's actions. The child engages in active search for objects that are completely hidden if he has witnessed them being hidden, whether he was in the act of reaching for the object or not. As indicated earlier, this is part of the new skill in subserving one action to another. There is, however, still a limit on the child's understanding of the permanence of an object and of its possible changes in space. The child of this age still searches where he *last found* the object. For example, one hides a toy under a pillow and has the child find it. If one again hides it under the same pillow but then in full sight of the child moves the object so that it is concealed under another pillow, the infant will search where the toy was last found. So, although the baby does have some understanding of the fact that objects continue to exist when they cannot be seen, he has not comprehended that while out of sight they can occupy a series of different places.

The child of this age also chooses to pay attention to slightly different things than before. Kagan (1971) suggests that the infant of 10 months or so begins to attend to things that are rich in "hypotheses." What he appears to mean by this is that the baby prefers to play with or manipulate things that offer many options for involvement or that involve several modalities. So, an infant will prefer a toy that makes noise, has several colors or patterns or textures, comes apart, and includes small and large parts—as opposed to a toy that is a single color and simpler in construction. This preference may be simply an extension of the discrepancy principle. The infant may still be preferring things of moderate complexity, except that now complexity is defined in terms of what can be *done* with the object rather than merely in terms of its perceptual richness.

Imitation also undergoes a significant change at this age. For the first time the infant is now able to imitate something novel.

Instead of being limited to imitating only those responses that are already in his repertoire, he will copy new sounds and make new body movements as a direct imitation of an adult or other child. Thus, what one observed in the younger infant was not strictly imitation. Rather, the adult's action seemed to serve as a kind of trigger that set off an equivalent behavior in the infant. Now, however, "real" imitation occurs, in which the child appears to add new responses to his repertoire. The development of such true imitation makes possible a whole new range of teaching strategies in language and in many other areas.

STAGE FIVE: 12 TO 18 MONTHS. The child begins at this age to show what might legitimately be called curiosity. The baby of 12 months or so will explore objects in an experimental way, as if to discover all the things that can be done with it. Piaget describes an example of this from his observations of his own child. The baby was playing with the soap dish while in the bath. In a younger infant one might have seen some repetition of a single dropping motion. But at this age Piaget noted multiple experimentations, with the infant dropping the soap dish at different angles, from different heights, over the leg, under the leg, down the back, and so forth. This trial-and-error procedure—for the explorations are not yet systematic—inevitably results in the child's experiences being broadened still further. He now knows much more about dropping things, about the behavior of objects when dropped, and about the ways in which his body and the object relate to each other. One of the consequences of this broadening of experience is that the infant now knows many more strategies, more ways to get things done, and this in turn is information that can be used by the infant in the service of other goals on other occasions. Note also that the infant's focus of attention has shifted from his own actions to the actions of the object, which is a kind of "decentering" of attention. This focus upon the object, rather than on his own action, in turn makes possible new strides in the development of the object concept. Objects begin to have an increasingly singular and permanent identity.

Recall that in stage four the infant searched where he last *found* the object—that is, it was his action of searching and finding that dominated. Now, in stage five, the toddler searches for a missing toy where it was last *seen,* even if this is not the place where it was last found. So, if one hides a toy under a scarf, has the child search for it, and then on the next trial hides it initially under the first scarf and then under a second, the 1-year-old child will search under the second scarf. However, the infant does not yet have full understanding of the object's existence in space, and he does not have a sense of the possible places the object might be. For example, if one lets the baby see one hide a toy under a pillow, then without the baby's seeing it hides the toy under a box, the infant will search under the pillow and then stop searching. An infant of this age does look puzzled, as if he knows that the toy is there somewhere; but he does not begin to look in other likely places.

The child's conception of causality also has become more sophisticated. Just as he now pays more attention to objects than to his own actions on them, so he now understands that there are causes for actions that are outside of himself. For example, the child of this age will put a ball on top of an incline and sit back waiting for it to roll down, thus showing that he has some understanding of the fact that the ball will roll without his having to do anything more to it.

Imitation does not undergo any major changes at this age. The biggest change took place during stage four, when the child was first able to imitate something that was not already in his repertoire. But this response becomes more sophisticated in stage five. The infant now does slightly better on his first try at imitating a new response. Instead of being satisfied with the first try, he will often persist with several tries until he has it more nearly correct. However, the infant of this age still has some difficulty imitating body movements that he cannot watch himself carry out, such as rubbing his forehead or touching his nose. Such imitations can be learned at this stage, but they are more difficult for the child.

Classification is still very rudimentary, but it does exist and appears to be based primarily on the shape, function, or action of objects, and not on the basis of color. Piaget has not placed much emphasis on the classification skills of children of this age. Reading Piaget's descriptions of this stage one gets the impression that he saw the 12- to 18-month-old child as still quite primitive in thinking and in the representation of objects. But more recent work by Nelson (1973a) suggests quite strongly that once again the young infant may have been underestimated. The study is an inventive one and worth describing.

Nelson argues that the young toddler develops categories based on actions, that is, on things that can be done to objects; and when he encounters something new, he "categorizes" it on the basis of its form. For example, the child may develop some very primitive category of "things that can be sat upon," based on all sorts of trials and experiences. But then perhaps the child extracts from this some "typical form" for things that can be sat upon, and when he sees something new that is shaped like the other things that can be sat upon, he assumes it belongs in that category. So, Nelson is suggesting that the categories are based originally on actions but are stored mentally on the basis of form. Younger children would have to try out the action before they could categorize the object, but the 12-to 18-month-old child is just beginning to be able to abstract in a very rudimentary way to create some kind of categorization system.

To test this notion, Nelson gave infants of 15 to 20 months of age a set of ten objects: one round rubber ball, three objects like a ball in form but unlike it in function (a heavy black ball of hard plastic, a rotating cork sphere on a stand, and a spherical rattle that was attached to a flat stand), three objects like a ball in function but unlike it in form (an oval shaped block covered in soft plastic, a small rubber football, and a hard plastic "whiffle" football with holes), and three objects unlike the ball in both form and function (a small frisbee, a small square block, and a cylindrical rattle). The infant was shown the set of ten and told, "Give me the ball." Generally, children of this age are able to respond correctly to this kind of request. After the child had handed over the ball, the experimenter once again said, "Give me the ball." This procedure was then repeated until five objects had been selected by the child.

The results indicated that infants of this age show some tendency to pick on the basis of form, suggesting that some kind of primitive category had been developed. However, after they had been given a chance to play with the ten toys, their selections were based on similarity of action. They then picked things that can roll or things that can be thrown, rather than things that look round but do not have similar action properties. So the preverbal, or beginning verbal, child does form categories, including categories for which there are no existing words in the child's very early vocabulary. This finding strongly suggests the independence of thought and speech. The child need not be able to form words in order to form categories.

The several advances in cognition and in perception at this age result in a number of new self-help skills. At around 1 year, for example, the baby begins to assist in dressing by holding his arms out at the sight of his shirt, thus indicating his association between the visual configuration of his shirt and the fact that it relates to his arms. The child of this age still does not recognize specific things about the shirt, such as that the left arm goes in a particular hole or the head in a particular place. But he does recognize in some sense that it is something that goes on his arms and torso, rather than on his feet.

The child's play with objects is heavily dominated by trial and error, by the kind of experimentation described above. However it is important to emphasize that at this age the child is not systematic and is not heavily guided by the perceptual input. For example, in nesting boxes or pots and pans, the child may try out several different combinations and methods of attack. But there is no inspection of the boxes to see which one should go next—that does not occur until stage six at the earliest. Nevertheless, experimentation is an important part of the play of the child. He experiments now with taking rings off a ring stack and tries to get them back on again; he fills things up and empties them; and he begins to stack blocks on top of one another—although at this age he is ordinarily able to stack only two blocks, perhaps due to limitations in his fine motor control for release activities.

STAGE SIX: 18 TO 24 MONTHS. Piaget saw this stage as a critical one for the beginning of *internal representation,* although Nelson's work might lead to the process being identified with an earlier age. Nonetheless a new element appears that seems to suggest that the child has indeed been able to internalize some of the actions. Where, in stage five, the child used trial and error with objects to discover new properties and new means, in stage six he is able for the first time to do some of that trial and error in his head. It is as if the child were now able to picture to himself the actions and thus need not perform all of them. It may seem a small step, but it is an immense one for the child and critically important for the development of cognitive skill.

For example, now that the child is able to represent actions to himself in some internal fashion, new kinds of imitation become possible. The child can watch someone do something and then practice it *later*. Piaget calls this *deferred imitation,* and it obviously requires the ability to hold the action in mind in some way. The child's imitations also become better on the first try, presumably in part because he is now able to try out some of the versions in his head before he tries them overtly.

The object concept is now fully developed as well. The child continues to search, after a first failure, and can successfully follow a series of moves of the hidden object. The child can even make some beginning deductions of where the object might be.

The child's attention appears to continue to be drawn by things that move, things that provoke action. Studies of language development (Nelson, 1973b) suggest that the child's earliest words are likely to be words for actions or words for objects that involve action. So, movement and activity seem still to be dominating deployment of the child's attention.

The child's understanding of causal relationships becomes more sophisticated as well. In particular, he appears at this age to understand that there may be several ways to bring about the same result. If one strategy fails, he turns to another, rather than persisting with the unsuccessful one. For example, a $1\frac{1}{2}$- to 2-year-old may point to a toy he wants while eating in a high chair. When the caregiver says no, he drops a spoon on the floor; when the caregiver bends down to pick up the spoon, the baby points to the toy again. So, when the first strategy—asking—did not work, a second strategy was developed.

All of these developments are represented in his play with objects. A child will now recognize a picture as a representation of an object and will pat the picture of a familiar object in a story book. The newly developed attention to the shape of objects is also reflected in greater skill in fitting shapes into form boards. When playing with a narrow-opening, plastic milk container into which clothespins may be dropped, the child demonstrates his understanding of the spatial and positional elements of the task by aligning the clothespins correctly before dropping them into the container.

*The Preconceptual Period: 2 to 5 Years**

The six stages of the sensorimotor period are completed by age 2, with the beginning of internal representation of objects and actions. What begins at about this age is a long period—which goes by various names—that appears to be a kind of consolidation of the various gains already made. The child begins to use words and images as methods of internal representation and uses them more and more effectively and efficiently.

These are the rudiments of a *symbolic* system that forms the basis for all later, more sophisticated, types of cognitive skill.

The symbolic characteristic of thought is the most critical feature of the child's cognitive skills at this stage. The child is able to use some image, some word, to *stand for* something else. The ability to do this introduces a whole host of new possibilities. The child can think about things that have already happened; he can engage in fantasy play, in which an object is used to stand for another object—a stick may become a witch's broomstick, or an arrow, or a bow, or any of a thousand other things; he can defer imitation, a skill that first appeared at stage six with the first rudiments of internal representation.

It is not at all clear that words are needed for this kind of symbolic representation. Bruner has suggested in fact that the early representations are heavily dominated by images and that language plays quite a small role at this stage (Bruner, Olver, & Greenfield, 1966). In much older children (6 or 7 years of age) some formal language system appears to be useful. But in the younger child it is certainly not necessary and probably not very helpful. (This is not to suggest that oral language is not helpful to the child in other ways; only that it is not necessary for internal symbolic representation.)

The child's internal symbols at this stage are highly idiosyn-

*Although Piaget's preconceptual period is from 2 to 5 years, discussion here is limited to the earlier part of this cognitive period, since this program guide focuses on children up to 3 years of age.

cratic. Each child will use different images and different small notions to represent objects or actions. In part, internal imagery remains individual throughout life. Our "mental shorthand" is composed of a whole range of highly personal symbols. But one of the things that happens with age is that many of the child's symbols become more public, or common, through the use of a common language.

Logic is still very primitive, but there are some signs that the child attempts to relate one experience with another in some logical way. For example, the child calls to his father and the father does not answer. The child concludes "Daddy didn't hear." Presumably what the child is doing in this instance is extrapolating from previous experiences in some way; he is assuming that a connection between events he had observed before holds in this instance. He believes or thinks that what he wants to happen or to be true is going to happen or be true.

Attention and habituation undergo a further change, resulting from the child's burgeoning ability to classify and to treat sets of objects as classes. In the young infant, habituation occurs for each object individually. But at this age, the child shows some signs of habituation for *classes* of objects (Faulkender, Wright, & Waldron, 1974). So, if one repeatedly shows the child a picture of a dog, he will demonstrate habituation. That is, he will look at it for shorter and shorter periods of time. Now if one shows a picture of *another* dog, it takes fewer presentations before the child it totally bored, suggesting that the child considers the two pictures to be the same in some sense.

As was true in the early periods, classification is still based heavily on form rather than color. But 2- to 3-year-old children do not do well at grouping or classifying abstract forms such as circles and squares. They do better with real objects or with pictures or small replicas of real objects (Denney, 1972a, 1972b).

Again, the child's play reflects many of these changes. He is immersed in play that requires conceptual judgments of form, color, position, detail, and size. He now recognizes photos of familiar adults, and by the age of 3 will recognize photos of himself. This visual understanding of body concept is also demonstrated by his ability to differentiate and identify the facial features on a stylized drawing of a face. The child of this age generally shows that he understands the relationships between objects and pictures (symbols) of objects. His fine motor coordination and conceptual skill also make possible the nesting of four different sizes of containers and the matching of geometric forms to their appropriate holes in a form board. In both cases, the preconceptual child approaches the task by looking it over carefully first, rather than starting right off with trial and error as the younger child is likely to do.

Other play skills observed in the 2- to 3-year-old child include positioning coins in the correct spatial orientation to fit into a penny bank or correctly aligning vertical pegs to fit into a pegboard. Block building now includes horizontal construction—with the blocks placed side by side. When playing with popbeads, he now is able to judge which ends go together.

Obviously, a great many changes occur in cognitive functioning from birth to 3 years of age. But the development is continuous, in small steps, and it appears to be heavily based on the child's opportunities to experience and manipulate objects, environments, people, and events. At each step the child repeats and practices skills he has acquired. In the repetition and practice, new modifications enter, new arrangements are understood, and in this way the child makes progress. Language spoken to the child by others may make some difference, but the critical factor appears to be the child's own opportunities to explore and experience.

The general principles of normal cognitive development outlined in this section are summarized in Table 8.1.

Cognitive Development in Atypical Children

Some physically disabled or otherwise atypical children are also "mentally retarded." For example, among the children seen in the first 19 centers involved in the National Collaborative Infant Project, the mean scores on the Denver Developmental Screening Test at the time the infants entered the programs ranged between .45 and .65 on the four scales of the test—personal–social, language, fine motor, and gross motor development. To be sure, there was a wide range of scores, with some children testing as essentially normal, but the large majority of the children who entered infant programs were functioning at a retarded level in all four domains.

To be mentally retarded need not mean that the process or

TABLE 8.1

General Principles of Cognitive Development*

FROM	TO
Global	Differentiated
Known, familiar	Unknown, unfamiliar
Percept	Concept
Reflexive	Voluntary
Trial and error	Foresight, planning schema
Unstructured	Structured
General (diffuse)	Specific
Transitory	Permanent
Inductive	Deductive
Sensorimotor	Symbolic
Concrete (direct)	Abstract (indirect)
Physical	Mental
Personal (proximal)	Vicarious (distal)
Idiosyncratic	Formalized (norm)
Egocentric	Socialized
Subjective	Objective
Gross	Fine
Simple	Complex
Disparate sensory experiences	Integrative sensory experiences
Immediate	Delayed
Discrete	Categorical

*By Lillian Shapiro with Gloria Boylan and Carol Hosaka.

progress of cognitive development is different in kind. Piaget's work, and that of others in the area of cognitive development in infancy, suggests strongly that in the sequence and process of mental development there are basic commonalities among children. Unless and until research demonstrates otherwise, it is reasonable to assume that atypical children share these basic processes and sequences of cognitive development.

There is evidence from several sources that the slowing of cognitive development in the atypical child is heavily influenced by experiences after birth and may not necessarily be a result of the basic disorder. For example, a number of researchers have reported that the low birth weight infant is likely to show normal rates of development if raised in a middle class family but will be somewhat retarded in cognitive development if raised in a poverty-level or working-class family (Scarr-Salapatek & Williams,

1973). Willerman, Broman, and Fielder (1970) have also found that infants under 1 year who show very slow early cognitive development are far more likely to show continued retardation if they are raised in a working-class family; equivalently developmentally delayed children raised in a middle-class family are likely to show quite normal intellectual development by age 4. Such evidence suggests that there are environmental factors at work that can affect the rate of cognitive growth in children during the years of infancy, and that these environmental factors interact with or even override the child's physical disorders.

There is also accumulating evidence from studies of some groups of atypical children that the early stages of sensorimotor development are very similar to the patterns seen in normal children. Fraiberg, for example, has shown that the patterns of early sensorimotor development are essentially the same in blind children as in sighted children (Fraiberg, 1968, 1974; Fraiberg, Siegel, & Gibson, 1966). Divergencies in development do occur later, but it is not entirely clear whether these differences in the sequence or pattern of growth are due to the physical disability or disorder or to differences in the pattern of experience that is available to the child.

At the same time, there is some information to suggest that the form, as well as the rate, of growth may be different for some groups of atypical children. For example, a number of researchers have reported that habituation to repeated stimuli does not occur as readily among young premature babies (Sigman & Parmelee, 1974) and among Down's syndrome infants (Miranda & Fanz, 1973, 1974). The premature babies, who were approximately 4 months old in this study, also did not show any clear preference for novel stimuli, although they did show an apparently normal preference for stimuli of moderate complexity. Whether these differences in the pattern of cognitive development are due to differences in central nervous system functioning, or whether they result from some systematic differences in experiences resulting from the primary disorder, or both, is not at all clear from data of this kind. Further research on the patterns of cognitive development in other groups of atypical infants will be needed before one has a very clear picture of the qualitative differences in development that may be related to disorders of various kinds. Lacking such evidence, it seems most reasonable to assume that the basic processes are the same, or very similar, and that what is needed by the child is the maximum possible opportunity to explore and manipulate.

All of the accumulating information about cognitive development in infancy underlines the fact that the infant makes cognitive progress through continual interaction with and action upon the environment. Assuming that this is a correct analysis of what is happening, then two factors will influence the quality and rate of the child's cognitive development: (*a*) the extent to which the infant is capable of interacting with the environment; and (*b*) the nature of the environment with which the infant is interacting.

For many visually or auditorily impaired, physically disabled, abused, addicted, premature, or multiply handicapped infants, the capability of interacting freely with the environment is attenuated. For example, when, in the second stage of the sensorimotor period, a severely spastic infant attempts to coordinate sucking with arm movements, the tightness of his arm muscles makes this coordinated movement impossible. If difficulty is experienced with a large number of such intersensory integrations, there may well be some interference with the normal pattern of cognitive growth. Since other skills are hierarchically organized upon these early accomplishments, the spasticity may later affect a forward reach, prehension, feeding, and dressing. Or, to take another example, the distortion or lack of visual information in the partially sighted baby may markedly limit the variety and quality of experiences, and may affect the baby's ability to practice coordinated behaviors. Again, this will affect the development of later skills that build on these behaviors.

The hearing-impaired infant, to take yet another example, may be unable to use the usual auditory cues from the environment. Such a child is able to watch someone leave his field of vision, but he remains unaware of the other's continued presence because he cannot hear the sounds of movement (e.g., footsteps). The child's growing sense of object permanence may be affected by this limitation.

The normally functioning child in a normally adequate environment will find opportunities to explore and act on the world around him. These explorations and actions will help to build up step by step the complex understanding of the environment, of objects and their relationships to one another, that is the basis of the child's cognitive system. The physically disabled or other atypical child, lacking in many instances the ability to reach out to the environment, is inevitably going to miss some of the early stepping stones. The role of the staff intervening in the cognitive development of such a child is largely to make it possible for the child to experience as normally as possible, and to expand, those experiences or explorations that are available to the child.

A stimulating environment is essential to development. A child may have all the necessary capabilities, but if there is nothing there to reach for, explore, look at, or manipulate, no one to look at, smile at, or cry for, impaired cognitive functioning may develop. It is clear, for example, that physically normal children raised in the socially and emotionally impoverished environment of some institutions show markedly retarded cognitive growth (Bowlby, 1951; Provence & Lipton, 1962). The critical deficits in such institutions appear to be both a lack of sufficient animate stimulation (handling, stroking, and verbal interaction) and a lack of sufficient inanimate stimulation (toys, mobiles, and other things to look at or manipulate). The need for variety appears to be particularly critical during the stages of sensorimotor development, when the infant is coordinating and elaborating behaviors.

There is a motivational, as well as a purely cognitive, risk involved in an insufficiency of stimulation. Hunt (1961) has emphasized that while children may be born with a tendency to explore, manipulate, and examine objects and people, this tendency can atrophy to some extent if it is not used. The child who has explored and examined many new things will approach still newer things with less fear and more interest and curiosity than the child with more limited experiences. The risk, then, for the atypical child, with his consequent deprivations in experience and stimulation, is that the child may become apathetic or fearful.

The caregiver's attitude toward the child's handicap may also have a substantial effect on the sort of stimulation that is provided and the sorts of expectations for performance that are held for the child. There are two common reactions, both of them extreme. One is for the caregiver to have a falsely high level of expectation for the child's cognitive development, so that the child may be under continuous pressure to achieve unrealistic goals. For example, in the belief that the child may become normal, the caregiver may repeatedly present to a young quadriplegic infant with apparently normal cognitive ability the task of dropping objects into a container. Although the baby may understand the task and attempt to do it, his disability prevents him from coordinating his movements, resulting in continual frustration for both child and caregiver. As a result, the child may become fearful or withdrawn and be unwilling to experiment in other situations, which in turn may retard his cognitive development. Such an infant may tend to "fixate" at early levels of functioning, perseverating at strategies that are physically possible for him.

The other extreme reaction is for the caregiver's expectations for the cognitive development of the child to be so low that no attempt is made to motivate, encourage, or elicit behaviors appropriate to his developmental level. For example, thinking that the infant cannot hear or respond, the caregiver may not talk to the infant or present toys to him, thus giving the baby little or no chance to respond differentially or creatively to his environment. Both of these extreme attitudes on the part of the caregiver may result in children who exhibit perseverative or bizarre behaviors, or who may be unnecessarily slowed in cognitive growth. In this way the disabled child is rendered more handicapped than he need be.

It is important to emphasize that a great many of the generalizations and conclusions offered here about the cognitive development of the atypical child are based on clinical observation and on the intuitive conclusions of sensitive professionals. Research data on the patterns of cognitive growth in the atypical child are scarce and tend to be heavily focused on several specific groups of the atypical—most notably the premature (or low birth weight) infant and the Down's syndrome infant. Piaget's theory has also been strongly influential. The basic assumptions that underlie all of the suggested interventions are (*a*) that the cognitive growth of the atypical child is more like that of a normal child than it is unlike; and (*b*) that cognitive growth in any child is heavily based on the child's own opportunities to explore and manipulate the environment. What is not known is what happens to the whole developing system if one or more modes of exploration is restricted. Can the child compensate through other modalities? Are some modalities, such as tactual exploration, more important than others in the child's growing understanding of objects and the total environment? Or can visual exploration be substituted in part for tactual exploration in those children for whom tactual manipulation is difficult? These are important questions for future research. Lacking answers to them, it remains only to emphasize the importance of the richest possible variety of stimulation and exploration.

Intervention

As with a young plant already unique, growing, and interacting with its environment, intervention should be like enriching the soil that surrounds the seedling, strengthening its ability to grow. Too often the intervention is like a grafting, an adding on, instead of an enhancement of the maturing organism. If those who work with babies understand what the child is attempting to do, at which stage the child is functioning, and what steps are needed next, they are better able to facilitate growth by providing the bridge between what the infant can do and what he cannot do.

Unfortunately, structured didactic lessons are often the only means of cognitive intervention presented in a child's program at home or at the center. In this approach, emphasis is generally placed on the finished product (i.e., the child returned the rings to the ring stack in the appropriate order, finished the puzzle, or copied the vertical line drawing), rather than on the actual learning process. Thus the young child spends a disproportionate amount of time sitting at a table manipulating toys.

In such a setting the adult usually assumes the role of a traditional "teacher"—showing the child how to place the pieces into the puzzle, handing him the correct ring size to be placed on the stack, or taking his arm through the movement required for copying a vertical line. Demonstration (visual modeling) and guiding the child through the task are often necessary and appropriate when teaching the young child. However, when these are the sole teaching strategies, they limit the infant or toddler's opportunity to engage in independent problem solving. A problem-solving approach that is process oriented, rather than task oriented, allows for the free exploration of objects. Particularly for children in the sensorimotor period, there is a need for experimentation through trial and error. The child should be given the freedom to investigate the object in the manner of his choice—such as mouthing, squeezing, throwing, or banging it. These opportunities allow him to explore the various sensory components of the experience as well as its potential possibilities for play. For example, round puzzle pieces not only fit in a puzzle; they may also be spun on the floor or rolled off a table top, or they may serve as a cookie to be fed to a doll.

Interventions to facilitate cognitive development can be incorporated in a natural fashion into the daily life of the child and his family. For instance parents can be encouraged to play "hide and seek" games when the child is cognitively at or past stage three, thus fostering the acquisition of object constancy. It is important to allow older children a chance for fantasy play, which requires time alone with plenty of materials or toys within reach. Frequently the physically handicapped child must be positioned properly to make such play possible.

A broad range of strategies is required to allow the child to experience success and to engage in situations that allow him to feel he has an effect on his environment. This may involve adaptation of materials, visual demonstrations, verbal directions, precueing, or actively performing the task with him. In the child whose physical disability is quite severe, having someone "demonstrate" hiding and searching, stacking, and the like may be helpful. Another strategy is to accompany some activities with verbal stimulation; for example, labeling the toys or objects involved, describing their features, and talking about the actions performed.

In program planning, staff members and parents need to evaluate carefully the current level of cognitive functioning of the child and the likely next steps in the developmental progression. Then efforts can be made to provide the child with the sort of opportunities and experiences that will help him achieve the next sequence toward an understanding of the world around him. In implementing any intervention, it is vital that the young child be properly positioned to maximize his abilities to interact with his environment. This may necessitate modifications in carrying and handling, special materials, and adaptive equipment such as bolsters, prone boards, and floor seats (see Appendix A).

Staff members need to be aware of their own teaching style as well as the nature of the teaching–learning interaction of parent with child. Available studies show great variability in the way that mothers teach their children (Bee, Van Egeren, Streissguth, Nyman, & Leckie, 1969; Hess & Shipman, 1965, 1967, 1968; Steward & Steward, 1973). The researchers delineate the elements that seem to maximize learning. For instance, instructions should be presented with clarity, so the learner knows what is expected of him. A positive pattern of feedback is indicated, with praise outweighing criticism. Optimally, feedback should be in the context of what the learner is doing; if random or delayed, the child may have difficulty deciding what it was that he did correctly or incorrectly.

The learner needs permission and encouragement for independent action. In a study by Bee and her associates (1969), some mothers physically interfered in the child's task behavior. The mothers were asked to teach the child how to build a particular house out of blocks. Some of the mothers built the house for the child, rather than helping him to learn how to build it himself; but other mothers made helpful suggestions to the child, such as "Look at the model" or "Think about what you should do next." Orienting comments of this kind or questions such as "Do you want to start at the back or at the front?" help to focus the child on the *way* to solve a problem and thus foster problem-solving skills. However, in some cases simple directions may be more appropriate.

Other considerations include the overall sensitivity of the teacher to the learner's needs, the use of physical space so that everyone is comfortable and can participate in the task, and the tempo or pacing of the learning experience with respect to the amount of instruction and learner involvement. It is also important for the caregiver to determine if the learner has a preferred sensory channel or mode of learning. There is a cyclical, give-and-take quality in a good teaching–learning interaction in which teacher and learner interchange dominant roles.

Parents have varied teaching styles. Staff members need to be attuned to these differences in style and may have to work directly on modifying them. For example, if a parent's natural inclination is to overlook good performance and focus on errors, then time may have to be spent with the parent to explain the function and value of praise in teaching. Of course, all the variations of teaching style that are found in parents are also found in professionals.

And the effects of those teaching styles are equally relevant when the parent is the learner. Staff members should analyze the interactional pattern used when instructing a parent as well as a child. Is one providing positive feedback about what the parent does with the child? Or is attention so focused on the child that all reinforcement is directed toward him and none to the parent? Are the principles of learning theory being applied to both parent and child?

Sample Activities and Interventions

■ *Visual Attention.* Designing interventions to develop visual attention requires that the status of the child's visual system be known. Few of the young babies presently involved in programs of early intervention have had a thorough visual evaluation. In the absence of such evaluation, a general screening tool may be utilized to determine the gross status of visual attention, visual acuity, visual tracking, and the like (Sheridan, 1973). If inattention is a significant characteristic of the young child's behavior, it is important to ascertain whether the attentional limitation is organic or developmenal in origin.

Practitioners need to be aware of the appropriateness of the visual environment in relation to the infant's stage of cognitive development. For example, one of the first objects babies are expected to attend to is an overhead crib mobile. These mobiles, while aesthetic to the adult eye, have mostly been designed in ignorance of the principles of visual preference, discrepancy, and perception. Thus they consist of small wooden figures or pastel-colored objects which hang 3 to 4 feet away from the baby. It is not surprising that they are ineffectual in eliciting visual attention in the infant, who is described as looking off into space or of selectively attending to overhead bright lights or busy wallpaper. For infants in stages one and two, a more appropriate mobile may be achieved by wrapping black electrician's tape around the pastel objects to delineate more interesting patterns and contours. Paper plates decorated in red, white, and black contrasting patterns may be added to an existing overhead mobile by simply stringing a shoelace or ribbon through the plate. Or a mobile may be constructed of shiny silver objects such as teaspoons and small tin cans.

For an infant who has reached stage five, and is beginning to recognize pictures, a more appropriate mobile would be one constructed of large photographs of familiar objects. At stage four, it would be more appropriate to have the real objects themselves attached to the mobile. At the preconceptual stage of development, letters or words could be printed on cards and tied to the mobile.

Since many motor interventions for the atypical child require the utilization of specific recommended positions (lying prone propped over a wedge, sitting in an adapted chair, standing on a prone board), the staff is responsible for creating an interesting visual environment individualized to the positioning and the cognitive level of the child. Lying in the prone position over a bolster, an infant's visual environment may be limited to the rug, furniture legs, human feet, the lower portion of a wall, and the objects that have been placed in front of him. Appropriate adaptation of the surroundings in this instance would include decorating the floor surface or lower two feet of the wall. Again, the type of decoration (bright geometric shapes, magazine pictures, or letters of the alphabet) would depend on the cognitive level of the individual child. The toys and other objects placed in front of him could provide visual as well as tactile and motor stimulation—for example, a shiny cookie sheet on which to smear yogurt.

Habituation to stimuli necessitates frequently changing the infant's visual environment. What is observed as inattention may just be boredom. However, one must also be aware of the possibility of visually overloading the child. Busy patterns on crib sheets and bumper guards, wallpaper and curtains can visually overwhelm the child, increasing his inattentive behavior as he tunes out his distracting environment. Sensory bombardment of a child is usually contraindicated; whatever the sensory modality, input should be selectively graded to facilitate perceptual and cognitive integration.

■ *Object Exploration.*   According to Piaget, the various stages of cognitive development are characterized by variations in the child's manual exploration of objects. During the very earliest stage of cognitive development the exploration of objects is characterized by "holding" behaviors—not surprisingly, since this parallels the time at which the baby demonstrates the grasp reflex. Initially the baby does not look at the object in his hand, nor does he manipulate the object to discover its tactile components.

The ability to sustain a grasp appears essential to many higher-level explorations such as mouthing, dropping, throwing, and showing objects. A baby that cannot maintain a grasp due to motor dysfunction is hampered in his further explorations. To help overcome this problem, objects may be secured to the infant's palm with surgical tape, thus allowing him to engage in the more advanced skills of banging and hitting. The child whose hands are fisted—the thumb held against the palm of the hand and the fingers flexed around the thumb—is likewise limited in his handling of objects. Flexing the child's wrist can often reduce tension and facilitate partial extension of the fingers.

Some children seem unable to tolerate grasping objects that have particular tactile properties. While muscle tone is normal, certain tactile experiences are seen as threatening and the child withdraws his hand.* The clinician should try to determine the nature of the experiences that are perceived as loathsome and provide activities that will decrease the child's hypersensitivity and tactile defensiveness. For example, if the child withdraws from contact with such materials as carpeting, fuzzy stuffed toys, or sweaters, the practitioner can begin with such nonthreatening activities as the child rolling on differently textured firm surfaces, gentle blanket swinging, or rocking**—followed possibly by brisk rubbing. Rubbing the child's body with terry cloth should be done with pressure, since many of these children respond negatively to a light, tickling touch. Encouraging the child to participate in the activity by having him rub his own arms and legs may be less threatening and may ease in the transition to his handling of other materials.

The manipulative play of the infant who is cognitively in stage three often involves object explorations that result in the production of sound—banging toys up and down, hitting objects against one another, and shaking them from side to side. The production of noise delights and encourages the child. If no noise results, the frequency of shaking and banging behaviors usually declines. Thus, the child who is unable to hold objects or is

---

*This is not to be confused with a neurologically based avoidance reaction.

**Vestibular stimulation must be used with caution if the child has a history of seizures.

restricted by marked spasticity may be considerably limited in his play repertoire. Such a child may be placed in a side-lying position with a toy secured by suction cups on the floor or crib. Then, even a grossly directed reach or swipe may activate an auditory and/or visual result. In addition, bells or rattles loosely tied to a wrist or ankle stimulate shaking or banging movements of the arm or leg. If noiseless toys (sponge, sock, powder puff, cotton ball) are also available for the child to "bang at," he may begin to develop primitive classifications—some objects when manipulated result in noise production, others do not.

Experimentation with the numerous properties and functions of objects as discovered through trial and error particularly characterizes stage five of cognitive development and is the foundation for beginning skills in classification. At this stage a wide variety of toys or materials should be made available to the child. As he begins to demonstrate his understanding of various concepts of himself and his environment, numerous occasions can be provided for such concepts to be generalized to new situations and materials.

At any age it is important *not* to give the child his favorite toy all the time. Far too frequently practitioners use a preferred toy as a pacifier when interventions are being done. For instance, the same toy is always presented when the young child practices kneeling or standing at a small table. Within reason, the child will benefit from being challenged and encouraged to widen his horizons, rather than being too often pacified.

CHAPTER 9

SOCIAL–EMOTIONAL DEVELOPMENT

O F ALL the areas discussed in this program guide, the child's social and emotional development has probably been the least systematically studied.

Normal Social–Emotional Development

Except for some good research on the development of attachment (which is fully discussed in this chapter), little work has focused on the sequential development of social skills or emotional patterns. The studies that are available tend to be fairly narrow in scope. For example, researchers who have studied the development of attachment in the first years of life have not simultaneously looked at the growth of self-concept or at changes in emotional patterns. Due to the somewhat splintered quality of the information on which the discussion is based, it seems reasonable in this instance to present the material in a topical, rather than purely developmental manner. However the simultaneity of the processes is suggested by the accompanying developmental chart (Table 9.1).

The Development of Attachment

The development of an attachment by the child to the caregiver and by the caregiver to the child is beyond any doubt the most important and the most pervasive early social and emotional

The major contributor to this chapter is Helen Bee Douglas assisted by Helen Hoffman.

TABLE 9.1
Social–Emotional Development

AGE	ATTACHMENT	SELF-CONCEPT	EMOTIONAL DEVELOPMENT	INDEPENDENCE–DEPENDENCE
0 to 6 months	Diffuse attachments Social smile	Little separation of self and not-self	Differentiation of delight and distress	
6 months to 1 year	Specific attachment	Formation of concept of constant self	Fear, disgust, anger	
12 months to 18 months	Multiple attachments		Affection, elation	Beginning of strong independence strivings; independent loco-motion
18 months to 2 years	Some continuing dis-tress at separation, but multiple attachments and better coping	Response to own name	Verbal expression of feelings	
2 to 3 years	Better coping with separation; still some distress if left with strangers	By 3 may know own gender		Major time for concern of autonomy versus shame and doubt (Erikson)

event in the child's life. The quality of this earliest attachment appears to have pervasive effects on the child's later interactions with others and on his developing sense of self. There may be as well some important ways in which the child's sense of security in his attachment to the caregiver affects his cognitive development.

There are several good developmental studies (Schaffer & Emerson, 1964; Ainsworth, 1963, 1964) that suggest a consistent developmental pattern in the growth of all achievements, more or less independent of cultural variations.

Phase One: Indiscriminate attachment.   This phase is from birth to approximately 5 or 6 months of age. During this period the child appears to enjoy being handled, approaching or being approached by people, and responding to social situations. The child may be quite happy being held by any one of several people and ordinarily is quite content to be handled by strangers. There is no special responsiveness to the major caregiver. The social smile appears at about 2 months of age, but the child smiles at many people, not exclusively at the caregiver. (It should be noted, however, that there may be earlier signs of specific attachment to the caregiver than have been studied by these researchers. For example, it is possible that the baby can discriminate between the caregiver and others on the basis of smell or touch and may respond in subtly different ways to the caregiver before 5 or 6 months.)

Phase Two: Specific attachment.   Sometime between 5 and 7 months, most children show a marked change in their behavior toward the adults around them. Instead of contentedly responding to any number of caregivers, they begin to show strong attachment to a single person—usually the one who is the major caregiver. A child visually follows that person around, fusses when she leaves, smiles more to her than to others, makes pleased noises when she is nearby or picks him up, and so forth. Others may be summarily rejected; no longer will the child allow himself to be held by strangers. Indeed at about 8 months or so many children develop a very strong fear of strangers.

Phase Three: Multiple attachments.   At about 1 year of age, the child's single specific attachment has begun to spread, so that there are now two, three, or perhaps more people to whom the child may show strong attachment. These are not diffuse attachments; rather, there is simply an increase in the number of people to whom the child shows strong specific attachments. Usually the spread is to the other parent, to a frequent baby-sitter, to a grandmother, a day care worker, or someone with whom the child has frequent contact.

Of course there are some individual differences in these patterns. Some children go directly from indiscriminate to multiple attachment apparently without ever going through a phase of a strong single attachment. Also, there is some reason to suspect that a more rapid shift to multiple attachments is more common in children who have had several caregivers, such as a child in a day care or treatment center or one with a steady baby-sitter (Schaffer & Emerson, 1964). Children also differ in the age of onset of the specific attachment; some infants show quite a strong attachment as early as 22 weeks, others not until about 1 year. Still, the sequence of development seems to be quite consistent, and the consistency has been found in studies in several cultural milieus.

But the attachment process is not always smooth. Ainsworth has noted quite striking differences in the *security* of the child's attachment to the mother. She describes the insecurely attached infant as a clinging, weeping child, who seems to be greatly distressed by separation from the mother but at the same time not easily comforted by the mother. These are children who fuss to be picked up and then fuss to be put down again. They stay near the mother but do not use her as much for a "safe base" from which to explore the world as do more securely attached infants, who show many more of the positive signs of attachment, including smiling, cooing, following, and holding out the arms to be picked up. These more securely attached children fuss less at being left and stop crying more quickly after the mother's departure. Some follow-up research (Ainsworth, Bell, & Stayton, 1972) suggests that the pattern of secure attachment may be the result of affectionate interaction, of noninterference by the mother in the child's activities (for example she waits until the child is ready before she picks him up to change his diaper), and of relatively infrequent but long and pleasant physical contacts. The insecurely attached infants may come from families in which the mother's handling of the child is more abrupt, more interfering, and less affectionate. Mothers of the insecurely attached infants pick up the baby often during the day but mostly for routine care. They are not likely to cuddle the baby just because it is pleasant for both of them.

The pattern of interaction continues to change in older children. By about 2 years of age the child is able to explore the world using the mother as a safe base. But he will still show distress if left alone in an unfamiliar place or with a strange person and may fuss a lot at being left at a day care or other alternative care center. So, even though the child may have many attachments, the attachment to the mother (or other major caregiver) is powerful throughout the second and third years of the child's life, particularly in strange situations. It is not until about age 4 or $4\frac{1}{2}$ that the child's attachment to the mother weakens or his sense of security has developed sufficiently for him to be able to cope with being left alone in a strange setting without much distress (Maccoby & Feldman, 1972).

Explanations of Attachment

While there is considerable agreement on the basic sequence of the attachment process, there is substantial disagreement both on the factors that influence it and the proper explanation of the sequence itself. Perhaps the simplest way to conceptualize the problem is to consider separately the child's contribution to the process and the caregiver's contribution. An attachment is not a one-way phenomenon. Normally there are at least two people involved, and the eventual security, strength, and perhaps rate of development of the attachment pattern seems to be heavily influenced by both.

The child's contribution to this social interchange is of several kinds. First, babies differ from one another in important ways from the day of birth onward. There is good evidence that babies at birth differ from one another on at least the following dimensions: irritability, soothability, cuddliness, the amount of sucking and mouthing they do (which may be an indication of self-soothing ability), and attentiveness to stimulation (Korner, 1973). In addition, there are some basic differences between boys and girls in level of physical maturity and in a kind of "vulnerability" to stress. Boys are both more vulnerable to virtually any kind of external stress and less physically developed at birth, being perhaps 6 weeks behind girls in maturation (Arganian, 1973).

These variations in temperament, responsiveness, and maturation rate may be inherited (Freedman, 1965), may be the result of prenatal hormonal or other chemical influences, or may be in part the result of medications given to the mother at the time of the child's birth. But regardless of their origin, they appear to be powerful behavioral patterns that the infant brings to his social encounters. For example, cuddliness (the child's physical adjustment of his body to being picked up and his apparent pleasure in being held) has been found to be a consistent trait of children throughout at least the first 18 months of life (Schaffer & Emerson, 1964), almost without regard to the kind of handling they have received from their parents.

Results from the best-known work on temperamental differences in babies (Chess & Thomas, 1973) suggest three quite distinct types of response patterns:

1. *The easy child*:   This child has good biological rhythm, responds positively to new things, adapts easily to change, is usually in a good or positive mood, and reacts to things in a moderate rather than extreme way. This child rarely has tantrums, adapts to strangers fairly easily, and would likely manage the shift from single to multiple attachments with little fuss or bother.

2. *The difficult child*:   This child has irregular body rhythms, reacts negatively to new things, and reacts strongly in any case, whether positively or negatively. His adaptation to new experiences is very slow, and he is often in a bad mood (cranky, whiny, crying). Such children have a hard time adapting to strangers or strange situations and will cling to the mother, rather than approach something novel.

3. *The slow-to-warm-up child*:   This child is in many respects between the other two. He has a usually negative response to new things. But the response is mild rather than violent, and the prevailing mood is somewhat passive, neither overly happy nor clearly distressed. The body functioning is fairly regular, and after this child adapts to new things he can approach them positively. Thus this child does not reject new things; he just approaches them cautiously.

There is quite a striking parallel between the descriptions of easy and difficult children and those of securely and insecurely attached children. Although Ainsworth's research suggests that the security of the child's attachment to the caregiver is influenced by the caregiver's behavior, the studies of temperamental differences in infants point to the importance of the child's own characteristics as well. Some children, then, may be "predisposed" by temperament toward behavior that looks like secure attachment, while others may be predisposed toward behavior that appears insecure.

A quite different way to look at the child's contribution to the attachment process is to think of the ways in which the child signals to the mother that he is in some kind of need. Bowlby (1969) has suggested that the beginnings of attachment are rooted in an innate series of cues and responses between mother and child. Just as the mating rituals of many animals are composed of a series of cues and responses, so attachment too may be a kind of ritual dance. Each partner signals the other that the next step in the process is needed.

The baby signals his need for some kind of caretaking by crying or fussing; the mother responds by picking up the child; the child responds in turn with some kind of bodily reaction such as cuddling. The baby's bodily adjustments signal to the mother that he is ready for the next step, be it diapering, feeding, bathing, or just cuddling and stroking. The baby responds to the caregiving by quieting, which reinforces the mother's caregiving. Bowlby suggests that these linked responses are innately programmed. But whether one accepts this notion or not, it is clear that there are important chains of cues and responses in the normal infant–caregiver interactions which shape those interactions.

Mutual visual regard is one of the important linkages in the early chain of cue and response, which suggests that it is one of the earliest and most important components of mother–infant bonding. For example, many mothers report that the time they first felt love toward their baby, the time when they ceased to feel strange with the infant, was when the infant first looked at them. Eye contact, then, is part of the chain of cues between mother and child that helps to maintain their contact with each other and strengthen their bond to each other. Eye contact is also important because it is a necessary condition for the development of prolonged social smiling (Freedman, 1965) .

Since any breakdown in this signaling system or any lack of appropriate response by one member of the pair is going to affect the whole bonding or attachment process, the child's ability to signal for help, adjust to the care that is offered, and maintain emotional linkage through eye contact is as important as the mother's responsiveness to the child's signals. In fact there is good reason to suppose that mothers may *require* good signals from the child in order to become properly "hooked" or attached to the child at all. Mothers of blind infants, for example, frequently have difficulty in feeling attached to and loving toward their infants because of the lack of eye contact and the lack of development of the social smile (Fraiberg, 1974).

The mother has an independent contribution to make to the interaction as well. In the first instance, there is some suggestive evidence that mothers during the first days after delivery are perhaps physiologically "ready" to become attached to their infant. For example, mothers who have had extensive opportunities to handle, fondle, hold, and cuddle their infants during the first days after birth show stronger attachment to the infant during the entire first year of the child's life than do mothers who have experienced more routine hospital contacts with the child (Kennell, Jerauld, Wolfe, Chesler, Kreger, McAlpine, Steffa, & Klaus, 1974). Also, mothers of low birth weight infants, who usually do not have much chance to handle and fondle their infants during the first days and weeks after birth, frequently report feeling less confident about their ability to care for their babies. Perhaps more importantly these mothers smile at their infants less and have less "verbal contact" with the baby than do mothers of full-term infants (Leifer, Leiderman, Barnett, & Williams, 1972). Thus, mothers appear to be particularly ready to become involved with the infant immediately after birth.

The work of these researchers should not be taken to mean that attachment must be accomplished within the first few days of the child's life. That is clearly not the case. Later mutual interactions of the type already described (such as eye contact, smiling, and the linked giving and receiving of care) are all important elements in the formation of a strong bond between caregiver and child, and they can occur with caregivers other than the child's biological mother. But there does appear to be a special readiness for bonding that exists in the mother immediately after giving birth. If this period is skipped for some reason (such as illness in the child), bonding is still possible but it may be more difficult.

The mother or other caregiver also contributes her/his own unique attitudes, temperament, and nurturing skills to interaction with the infant. Caregivers differ in their inclination to be affectionate with their children, in their tendencies to talk to their infants or play with them, in their confidence in their own caretaking skills, and in myriad other ways. These variations in caregiving appear to make some difference in the quality and strength of the child's developing attachment.

Of particular interest is the mother's response to the baby's crying. Many parents—and many professionals—have been concerned about "spoiling" the child by responding too quickly to the baby's cries. In this case, the research evidence runs counter to the "common sense" expectation. Babies whose mothers respond quickly to their cries cry less frequently than do infants whose mothers wait longer to respond (Bell & Ainsworth, 1972). Crying is one of the few ways the young infant has of signaling that he is in need. If this signal is ignored, there are a number of undesirable consequences. First, the child's attempts at communication are not encouraged. Second, the child's sense of being able to make things happen and his sense of trust that the world around him is responsive may both be inhibited. Finally, since the "ritual dance" of cue and response is not being completed when the mother does not respond to the child's cry, the early development of mutual attachment may be disrupted in important ways, resulting in an insecurely attached child.

The eventual pattern of social interaction between infant and caregiver is inevitably a result of the several forces discussed above: the child's temperament, the effectiveness and strength of the baby's signals to the mother, the caregiver's own style and behavior, and possibly some hormonal or physiological triggering system in the mother, which may be stronger for some mother–infant pairs than for others. The resultant attachment pattern is *not* the sum of these forces; it is some interactional end product. For example, if a temperamentally difficult child is cared for by someone who is slow to respond to his cries and lacking in confidence and affection, he may develop an extremely insecure attachment accompanied by excessive fear of strangers and lack of exploration of the environment. The same child cared for by a more responsive and affectionate adult might have a more secure (although not untroubled) attachment. On the other hand a temperamentally easy child may be much more immune to differences in caregivers and may develop quite secure attachments to any of a variety of types of caregivers.

Attachment in Relation to Other Developing Systems

The growth of attachment does not occur in a vacuum. The child is developing other skills and concepts at the same time, and all are intertwined. For example, the development of a specific attachment cannot occur until the baby is able to discriminate the special caregiver from other people. As pointed out in Chapter 8, this kind of visual discrimination does not develop fully until 4 to 6 months of age. At the same time the baby is developing some rudimentary sense of the constancy and uniqueness of objects. He begins to understand that he has only one mother (and that it is the same mother from one occasion to the next), and later he understands that when she leaves him she continues to exist. A sense of security about the special person in the child's life requires that he understand that she still exists even when he cannot see her and that she will come back. There is a particular time in the growth of many children, after they have become attached to a single person but before they have grasped the permanence of objects and people, when the child may be particularly upset at being left. This intensified fear passes as the child grasps the fact that the mother is still around somewhere, even though he cannot see her.

So, to some extent the child's developing attachments are affected by, or perhaps limited by, the development of important cognitive concepts. However, the influence can work the other way as well. A securely attached child is more willing to explore by using the mother as a safe base and this extensive exploration enriches the child's cognitive development. Securely attached children thus show somewhat accelerated cognitive growth.

The Growth of Self-Concept

All of the child's social and emotional development is not contained in his attachments to others. The baby must also develop a sense of himself, where he begins and ends, what his name is, what sex he is, what he is good at and what is harder for him, and so on. The self-concept is a pervasive characteristic of everyone, and its growth begins in the earliest years of life.

Most theorists (including Piaget and Freud) believe that, at birth, the child does not understand that there is any difference between self and other. In this view, the newborn has little if any awareness of where his body begins and ends and no understanding of the difference between wishes and reality. This condition changes slowly during the first year. The social smile, which is clear in most babies from about 2 months of age, may mark the beginning of the child's awareness of self versus other. While, of course, it is always difficult to draw conclusions about internal ideas and emotions from merely observing behavior, it appears that by this age the child is smiling *at* someone. The smile is selective in that it occurs more when people are present than when they are not. This fact suggests that the baby at this age has some rudimentary idea or "schema" (to use Piaget's word) that "other people" are not the same as "me." However, the baby in the early months is still preoccupied with explorations of his own body. He looks at his hands, manipulates his fingers, and sucks his fingers and toes. By about 4 months the child's explorations move away from his body to things outside the self: toys, materials, people, and other objects that may be in reach.

Another cognitive accomplishment is necessary before the child's own self-concept grows further. Just as, for attachments to develop, the baby must come to understand that the mother and other objects remain constant from one occasion to another, so, for the development of the self-concept, the child has to understand that "I" is a continuous phenomenon. Piaget thinks that full object constancy is not present until about 18 months; presumably the idea of the constancy of the self develops along much the same timetable.

By about age 2, the child will respond to his own name fairly consistently and will often use his own name to refer to himself. At this same time the child is learning labels to go with his other concepts (such as "ball" or "cookie"), and he learns his name as a label for the concept or object "me." The child during the second and third year also begins to show considerable insistence on autonomy, the equivalent of "Mother, I'd rather do it myself!" Erikson (1963) suggests that, whereas the major developmental task of the first year of life is the development of a sense of basic trust (versus mistrust), so the major task of the second and third years of life is to develop a sense of autonomy (versus shame and doubt). The problem for the child is to begin to learn to balance his twin needs—for autonomy and for dependence and nurturance. Erikson further indicates that the child's ability to solve this second dilemma is going to be powerfully affected by the success of the first problem resolution. A child with a secure, trusting attachment should have less difficulty facing and coping with problems of autonomy.

One aspect of the self-image that is comparatively slow to develop, however, is the child's sense of sexual identity. A child younger than about 3 years of age rarely refers to himself correctly as a boy or girl and cannot identify the gender of others. Most 3-year-old children can use the correct label ("boy" or "girl") for themselves but still are unable to discriminate consistently between men and women or boys and girls other than themselves. The correct labeling of others does not appear until about age 4, but even then the child does not understand that gender is a permanent characteristic of themselves and others. The discovery of the "conservation of gender" does not occur until age 5 or 6, at about the same time as the child discovers other conservations (Kohlberg, 1966).

Thus, while the child's gender may be very important to the people around him, it appears to have little importance to the child until age 4 to 5 or perhaps older. There is little preference for "boys' toys" among boys or "girls' toys" among girls before this age, and little concern with the sex of playmates.

The Development of Emotions

While the unfolding of emotional patterns has been little studied, there is some evidence that there are quite consistent patterns of change over age. In the best-known study, Bridges (1930, 1931, 1932) observed in the newborn a sort of undifferentiated pattern of general excitement; the excitation seems to be the same, regardless of the stimulus. But rather quickly, around 3 weeks of age, a separate, more negative response pattern (distress) can be seen, in which the baby trembles, cries, and holds his breath. By about 2 months of age a clearer positive emotional response can also be seen, which includes smiles and cooing. Bridges called this early positive emotional response "delight."

The negative responses continue to differentiate further. By 6 months or so there appear to be somewhat different responses, which might be called fear, disgust, and anger. The positive emotion of delight differentiates somewhat later, at about 12 months, when affection and elation can be seen.

There is also a change developmentally in the form the emotional response takes. The young infant has few bodily responses available for expressing different feelings. But when the child begins to be mobile, and of course later when he begins to talk, the repertoire of possible emotional responses becomes vastly greater. The 2-year-old child can run away from something fearful instead of just crying; he can say "You big dummy!" or the equivalent to his mother when he is mad at her, and so forth.

Obviously the study of emotions in very young children is greatly complicated by the fact that the experimenter or observer is drawing inferences from the very small cues the child gives. It is not quite accurate to say that a child who shows smiling and cooing *feels* the same feeling that an adult would call delight. But one can note that the bodily responses have differentiated and that the expressions on the child's face and his bodily movements are similar to those of an adult who experiences a similar emotion.

The generality of the changes in emotional expression has been supported by studies of blind children (Goodenough, 1932; Thompson, 1941). Blind children and blind-and-deaf children show much the same facial expressions as do sighted children during the early months. They seem to develop new patterns of facial and bodily expression at about the same time as do sighted children. The differentiated facial expressions do not persist in quite the same way in this group however. By age 2 or 3, for example, there is less facial activity when the child smiles or laughs than there was earlier, suggesting that the response of the observer plays a part for the sighted child in maintaining and extending the range of facial expressions that accompany emotions.

Overview

Emotional and social development, like cognitive, motor, and language development, have quite clear developmental patterns, which underlie a great deal of behavior during the first 3 years of life. At the same time, the child brings his/her own temperament and individual responses to social interactions, as do the adults around the child. The resulting pattern of social interchange is an interaction of all the forces—maturational, cognitive, temperamental, and environmental. The major thread running through the progression of changes during the first 3 years is a transition from dependence to independence. The child consolidates his dependent attachment to caregivers and then moves from this physically and emotionally safe base to explore new relationships, new objects, new places. Although the child still has powerful attachments to caregivers, by age 3 he has achieved marked independence from them as well and receives important satisfaction from his independence.

Throughout the period, interactions with the parents (or other caregivers) are vital. Whether or not the parent can accept the child's unique qualities, encourage and enjoy the dependency, yet assist in the transition to independence—all such factors will affect how the child feels about himself as well as the child's degree of security in his attachment to his parents. The child with strong, satisfying, positive attachments to the parents during the early months may have advantages in cognitive growth as well. Thus the several developmental domains clearly affect one another from the very beginning.

Social–Emotional Development in Atypical Children

How is the normal process of attachment and socialization affected when the child is physically or mentally handicapped? So often, the tendency in programs for handicapped children is to focus attention on the physical disability, mental retardation, or other deficit, with little attention given to problems of the child's developing social and emotional patterns. But if Freud, Erikson, and others are correct, the earliest attachments and social encounters the child experiences may form the backdrop for all of his later emotional development. And these experiences in turn are going to have repercussions on cognitive growth and perhaps on physical development as well. A child without a sense of basic trust is more fearful of exploring new things and new people. He will have greater difficulty coping with the task of developing his maximal independence. Adult handicapped persons refer again and again to the problem of dependence versus independence as being a central concern in their lives as children and as adults. Obviously, physical abilities play a major part in determining how independent or dependent the atypical child may be. But there are important emotional components as well, which are rooted in the earliest attachments and in the later interactions with others, around the issue of independent functioning.

Since these two needs—the development of a basic and secure attachment and the development of a sense of independence and mastery—are so central to the social–emotional development of the infant and toddler, it seems useful to focus particularly on the disorders in these two areas that can occur in the families of atypical children.

Disorders of Attachment

As is true in exploring the development of attachment in normal children, it is important to begin by looking at the qualities the child brings to the interaction. It is too easy to fall into the trap of considering the parent somehow "at fault" if there are aberrations in the early attachments of handicapped children. As Battle (1974) has pointed out so eloquently, the child's contribution to the difficulty is probably as important as the parent's.

First, the atypical child may have deficiencies or dysfunctions in the signaling system that is part of the earliest, perhaps instinctive, "ritual dance" of attachment. As described earlier, a typical series of signals and responses includes the child crying, the mother picking up the child, the child adjusting his body to the mother's handling, her ministering to the child's needs, and the child's responding to the care by soothing or ceasing to cry. Any or all of these steps may be affected in an atypical child. The child's cry may be continuous or may have a particularly piercing or distressing quality. When picked up the child may be unable to respond physically in an appropriate way. The baby may arch his back, be floppy, or have other bodily responses that are not natural adjustments to the mother's handling. The baby may not be soothed in the end, perhaps due to some physical discomfort that is not soothable.

Eye contact may be particularly difficult for many atypical

children who have trouble either getting into or maintaining a head position that permits eye contact with the caregiver. And smiling, another of the keys to early attachment of mother to child, may also be absent or distorted in the atypical child. As noted, facial expressions do not develop in quite the normal way in the blind infant. In some children with athetosis or other motor disorders, a pleasing social smile may be physically difficult or impossible and may be replaced by unattractive grimacing or other facial movements.

If for any of these reasons the child's signaling system is deficient or distorted, the mutual interactions are less likely to be triggered or maintained. Thus the bonding of mother to child may be weakened. For example, Fraiberg (1974) has found that parents of blind infants are frequently emotionally indifferent to the child because of the child's lack of facial expression and contingent smiling. When these parents are helped to "read" the other bodily signals of pleasure and displeasure, the parents become more emotionally involved with the infant.

Second, due to the nature of his physical or mental disorder, the atypical child may more commonly be temperamentally "difficult," with poor bodily rhythm, a cranky disposition, negative reactions to new things, and intense reactions to most kinds of experiences. The child may not sleep through the night until very late in life and may not develop regular patterns of elimination or feeding. Such children, whether they are normal or atypical in other ways, are much more difficult to care for than is the child who rapidly develops good body rhythms. The parent must continuously adjust to the child's irregular patterns, and any kind of daily schedule is made more demanding. Similarly, a cranky, negative child is a great deal harder to handle and socialize with than is one who approaches daily living with more positive attitudes. As Chess and Thomas (1973) have pointed out, some children are just hard to raise, no matter how good the parenting may be. If such a difficult temperament is compounded with a physical and/or mental handicap, the strain on the parent's skills may be enormous.

Third, the child's physical disabilities may restrict the kind of experiences he can manage on his own. This aspect has been discussed extensively in Chapter 8 (in the section on cognitive development in atypical children), so it need not be labored here.

But, it is important to realize that the cognitive and emotional–social domains are linked in important ways. The development of strong attachments seems to require, as a necessary but not sufficient condition, that the child has achieved some ability to discriminate among people and has some rudimentary notion of object permanence. But these cognitive accomplishments are in turn affected by the richness and variety of the child's experiences. So, a child whose experiences are necessarily restricted because of physical limitations may also be delayed in social development.

For any or all of these reasons, the parent of an atypical child may feel indifferent or rejecting toward the infant. But, as with normal children, it is not a one-way street. The caregiver is part of the early mutuality as well, and his/her signals and responses also help to set the tone of the early relationship. In the early months of life when the pattern is being established, parents of handicapped children may be in a state of grief, anger, despair, or shame over the fact of having a handicapped child. These powerful emotions cannot help but affect the parents' responses to the child's cues. The mother may reject the child and not respond to his early cues at all. She may handle the child perfunctorily, she may isolate the child from others and from potentially enriching experiences, out of her sense of shame or grief.

Among physically normal children, those with mothers who are depressed and under emotional strain during the early months of life are more likely to have serious emotional difficulties later on. This fact may be due to the mother's inability to respond effectively to the child's signals (Broussard & Hortner, 1971). There is every reason to suppose that the early depression and emotional disturbance so common in the parents of physically handicapped children will similarly affect the child's emotional growth and stability. Of course, the more obvious and severe the physical atypicality, the more severe the parental reaction is likely to be.

One of the additional special difficulties in establishing a positive, trusting relationship between the atypical child and the caregiver is the frequent need for the child to be separated from the parents for various periods of time for medical treatment or therapy. What kind of impact does such separation have on the child?

Separation of child from parents immediately after birth, as is commonly the case in low birth weight infants or infants with physical difficulties requiring extensive hospitalization, can affect the early development of the nurturing–attachment relationship (Kennell et al., 1974; Leifer et al., 1972). As was pointed out in the discussion of normal development of attachment, some attenuation of the attachment seems to occur when the child has been separated from the parent during this period. In this case, the attenuation seems most likely to come from the caregiver, whose feelings of competence as a mother are affected. Leifer also found that mothers separated from their infants during these early months smiled less and held the child to their bodies less often— both responses that are part of the early mutuality of attachment. Since early separation of mother and child is more common for atypical than for normal children, another hurdle is created for the mother–child pair.

Separation for brief periods later, as for hospitalization for surgery or for other medical treatment, seems in normal children to have different effects, depending on the age of the infant. Babies who are separated for this reason during the time of most intense specific attachment (usually about 6 or 8 months to 1 year in normal children) show far greater disturbance during and after the separation than do children who are separated during the period of more diffuse attachments (Schaffer & Callender, 1959). Others have found that children separated for long periods from their parents go through a progression of responses, from protest at separation, to despair, to withdrawal or detachment. Since physically atypical children are again more likely to experience this type of lengthy separation from parents, there is added risk of withdrawal by the child from intensive or intimate social contact (Yarrow, 1964).

Finally, separation for brief periods, as for day care or for care in a facility for atypical children, also carries some risks. Children repeatedly separated from their parents sometimes show mild versions of the pattern of distress ranging from protest to despair (Blehar, 1974).

Such findings need not argue against any separation of parent and child for treatment or therapy, but they do argue for the involvement of the parent in the child's educational and therapeutic program and for sensitivity toward the impact of separation on the frequently tenuous or afflicted attachment patterns of the physically or mentally handicapped child. In sum, there is likely to be a sharply increased risk of disturbance in the development of secure attachment between parent and child in the case of the atypical child. This fact is related both to the child's characteristics and to the special emotional burdens associated with bearing and rearing a physically or mentally atypical child.

The prognosis, however, is not the same for all atypical children. Whether there is difficulty in establishing a good initial pattern of interaction will be heavily influenced by a whole host of factors, including the obviousness of the child's disability and the ease of caretaking. A baby who develops a good social smile, is capable of some cuddling, and has fairly good body rhythms and a generally positive attitude toward new experiences (or any combination of these and other positive reactions) is likely to elicit thoughtful handling, cuddling, and attachment on the part of the parent, regardless of any physical disability. As always, it is a mistake to lump "atypical children" together into one group and assume that the same difficulties will be present for all of them. There is likely to be some interaction between the type or severity of handicap and the quality of the interaction between the parent and child; it is necessary to diagnose or assess the parent–child attachment process in each family individually.

Disorders in Dependence–Independence

Whether or not the atypical infant and family have weathered the problems of the early attachment period, there are likely to be some additional stresses during the second and third years of life revolving around the whole question of the child's dependence and independence.

Again, there are contributions to the problem from both child and parent. Due to his physical disability, the child is usually incapable of the same degree of independent movement or action as an able-bodied child. The section in Chapter 5 on movement in the atypical child details the difficulties that various types of handicapped children are likely to encounter. Most multiply or severely impaired children are unable to achieve significant independent movement by age 3, and many have only limited ability to explore objects with the hands. So the child is, in fact, much more dependent on others for physical care, for locomotion, and for the presentation of experiences than is the able-bodied child. Whether or not this physical dependence on others attenuates or slows down the child's demand for independence is not entirely clear. In a normally developing child, by age 2 or 3 there is a very vigorous demand for independence in many areas. Presumably there is some aspect of this present in the physically disabled child, even though (or possibly because) his physical dependence is far greater. So the parent is confronted with a child with continuing physical dependence who nonetheless asks for and needs to be allowed scope for independent choices and independent action.

The parents, on their part, very frequently have a tendency to shield the handicapped child from experiences (in part as a protection of the child from potentially hurtful encounters) and in many cases to treat him as a much younger child as well. The parent may be so obsessed with the child's limitations that newly developed skills are overlooked. Activities that the child could undertake independently are thus not offered or available.

The inclination of parents to do things for their handicapped child and to keep the child at home in familiar surroundings does not arise entirely out of ignorance of the child's needs or developing abilities. In the short run, at least, it may be easier to do things for the child than to set up the environment so that the child can try things independently. Also, the parents have a quite understandable desire to shield the child from experiences that they can anticipate will be painful. But the result of the frequent overprotection is a lack of support for or encouragement of the child's natural and important independence strivings.

Disabled adults, in looking back on their childhood experiences and problems, nearly always list the lack of independence as having been a major problem. They suggest that they were not given the opportunity to try new experiences, to fail in small things so that they could learn to cope with failure effectively, to make choices and follow through on them. These are all things that *can* be done with the disabled child even at the age of 2 or 3, but they are frequently not part of the experience of the atypical child.

The roadblocks to the child's successful grappling with the dilemma of independence versus dependence are thus physiological, psychological, and social (Battle, 1974). Since the physiological limitations cannot in most cases be eliminated entirely, the focus of intervention must be on the psychological and social impediments to the child's sense of independence and competence.

In sum, the atypical child's social and emotional development is at special risk during two periods. During the first months there may be difficulty in establishing the basic pattern of give and take, of signal and response, that is fundamental to later attachment and security. During the second and third years of life, there is the beginning of a lifelong struggle with problems of independence versus dependence. Both the child's physical limitations and the psychological limitations imposed by the parents and by the child's own fragile self-concept may affect the child's ability to establish himself as an independently functioning human being.

Intervention

The first and in many ways the most crucial need is to have an assessment of the individual family's strengths and weaknesses in the social–emotional area. Obviously, it is important to be sensitive to the whole range of family problems in functioning that may affect the environment of the atypical child, including problems with siblings, with relatives and friends, and between husband and wife. Analysis of the potential problems in these areas and the potential interventions for them is beyond the scope of this curriculum guide, but they are clearly of basic importance and will require the attention of staff. The focus here is on interventions that are designed to deal with problems of attachment between infant and caregiver and problems of independence in the child.

There are no standard instruments available for assessing strength or security of attachment, or the child's sense of independence. Such assessment needs to be made on the basis of observations of the parent–child interactions in the home, during parent–child sessions in a center, or in whatever settings the family may be observed. In these observations, particular attention needs to be paid to such indicators as the following:

1. Is there evidence that the child shows a strong attachment to the mother or other caregiver?
2. Is the attachment pattern consistent with the child's chronological or mental age?
3. Does the mother smile at the child? Does the child have an effective social smile?
4. Is there frequent physical contact between mother and child?
5. Is there affectionate contact?

6. Is there eye contact?

7. Is the infant capable of maintaining eye contact in the customary holding positions? During feeding?

8. Does the mother report indifference to or distaste for the child?

9. Is the mother concerned about her inability to feel warm and loving toward this child? Does the father express such feelings?

10. Does the mother treat the child as if he were less capable than he really is?

11. Is the child offered choices? Do the parents follow through on the choices the child makes?

12. Is the child allowed or encouraged to try out new things, new toys, new foods, new playmates, new people?

13. Is the child sheltered from contact with others?

While many families will present complex combinations of problems in these areas, it may be helpful to think of the potential problems as belonging in one of several categories:

1. *The indifferent or rejecting parent.*   As already indicated, indifference or rejection may arise from several sources:

    a.   The child may lack the signals to "hook" the caregiver into an effective and satisfying relationship.

    b.   The child may be congenitally a temperamentally difficult child to raise, quite apart from his disability.

    c.   The mother or other caregiver may be experiencing significant depression or emotional turmoil, either about having a handicapped child or for quite separate reasons.

2. *The overinvolved or overprotective parent.*   Several types of parents might be classed here:

    a.   The parent who is unable or unwilling to leave the child alone for any period, who hovers over the child and does everything for him.

    b.   The parent who treats the child as if he were much younger, out of ignorance of the child's real abilities or out of a desire to simplify his/her own life with a stable routine.

    c.   The parent who shelters the child from encounters with others and from independent action, out of an ostensible or real desire to have the child avoid the experiences of failure or rejection by others.

INTERVENTION WITH INDIFFERENT OR REJECTING PARENTS.   If the indifference or rejection arises from the child's poor signaling ability, two types of intervention are useful.

■ The parents may be helped to "read" the child's body signals more effectively, so that they can tell when the child is pleased, fearful, uncomfortable, or whatever.

■ Parents may be given tasks or games to perform with the child, in the center or at home, that maximize the child's pleasure and responsiveness, thus "hooking" the parent into a more satisfied and satisfying interaction with the child. If the disorder of attachment is severe in a particular family, tasks of this sort may be, at least temporarily, the only kind a family is asked to do. Of course, over the long run it would not be wise to focus the family interventions exclusively on tasks the infant enjoys. There will inevitably be times when it is necessary to ask the family to undertake home interventions that are less pleasant and more neutral for the infant. But with families in which the initial need is to fortify the attachment of parent to child, tasks that display the child in the best possible light, with the most pleasing reactions, are in order.

If lack of attachment arises because the child is congenitally a "difficult" child, quite different interventions are in order.

■ The parents may be helped to understand that temperamental differences exist among normal infants as well as among atypical infants and that the child's cranky behavior or negativism has not resulted from anything they have or have not done.

■ The parent can be offered help in developing the skills needed to deal with the temperamentally difficult child such as:

1. Responding quickly when the child cries. Over time, this may help to reduce the number of crying occasions.

2. Organizing a routine that is stable and predictable from day to day.

3. If new experiences and encounters are planned or required, preparing the parent for the child's initial resistance. The child will eventually adapt to the new experience, and nothing is gained by backing off and trying again later.

If the difficulty in attachment arises from the mother's own emotional difficulties, yet other interventions are needed.

■ Respite care may be arranged for the mother or for the entire family on some fairly regular basis.

■ The mother may participate in a parent group, or she may require more specific therapy. In cases of severe emotional disorder, individualized therapy is likely to be needed, arranged either at the center or privately.

Intervention with Overinvolved or Overprotective Parents. Several general types of intervention are reasonable and useful for the parents who fall into this broad category.

■ Parents may be given information about the skills and abilities the child does have and help in redesigning the family routine so that the child can practice the new skills and abilities.

■ Parents may be helped to learn to offer choices to their child. For example, if there are two toys that are equally good for some particular purpose, put both within reach of the child. In an older child with good receptive language, ask the child which he would like to have. The child may also be offered choices of food to eat and clothing to wear.

■ A private time may be set aside for the child each day when he is awake and alert but left alone (in a good position for exploration) to play as he wishes.

■ The parents may be given instruction in ways to teach the child self-help skills, such as eating and dressing, where this is physically possible for the child.

It is worth reiterating that the most crucial part of intervention in this domain is a good assessment of the family functioning. Once the problems have been identified, most of the reasonable interventions become quite obvious. But the assessment itself may be time consuming and it may require the involvement of several staff members to observe family interactions under different circumstances and in different settings. In particular, some acquaintance with the family in their own home surroundings is probably necessary for a reasonable assessment of their social–emotional functioning with their atypical child.

PART THREE

CURRICULUM IN ACTION

CHAPTER 10

INDIVIDUALLY PLANNED PROGRAMS—
USING THE TRANSDISCIPLINARY
APPROACH

T HIS program guide attempts to deal with the scope and variety of components that must be considered if early intervention is to have maximal benefit for developmentally disabled infants and their families. At the same time it is assumed that readers represent a broad spectrum of skill areas and varied types of experience.

The traditional approach has been "the laying on of hands" by physicians, physical therapists, occupational therapists, early childhood educators—a succession of professionals, each devoted to applying his or her expertise toward alleviation of problems. Often the contact between them has been limited or absent. This volume suggests that such an approach is no longer appropriate.

Just as human development is the coordination and integration of a variety of physical, mental, emotional, and social processes, so must intervention to aid that development be a coordinated and integrated effort. A systematic, developmental approach to programming is required. We recognize that any division of human development is artificial and usually results in inappropriate fragmentation. However, we must analyze goals, strategies, and activities for atypical children. For the purposes of this pro-

The major contributors to this chapter are Frances P. Connor, John M. Siepp, and G. Gordon Williamson.

gram guide, it was arbitrarily decided to separate development into the components: movement, pre-speech, language, cognition, and social–emotional. But no one person can possess all the knowledge or skills required to do what may be needed to overcome or cope with deficits that may range over all of these areas. All professionals working with developmentally disabled infants—whatever their area of expertise—have the responsibility to call upon the knowledge of other professionals as the needs of each infant dictate, in addition to applying their own expertise.

The complexity of human development calls for the pooling of professional skills to design individual program plans. Examples of team efforts at problem solving are presented in this chapter. The purpose of including these sample plans is not to suggest final or complete answers to problems. The intention is, rather, to emphasize the need for a transdisciplinary approach: to make teachers aware of the need to seek out resources in fields other than education; to give physicians or nurses a perspective on the needs of the infant and the family that can be met by nonmedical personnel; to prompt physical, occupational, and speech therapists to find ways in which a social worker or teacher can be of help in serving the total child. The direct beneficiaries of this cooperation must be the family of the affected child, who will be helped to view their child as a unique, whole personality within a constellation of personalities, rather than as a detached bundle of problems interfering with family life.

The infant described in each sample plan is an individual unlike any others. The movement, pre-speech, langauge, cognitive, and social–emotional development of the infant are outlined, incorporating both strengths and needs. (Chapters 5 through 9 should be consulted for an explanation of the principles involved in each of these aspects of development.) A brief description of the family and its social–economic setting is also included. All of the diverse factors in the situation had to be integrated by the appropriate professionals before a plan for that child and his family could begin to be properly conceived.

Teams of professionals devised the sample plans in a transdisciplinary fashion. They reviewed the status data on each child, shared information, challenged and taught one another. The end product in each case was a program plan that incorporated the goals of all of them. As a result of the team's assessment of the child and the family, a number of concerns were perceived. Strategies were formulated for implementing the plan and alleviating these concerns. Each case thus comprises five elements: a description of the child and family, an outline of the child's developmental status, a list of sample concerns, a list of corresponding strategies, and a chart illustrating implementation of the strategies.

Implementation of an individual program plan will vary as dictated by the child's unique and changing needs and the nature of the interventions. It is also highly dependent on good communication between center personnel and home caregivers. This chapter therefore concludes with a discussion of the various ways in which a center may effectively communicate home program needs to parents and other caregivers.

Sample Plans

Each transdisciplinary team brings its own body of expertise and its own frame of reference to the design of a child's program plan. Four sample approaches of curriculum development are included in this chapter and are presented in somewhat differing formats. These approaches are identified as (*a*) sequential task analysis, (*b*) a major activity and its possible consequences across developmental areas, (*c*) integrated activities meeting multiple objectives, and (*d*) multiple interventions to meet a general behavioral objective.

The first approach focuses on a sequential task analysis and suggested intervention strategies. It is represented in the cases of Cindy and James (Plans I and II). In this method there is a step-by-step procedure delineated in sequential order for achieving a stated goal. For example, the task of bathing Cindy has been analyzed into its component steps in order to meet some of her educational, therapeutic, and nurturing needs.

A second approach for evolving a problem-solving plan is to choose a major activity for a child and differentiate the expected outcomes of the intervention in each of the developmental areas. In the plans for Terry and Sue (Plans III and IV), the major activity is listed first and then the developmental consequences resulting from the intervention are briefly enumerated. For instance, providing Terry with an adapted tricycle fosters the learning of many types of skills, particularly when specific additional strategies related to the activity are incorporated.

The third approach of curriculum development utilizes integrated activities that meet multiple objectives, as seen in the program descriptions of Kathy and John (Plans V and VI). The objectives of various professional workers are met through a number of simultaneous and related activities or interventions. In the case of Kathy, for example, a proper sitting position reduces abnormal movement patterns, jaw control facilitates feeding and vocalization, mother's conversation introduces the concept of "more," and use of the sound "m" encourages desired lip closure. Thus, related activities meet numerous educational and therapeutic objectives at the same time.

The final, sample approach is demonstrated by the case of Samuel (Plan VII). This approach employs multiple interventions in various developmental areas to meet stated goals; the team begins with a general behavioral objective and evolves various strategies to meet it. For example, in Samuel's case, one of the objectives agreed upon by the team is to increase his imitation of the sounds that he hears from his mother. Under each developmental category there appear different ways of meeting this single objective.

Each of the following problem-solving plans is an example of curriculum planning for a specific child, and each was revised as dictated by the child's progress. Due to the uniqueness of every infant, no program plan can be applied indiscriminately. It is hoped that these sample plans will serve to demonstrate how the areas of development of a child are interrelated and how interventions cross and recross the lines of traditional disciplinary boundaries.

Sequential Task Analysis: Plan I

Description of Child and Family   Cindy is an 18-month-old girl, a fraternal twin, who has athetosis. Her twin sister appears healthy and normal. In addition to the twins, there are two other siblings who attend school. The family is intact and lives in the inner city. Mother is employed as a nurse's aide; father is a construction worker. Cindy's grandmother resides in the home and is the major caregiver during the day. Cindy experiences frequent upper respiratory infections and a hearing loss is suspected. She has normal vision.

**Developmental
Status**

MOTOR

Cindy's muscle tone fluctuates from very high to very low. She has an asymmetrical tonic neck reflex to both sides, and this reflex dominates her posture when lying supine. Head control in the prone position is poor, and total support is required in sitting.

PRE-SPEECH

Tongue thrusting fluctuates with tone. Diet is limited to strained baby food. Cindy maintains her mouth open during feeding, and her grandmother scrapes food into her mouth.

LANGUAGE AND COGNITION

Open-mouth sounds are attempted. Her differentiation of sounds is difficult to assess. Sound production is associated with familiar people and objects in her environment, as well as being a behavior for gaining attention. She has a favorite soft toy. Cindy rarely leaves the house and spends most of the time in front of the television set.

SOCIAL–EMOTIONAL

Cindy is a good-natured child who smiles often. She is beginning to show signs of frustration when she wants to play with toys that she cannot control or when she tries to communicate with people unsuccessfully. With the exception of her relationship with her twin, Cindy is well integrated into the family. They play with her, talk to her, and sit with her in front of the television. Due to the amount of physical attention that Cindy needs, the other twin seems quite jealous.

Sample Concerns

■ Grandmother is experiencing great difficulty in the management of Cindy's physical problems, in relation to bathing, feeding, and transporting her. Adding to the difficulty is the fact that the grandmother is herself quite heavy and has trouble moving around.

■ There is general instability of Cindy's head and trunk in maintaining a sitting posture, as well as extensor thrusting of her arms and legs in response to stimulation from the environment.

■ The social–emotional interactions between Cindy and grandmother and Cindy and her twin are deteriorating because:

1. Cindy is a very aware child whose ability to comprehend appears to be greater than her ability to perform.

2. There is increasing hostility of the twin toward Cindy because of the attention given to Cindy's problems.

3. The grandmother is having greater difficulty coping with Cindy's management due to her own increasing age.

4. The parents are excluded from day-to-day relations with Cindy, due to the economic necessity of their having to work. Their understanding of Cindy's behavior is therefore limited.

Strategies

■ Using activities of daily living:

1. Through handling, facilitate increased trunk stability.

2. Make bath time physically and emotionally more comfortable for Cindy, grandmother, and the twin.

■ Assess the need for adaptive equipment to facilitate easier handling and greater independence for Cindy.

■ Through implementation of the preceding strategies, provide for more positive interactions in the home, by making activities of daily living more pleasurable and providing for more successful play experiences for Cindy and her twin.

■ Arrange home visits at a time when parents are present to discuss home management.

Sequential Task Analysis: Plan I

A. Bathing Activity

MOTOR	PRE-SPEECH	LANGUAGE	COGNITION	SOCIAL–EMOTIONAL
1. Select a quiet time of the day for a low-stimulus environment.		Prepare Cindy for bath by talking to her about what is going to happen.	Allow Cindy to choose two familiar toys to accompany her in the bath.	Involve twin sister in the preparation of Cindy's bath (e.g., carrying towels). Talk in a quiet, calming voice.
2. With small laundry basket in the kitchen sink stabilized against the sides of the sink, place Cindy in basket facing adult, with child's hips and knees flexed close to the body, shoulders and arms forward, head in midline slightly flexed to inhibit the total extensor pattern of the body. Cindy's twin sister	With terry facecloth, use firm but gentle strokes in washing. When washing the face, strokes should be in direction of the mouth, toward the midline.	While bathing, caregiver names body parts ("Here's your hand; now I'm washing your tummy") or sings quiet songs ("This is the way we wash your face"). Provide opportunities for twin to identify own body parts.	Cindy identifies several body parts by looking at them when named. She also feels the temperature of the water and the buoyance of it.	Proper handling, as well as eye contact between Cindy and caregiver, makes experience more enjoyable and secure for Cindy, caregiver, and twin. The kitchen sink provides optimal height for management and interaction.

Plan I: Bathing Activity (*Continued*)

MOTOR	PRE-SPEECH	LANGUAGE	COGNITION	SOCIAL–EMOTIONAL
could be placed in a high chair near the sink.				
3. To remove Cindy from sink, turn basket around so that child is facing away from adult. Lift child while she is held in a flexed posture.		Talk to Cindy, telling her the bath is finished, thus precueing her for being removed from basket.		Sink is drained after child has been removed from it. Twin may help to pull plug while Cindy watches.
4. Wrap Cindy snugly in a large towel, maintaining her in the flexed position.		Talk to Cindy, tell her what a good girl she was during the bath.		The easier it is to bathe the child, the less anxiety producing it will be. In a relaxed atmosphere, a warm relationship can be fostered between Cindy, caregiver, and twin.

Plan I: **Bathing Activity** (*Continued*)

MOTOR	PRE-SPEECH	LANGUAGE	COGNITION	SOCIAL–EMOTIONAL
5. Dry Cindy on kitchen counter, maintaining proper body position.	In drying, use the action described in Step 2.	Talk to Cindy as in Step 2.	Drying and powdering Cindy after bath gives caregiver the opportunity to rub her with substances of different texture, to increase Cindy's tactile experiences as well as provide further opportunity for identification of body parts.	The child experiences another pleasurable contact with caregiver.

Additional suggestions:
(a) Twin is provided independent bath time with grandmother while Cindy sits in adapted high chair watching.
(b) Staff to visit home on weekend to involve parents in bathing program. Mother may carry out the procedure in the quiet and privacy of the bathroom.

Plan I: Shopping Activity

B. *Shopping Activity*

MOTOR	PRE-SPEECH	LANGUAGE	COGNITION	SOCIAL–EMOTIONAL
		1. Grandmother tells twins about shopping trip.	Grandmother discusses items to be bought, giving real choices to the girls when appropriate.	All activities should be slowly paced, allowing for responses from the twins and minimizing the tendency for Cindy to go into extension. Involve the twin in preparation for outing by having her fetch coats and hats. Provide positive reinforcement for this participation.
2. Place Cindy in car seat (see Appendix A) in rear of shopping cart. Place twin in front seat of shopping cart.		Grandmother describes each of her actions as she places Cindy and her sister in the shopping cart.	Grandmother mentions several times which child is sitting in front and which is sitting in back.	Let twin climb in as independently as possible, with reinforcement for accomplishment. The girls take turns sitting front and back, reducing possible cause for jealousy.

Plan I: Shopping Activity *(Continued)*

MOTOR	PRE-SPEECH	LANGUAGE	COGNITION	SOCIAL–EMOTIONAL
Alternative position: Place Cindy in front seat of shopping cart, propped against a pillow and tied around the hips for safety. Place grandmother's large pocketbook in front of Cindy, to prevent her falling forward. Place twin in back of shopping cart. (Twin can now use Cindy's seat.)		3. Name items as they are taken off shelf for purchase. Explain supermarket processes at a level suitable to the children.	The girls' choices under Step 1 are now identified, and items handed to the twin in back of shopping cart.	Each twin is given equal opportunity to choose. Cindy learns she can meaningfully influence her environment.

Sequential Task Analysis: Plan II

Description of Child and Family   James is a 9-month-old infant with Down's syndrome. His general health is good. Vision and hearing seem normal. He is the youngest of three children (he has a sister aged 6 and a brother aged 4) in a two-parent, working-class family. The mother, who is the principal caregiver, is overprotective of James and handles him as a much younger child. For example, she habitually feeds him cradled in her arms in a semireclining position. She has expressed concern about this pattern but is at a loss for realistic developmental expectations for him.

Developmental Status

MOTOR

James has lower than normal muscle tone; he rolls in either direction; he is able to sit, supported, but with a rounded back.

PRE-SPEECH

Sucking and chewing patterns are slightly primitive for his age. The tongue is floppy and frequently protrudes from the mouth. James has a readiness to begin self-feeding.

LANGUAGE AND COGNITION

Skills are those usually associated with a 6-month-old baby. He visually recognizes familiar people; reacts to friendly and angry tones; gestures by holding out his arms to be picked up; looks for a fallen object; responds to a mirror.

SOCIAL–EMOTIONAL

James is a social, affable child but tends to be passive and accepting. He seldom initiates behavior to explore his environment actively. There is an affectionate relationship between mother and child, as well as a warm family atmosphere.

Sample Concerns   ■   Mother expresses concern regarding her lack of knowledge about ways to foster James's independence.

Sequential Task Analysis: Plan II
Feeding Activity

MOTOR	PRE-SPEECH	LANGUAGE AND COGNITION	SOCIAL–EMOTIONAL
1. While mother holds James facing her in a seated position straddling her leg with his back straight, she bounces him firmly to increase overall muscle tone, thereby improving head and trunk stability.		Mother provides a two- or three-word rhythmic-action song that describes what she is doing as she bounces James.	Mother and James smile and laugh while bouncing and singing. Mother "congratulates" him when he holds his trunk independently.
2. Mother places James in a high chair in a right-angled sitting position.	Mother uses James's hand in gently tapping his mouth to increase oral muscle tone and awareness of oral sensation.	Mother imitates whatever sounds James produces as his lips are tapped.	Mother fosters warm, playful interaction in making sounds as the mouth is tapped.
3. After putting a "sit-up" straw in bottle, mother places James's hands on the bottle and brings it to his mouth. After he has been drinking for a while, mother gradually removes her support from his hands for very short periods of time. The time is gradually extended until she sees that he is able to maintain the bottle in his mouth without her assistance.		Mother describes the action as James performs the task and acquires skill in drinking more independently.	As James gains independence in self-feeding, mother rewards him with praise for his efforts.

■ She feels it is important to begin with self-help skills in feeding, such as holding his own bottle.

Strategies

■ Increase muscle tone to foster independent sitting in a high chair.

■ Encourage James to place his hands on the bottle while he is drinking. Mother gradually to remove her support of the bottle.

■ Provide a "sit-up" straw for the bottle (see Chapter 6: Bottle Feeding), so that James will be able to drink without having to tilt his head backward and thus lose his sitting balance.

Developmental Consequences of a Major
Activity: Plan III

Description of Child and Family

Terry is a 3-year-old boy with left hemiplegia. He is from a two-parent, middle-class professional family. He has a 1-year-old sister, who is bright and competent. Terry's health is generally good. Hearing is normal; vision is affected by strabismus.

Developmental Status

MOTOR

Terry's left arm is generally held in a flexed position with fisted hand, which can be used assistively when he is motivated. He walks independently, but weight bearing on the left foot is restricted to the toes.

PRE-SPEECH

He independently eats finger foods and uses utensils.

LANGUAGE AND COGNITION

Terry is receptively age appropriate, but he uses only one-word sentences. He is apparently hyperactive, with poor attending behavior. He can play appropriately with toys but for only a few minutes at a time.

SOCIAL–EMOTIONAL

He has an increasing interest in peer play, especially play involving gross motor activities. He has temper tantrums when an attempt is made to have him do something he does not want to do.

Sample Concerns

■ Terry's need to affiliate with his peer group demands his being mobile. But walking increases the undesired flexion observed in the affected left arm.

■ The parents' lack of understanding of the nature of Terry's disability is fostering expectations that are a source of potential emotional conflict for Terry and his family. For example, Terry's achievement of independent ambulation has been so greatly satisfying to his parents that they are now talking about "Little League." Parents need help to deal with their expectations versus the realities of Terry's development, and their feelings about having a handicapped child.

■ Terry's short attention to purposeful activities and its possible relation to visual perceptual problems.

Strategies

■ Find alternate means of mobility for Terry that will satisfy his social–emotional needs but not increase his spasticity.

■ Expand Terry's language to lessen his dependence on temper tantrums.

■ Utilize Terry's enjoyment of and success in gross motor activities to increase his visual–motor proficiency.

■ Suggest the parents join a counseling group that includes some parents of older children with hemiplegia.

Developmental Consequences of a Major Activity: **Plan III**

MAJOR ACTIVITY	MOTOR	LANGUAGE AND COGNTION	SOCIAL–EMOTIONAL
1. Instruction in riding and use of an adapted tricycle (see Appendix A).	Bilateral hand use. Reciprocal leg movements.	Use of names and functions in talking about the tricycle. Imaginary play through assuming roles and taking trips.	Satisfaction of successfully riding the tricycle. Tricycle offered as a present and source of fun. Increased mobility for relating to peers through use of the tricycle. Parents view tricycle as an accomplishment rather than a setback to mobility.
2. Symmetrical sitting and riding on a rocking horse.	Bilateral hand use. Bilateral integration of movement.	Imaginary play, such as rocking games and "cowboys." Use of action words (e.g., "fast," "slow").	Pleasurable gross motor activity provides an outlet for hyperactivity. Opportunity for self-initiated and independent use of rocking horse.
3. Finger painting on an easel in a group setting.	Bilateral hand use.	Experiencing a new medium. Sustained attention to a satisfying task. Exploration and use of concepts related to color and texture. Meaningful play activity fostering creative expression.	Opportunity for peer group activity. Opportunity to indicate desire to stop activity without resorting to temper tantrums.

Developmental Consequences of a Major Activity: Plan IV

Description of Child and Family Sue is a 4-month-old spastic infant, the first child of teenage parents. The father is a fireman and the mother is a housewife. Informal hearing and visual testing suggests that these senses may be within normal limits, although formal testing is impossible at this time. Most of Sue's waking hours are spent crying or fussing.

Developmental Status

MOTOR

In supine, Sue is in severe extension—retraction of shoulders and head, arching of back, and scissoring of legs. In prone, she is unable to lift her head against gravity. Due to the hypertonicity, she demonstrates minimal movement. Sue spends most of the time in the supine position in the crib.

PRE-SPEECH

Sue's major source of nourishment is milk and cereal through a bottle, at least seven times per day. The nipple hole has been enlarged, so that the thick substance pours into her mouth. Supplemental spoon feedings of strained fruit are presented, usually at the noon meal. Spoon feeding is accomplished by scraping the fruit into Sue's mouth while she is held in a supine position in mother's arms. The rooting and suck–swallow reflexes are observed strongly upon any stimulation near the child's face. A violent gag reflex is observed when the examiner touches Sue's upper gum ridge. Her respiration pattern is shallow, rapid, and arhythmic.

LANGUAGE AND COGNITION

Sue does not attempt eye contact when mother speaks or sings to her. She does, however, stop fussing when she hears mother's voice. Sue displays limited differentiation in sound production. Crying and fussing can be characterized as whiny, open-mouth vowel sounds.

Developmental Consequences of a Major Activity: Plan IV

MAJOR ACTIVITY	MOTOR	PRE-SPEECH	LANGUAGE AND COGNTION	SOCIAL–EMOTIONAL
1. Mother is taught to carry Sue in an upright position, facing outward, with hips flexed less than 90°. Sue's retracted shoulders and arms are brought forward toward her midline.	This position reduces extensor tone and improves head and trunk alignment. Spastic pattern of arms is inhibited. With improved arm position it is now possible for mother to assist in bringing Sue's hands to her mouth.	As a result of decreased tone, there is a tendency toward bilabial closure. Due to the improvement in head and trunk alignment, Sue's respiration becomes deeper and more regular.	As a result of the more upright position, Sue has the opportunity to attend visually to her environment and her mother in a more natural way. Now that mother is more comfortable, she spontaneously talks more to Sue.	Sue and mother feel more secure and relaxed. Mother no longer expresses the feeling of being "pushed away." Thus, mother holds and cuddles Sue more and is able to comfort her when she cries.
2. When Sue has increased head control and trunk stability, an alternative carrying position is introduced. Sue straddles mother's hip with abducted, externally rotated legs, and flexion of the hips. Sue's trunk is rotated so that she is looking forward. Her arms remain in front of her in midline.	This position improves head and trunk control and body rotation. The independent hand-to-mouth pattern is facilitated.	Due to the more upright position with body rotation, Sue is able to produce more vocal resonance during babbling.	There is improved attending behavior to visual and auditory stimuli.	Mother says that Sue "looks more normal." Mother is willing to take her to public places such as the supermarket. Thus mother is less isolated and able to engage in a greater variety of activities. Mother expresses less frustration and anger about her life style.

SOCIAL–EMOTIONAL

Mother reports extreme depression and frustration inasmuch as she is unable to comfort Sue by holding her. She feels that the baby "pushes her away" when she tries to cuddle her. Since mother finds it difficult to carry Sue, she leaves her in the crib for long periods of time. The mother also reports that she feels confined to the house by the baby and this makes her angry.

Sample Concerns

■ Mother's frustration over inability to handle and comfort her child.

■ Mother's need for an outlet for her feelings of anger and frustration.

Strategies

■ Provide an alternative carrying position that may reduce the spasticity of the infant and thereby reduce the feeling mother has of being pushed away when holding her.

■ Arrange for supportive counseling (individual and/or in group with other mothers of severely handicapped babies), where the mother is encouraged to express her feelings of resentment and is shown how to deal constructively with her anger.

■ Attempt to bring the couple together to discuss their feelings and mutual concerns; eventually introduce them to other young couples who share some of the same problems.

Integrated Activities Meeting Multiple Objectives: Plan V

Description of Child and Family

Kathy is a 20-month-old child with athetosis. She has two older siblings. She and her two-parent, middle-class family live in a suburb near the grandparents and other relatives. The father is an accountant for the city. Kathy has a mild hearing impairment but is not required to wear a hearing aid at the present time. Her visual acuity is apparently normal, although she has extraneous eye movements that are probably associated with the athetosis. She is average for her age in height and weight. General health is good, except that Kathy is frequently constipated.

Developmental Status

MOTOR

Kathy has a bilateral asymmetrical tonic neck reflex and her muscle tone fluctuates from very high to very low. She has limited ability to bring her head or hands to midline. Her head and trunk alignment is poor in supported sitting, and there is occasional extraneous movement of hands and arms. There is no means of independent mobility.

PRE-SPEECH

Kathy presents rooting, suckle–swallow, bite, and hyperactive gag reflexes. There is no hand-to-mouth activity. Constant drooling and involuntary oral movements with accompanying tongue thrusting in supine are evident. Tongue thrusting increases upon any oral stimulation.

LANGUAGE

There are frequent vocalizations consisting of low, back vowel sounds; smiling; vocalization in response to people; laughs (low throaty sounds). Her fussing leads to crying in order to attract attention. There is a limited but effective repertoire of facial expressions to communicate emotional state (smiling when happy; frowning, pouting, lip quivering when upset; perplexed expression in new situations). She attempts visually to locate familiar people in response to a verbal request, for example, "Where's Mommy?" The general impression is that she demonstrates some response to language from her mother within certain situational contexts, for example, "It's time to eat."

COGNITION

Kathy enjoys the social approaches of all family members, including brother and sister, and responds to peek-a-boo and having arms moved for pat-a-cake. Although she enjoys being tickled, she responds with increased abnormal body postures and extreme hypertonicity.

SOCIAL–EMOTIONAL

Kathy is an integrated family member. Her siblings play with her, as during her waking hours she is brought into the same room as other family members. Attachment to mother is strong but appropriate for her age and physical dependency. Mother and father hold and cuddle her often but tend to relate to her as though she were a much younger child. Although much of mother's time is spent attending to Kathy, other children in the family are also given individual attention.

Sample Concerns

■ Abnormal movement patterns.

■ Inappropriate feeding behaviors and lack of appropriate oral stimulation.

■ Inability to communicate personal needs consistently.

■ Parents' interaction with Kathy is inappropriate to Kathy's developmental level.

■ Mother is apparently unaware of the need to expand Kathy's vocalizations.

Strategies

■ Positioning to reduce effects of abnormal movement patterns.

■ Feeding intervention to normalize oral sensorimotor patterns.

■ Establish Kathy's smile as a consistent "yes" response.

■ Demonstrate to mother ways of expanding Kathy's vocalizations.

Integrated Activities Meeting Multiple Objectives: Plan V

MOTOR	PRE-SPEECH	LANGUAGE	COGNITION	SOCIAL–EMOTIONAL
1. Place Kathy in an upright, symmetrical sitting position in an infant seat, pillow at nape of neck to provide flexion.	Use jaw control (see Chapter 6) to encourage lip closure over spoon presented in midline. (Caution: Initially, jaw control should be used only once during the day to avoid frustration for mother and child. Later it may be gradually increased until it is used for each meal.)	Introduce concept of "more" by saying the word just prior to moving the food toward her mouth; talk to Kathy about the food and her eating during the meal.	Move Kathy's hands so that she feels the food and utensils; help her to handle food, bring food to mouth.	Encourage mother to use mealtime to establish interaction with Kathy and to note Kathy's evidences of pleasure (e.g., smiling, eye contact) upon eating food of various textures, consistencies, and flavors.
2. Position Kathy in prone over wedge, to achieve head-to-midline orientation.	Three or four times a day, guide Kathy's hands to her face.	Name parts of the face as she touches them; use song or labeling game.	Affix toys to the floor in front of Kathy. Help her to touch and stroke toys of different textures. She can be left alone with toys and objects to look at and listen to, or to watch television.	With Kathy in prone over wedge and provided with toys, mother moves freely about the room and speaks to Kathy. Distance from Kathy is gradually increased and frequency of oral communication diminished, as mother encourages independence and separation for short periods of time.

Integrated Activities Meeting Multiple Objectives: Plan V (*Continued*)

MOTOR	PRE-SPEECH	LANGUAGE	COGNITION	SOCIAL–EMOTIONAL
3. Place Kathy in infant seat, upright symmetrical position, pillow at nape of neck to provide neck flexion.		Show pleasurable objects (e.g., musical toys) to Kathy to initiate her smile as a consistent "yes" response. Toy will be presented to Kathy upon a smile from her and accompanied by a verbal "yes" from mother.		Mother will record the number of times Kathy smiles indicating a "yes" response during interactional situations.
4. Mother sits in cross-legged position in front of mirror with Kathy sitting in the valley of mother's lap (this replaces Kathy's former supine dressing position).		Mother names clothing items and actions while dressing and undressing Kathy (e.g., "Touch the sock," "Where is the shoe?" "Look at the shoe.").		Mother and child in close physical proximity to foster intimacy. Eye contact is still possible in mirror.

Integrated Activities Meeting Multiple Objectives: Plan VI

Description of Child and Family

John is an 18-month-old child with spastic diplegia. He is the youngest of three children in an intact, professional family. He was 6 weeks premature and remained hospitalized for 2 months. The parents became concerned about his development at 9 months of age and sought special services. Vision and hearing appear to be within normal limits. John is small but seemingly well nourished.

Developmental Status

MOTOR

John rolls with no segmental rotation. He sits without support but has poor balance due to limited trunk rotation. Protective extension reactions are present forward, but not backward or toward the side. He is nonambulatory but takes some weight on his feet when supported and attempts to take reciprocal steps. There is incoordination in his forward reach, due to the mild flexor spasticity. A palmar grasp and release is present, but limited prehensile patterns are used in play activities.

PRE-SPEECH

John has inadequate lip closure and a slight tongue thrust. He still drinks from a bottle and resists cup drinking. John is a fussy eater; he accepts some soft, lumpy foods, will self-feed when presented with a Graham cracker.

LANGUAGE

He responds to his name and to familiar phrases related to daily activities. Some deliberate vocalization is demonstrated in relation to objects and beginning socialization. Vocalization is used to express pleasure; it increases in intensity to express discomfort.

COGNITION

John shows the beginning of object permanence by searching for objects where they were hidden.

Integrated Activities Meeting Multiple Objectives: Plan VI

MOTOR	PRE-SPEECH	LANGUAGE	COGNITION	SOCIAL–EMOTIONAL
1. John is placed in prone over a large beachball. Holding him at ankles, mother gently rolls ball forward toward a toy on the floor. She encourages him to raise his head and reach forward as he approaches toy. Movement over the ball helps to normalize muscle tone.	Mother rolls John forward over a large beachball until his extended hands touch floor. Father facing baby says "Boom!" Mother moves ball back, then rolls it forward again. Father repeats "Boom!" each time baby's hands touch floor. He reinforces John whenever he makes a sound as a response to stimuli.	With John over ball, father says "Johnny touch" each time he is moved within reach of toy. Father reinforces John with loving reaction whenever he touches a toy.	Toys placed near the beachball vary in color and texture to attract and hold John's attention. Parent guides John's hand to touch and manipulate sensorily varied materials. While on ball, John attends to a wind-up toy as it enters a small tunnel and reappears on other side.	Caregivers offer positive reinforcement (happy loving reactions) to John's vocalizations or purposeful movements in response to the environment.
2. John sits upright straddling a bolster, with his arms on a table in front of him. Large objects requiring two hands to lift are placed to the left and to the right of him on the table. Trunk rotation is therefore elicited as he reaches for the objects.	A tape recording of John's vocalizations is played for his imitation. He is reinforced each time he reproduces the sounds.	Astride the bolster, John follows verbal directions, e.g., to reach for the big yellow clown or the large balloon at either end of the table.	Astride the bolster at the table, John is encouraged to swipe a light inflatable ball and knock it to the floor. Parent picks it up and says "Here is the ball" and returns it to John. The process is repeated to extend John's concept of object permanence.	On John's irritable days, mother introduces only those activities in which his success is guaranteed.

This action is brief and unsystematic. He does not look for dropped objects that are out of sight. He mouths objects, shakes and bangs them, is beginning to rotate objects to inspect them, and hits at suspended objects. However, for his age, he is generally passive regarding his environment.

SOCIAL–EMOTIONAL

John swings markedly between high irritability, fussing, and crying on some days, and days when he is quiet and complacent. Mother finds it very difficult to cope with this fluctuating pattern and his inconsistent response to her.

Sample Concerns
- Inadequate trunk control and rotation.
- Limited forward reach patterns and manipulation.
- General disinterest in his environment.
- Delayed meaningful vocalization.

Strategies
- Facilitate trunk rotation and postural support against gravity.
- Promote successful reaching and manipulation of objects.
- Promote responsiveness to environment.
- Encourage production of sound as a response to stimuli.

Multiple Interventions to Meet a General Behavioral Objective: Plan VII

Description of Child and Family
Samuel is a 9-month-old boy with delayed development. His bilateral cleft palate has been surgically repaired, and his seizures are controlled with medication. He is the only child of parents who separated when he was 3 months old.

Developmental Status
MOTOR
Samuel's motor development is estimated at the 2- to 3-month level. He can raise his head up for brief moments in supported sitting or prone.

Arm movements are limited to crude swiping of brightly colored or noisy objects.

PRE-SPEECH

Samuel makes a variety of sounds in spontaneous babbling. He can tolerate only pureed foods; he drinks from a bottle.

LANGUAGE

He smiles when his mother makes sounds which he associates with pleasurable experiences such as feeding. He seems to recognize his name and attempts to look in the direction of the voice. He has clearly differentiated qualities and variations in crying by which he communicates his needs and emotions.

COGNITION

Samuel cries when objects drop out of sight, but he does not visually search for them. When sitting in a semireclined position, he visually tracks objects without differentiating head and eye movements. He is beginning to anticipate events through association of objects. For example, he sometimes coos and chuckles when he sees his bottle.

SOCIAL–EMOTIONAL

Samuel responds easily to being handled by a variety of caregivers. He does not become upset when his mother leaves him periodically with a baby-sitter. There seems to be good interaction between Samuel and his mother. She is reassuring and supportive; she appears to enjoy him. She speaks to him calmly and in a soft voice.

Sample Concerns

- Lack of head control.
- Disinterest in exploring objects.
- Limited imitative vocalization.

Strategies

- Facilitate head control in the prone position.
- Encourage imitation of sounds.
- Increase awareness of objects and sounds in his environment.

Multiple Interventions to Meet a General Behavioral Objective: Plan VII

A. *To Increase the Number of Imitative Vocalizations*

Objective: When the mother utters a sound already in his repertoire, Samuel will produce the same sound in response a gradually increasing proportion of the time: (*a*) 25% of the time, (*b*) 50% of the time, (*c*) 75% of the time, in the ensuing 6-month period.

MOTOR	PRE-SPEECH	LANGUAGE	COGNITION	SOCIAL–EMOTIONAL
When mother is serving as the speech model, she positions Samuel facing her on her lap or in an infant seat. He is semireclined at a 45° angle. To facilitate increased vocalization through controlled exhalation of breath, mother pushes his legs against his stomach; or she raises his arms and then lowers them to his chest.	During mealtime mother makes pleasurable sounds for imitation (e.g., "mmm").	Mother tape records Samuel's sounds and plays them back for him to imitate. Mother says "up" as his arms are raised and "down" as they are lowered, when involved in the **motor** procedure.	Mother exaggerates selected sounds in the context of a song or as an animal response in play situations.	Mother smiles at Samuel and pats him when he attempts to imitate a sound.

Multiple Interventions to Meet a General Behavioral Objective: Plan VII (*Continued*)

B. *To Increase Samuel's Head Control in the Prone Position*

Objective: When in a prone position, Samuel will raise his head in midline and hold it for increasing durations: (*a*) 15 second, (*b*) 30 seconds, (*c*) 45 seconds, in the ensuing 4-week period.

MOTOR	PRE-SPEECH	LANGUAGE	COGNITION	SOCIAL–EMOTIONAL
Mother places Samuel in prone position over a small wedge or bolster, or over her lap when she is sitting on the floor with her legs extended (long sitting).	During snack time, with Samuel in prone position, mother dips the spoon in applesauce (or some other favorite food) and places it on Samuel's tongue each time he raises his head.	With Samuel in prone position, mother says "Head up" as she dangles a string of bells in front of him at midline. Other phrases such as "Look, Samuel, see the bells" are offered to get his attention.	With Samuel in prone position over wedge or bolster, mother plays peek-a-boo with him.	Mother smiles at and talks to Samuel each time he raises his head.

Communicating Home Program Needs to Parents*

Since the parent or caregiver is the most important person in the baby's life and the baby spends the greatest amount of time with that person, it is essential that there be effective communication between the center's professional personnel and parents. What follows is an outline of the various methods of communication used by the different centers involved in the National Collaborative Infant Project.

The means by which staff may communicate with caregivers regarding home program elements include demonstration, verbal and written instructions, and modeling. All of these depend on the staff member's ability to articulate clearly what is intended and on the understanding that staff member and caregiver have of each other's language. The centers evolved a variety of ways—some of them quite unique—to measure the degree of comprehension and the level of cooperation in carrying out what had been communicated.

The most uniformly noted method was demonstration by a staff member to a parent of the desirable way to carry out an "exercise" that was to be performed regularly at home. Usually, but not always, this was followed by a period during which the caregiver could practice under supervision. In the absence of reinforcing methods, parents were often unable to follow through on all the activities, forgetting some by the time they arrived home. Where the demonstration and practice sessions were reinforced with written instructions, there was a marked increase in participation and follow through. In one center, recommendations were demonstrated and, in addition, a written version with line drawings of the required positioning or equipment were provided.

In another center, parents kept their own notebooks, writing down things as they were observed or discussed, and keeping a weekly log which they brought with them to the center. Every 3 or 4 months, parents were asked to leave these notebooks with staff for updating, so that aspects of the home program no longer necessary could be crossed off. In yet another center, "pink sheets" of written instructions were prepared by each individual therapist and teacher on the day the child came to the clinic. A social worker conferred with parents before they left the center, to be

*The major contributor to this section is Margaret Schilling.

sure that what appeared on these sheets was well understood. Parents took home one copy, the center kept the other on file. The child's records at the center thus contained all past and current recommendations, and provided a running commentary on the child's progress.

One center devised two colors for home program recommendations—one being for parents to take home (green sheets), the other being for "in-center" use (blue sheets). The two sets of sheets contained the same general information but were more simply written for parents, more precise and technically detailed for staff. Parents brought back their green sheets each week, with check marks placed against those activities that had been attempted or successfully accomplished each day.

Another plan for promoting understanding between staff and parents was devised by a center where a group of parents were in need of reinforcement and approval. Each parent participated in writing plans to take home each week. A copy of these in simple form was kept at the center. On the date of the return visit, the duplicate was put on the bulletin board. The parents' first activity on arrival was to cross out those activities the child had accomplished during the past week while other parents watched approvingly as items were crossed off, offering support if none had been accomplished. Staff were alert and would change an activity or break it down into smaller segments for the next week to ensure some success.

A variation of the method in which the parents kept notebooks is one that had the parents writing down suggestions in their own language as they were given. If the intervention was complex, a staff member reviewed the parent's notes "to help you be sure" and expanded upon or altered them where necessary. These sheets were in duplicate form—the top tear-off copy going to the parent, the carbon copy going into the child's records at the center. On the bottom portion of the sheets reminders or plans for the next visit were written.

One method, more sophisticated than those mentioned so far, was devised by a center that follows children in direct programs from birth through age 5 and, after transfer to public school, continues to provide therapy if needed. Project visitors who interviewed the parents of children aged 3, 4, and 5 found that the parents were vague about the agency goals and had no clear concept of what future was envisaged for their children. Selecting a group of parents and children whom they had followed closely for several years, the staff created a personal notebook for each family. The book contained background data from each of the staff members about the child: discussion of his diagnosis, line drawings of the brain to illustrate affected areas, and summaries of current status and realistic goals. (Great care was taken to explain the purpose of compiling such a summary—to assure the family that it did not mean that the center was going to stop trying to achieve the highest possible goals for the child.) The compilation of such reports is time consuming, and it can only be undertaken where the staff are highly skilled and transdisciplinary in approach and have followed the child over a considerable period of time. An adequate amount of time also must be allowed for interpretation to the family. Not all staffs are ready for this process, not all families are ready to hear the reports; but it is one means of conveying to the major caregivers how the staff sees the future for the child at that point in time.

An important element that is common to many of the methods outlined here is the opportunity provided by centers for the family to assess various parameters of the child's functioning at home. Serious consideration is given to parents' reports: The parent and the team facilitator (with other staff present) together go over the report, review the status quo and the overall objectives developed cooperatively on the child's behalf, and discuss any constraints that may apply (such as lack of time, lack of money to buy recommended dietary supplements, objections by the child's grandmother to the exercise of discipline, or any recommendation that conflicts with the family's life style). Appropriate adjustments are made, and the parent and staff then cooperate in drawing up the home program for the next week or month.

CHAPTER 11

MODES AND METHODS OF
SERVICE DELIVERY

T HE purpose of this chapter is to convey a clear picture of the various modes for delivery of services to atypical infants and their families. Most of the individual and group models described were actually observed in operation (in part or in whole) at the various infant centers participating in the National Collaborative Infant Project, and the examples have been drawn from the curriculum sheets specifically designed for the infants and toddlers within these programs (see Appendix E for sample forms used by the centers).

There are probably many other types of service delivery systems that might be added to the ones described here, to meet the needs of particular infants and their families. The appropriate professionals, along with representatives from consumer groups, should study these examples and plan a service delivery system (which may be a combination of two or more of the models outlined here) that is based upon the needs of the particular infant, his total family, the resources of the agency, the cultural, ethnic, and social mores of the population to be served, and the current practice of the professional community in that geographical area.

The major contributors to this chapter are Margaret Schilling and John M. Siepp.

The service delivery models that follow have been divided into three major types: individual oriented, group settings, and residential care.

Individual-Oriented Delivery Systems

Four of the models are more clearly identified with an individual-oriented delivery system, designed to meet specific needs: the arena, the consultation, the slot machine, and the home call. The primary purpose is usually to reach a diagnosis and outline a method for treatment. The following characteristics are usually associated with the models in this group:

1. A full complement of staff is available at the center (or systems exist in the community that can be drawn upon) capable of providing the medical, social–psychological, educational, and other expertise necessary for complete, comprehensive evaluations and/or services.
2. Responsibility for the delivery of service is usually center based and center funded.
3. The status of the agency in the community is usually well established.
4. Unit costs of care (e.g., cost of electroencephalogram, doctor's examination, etc.) are more easily identified and consequently more readily understood than in group models.
5. The age of the child is an influential factor in the selection of one of these models, e.g., babies are better served by home calls.

The Arena

In an arena system the child, the parent(s) or principal caregiver(s), and the primary facilitator are the center of focus for the group, with the staff immediately concerned seated around the triad. (However, the family may feel more comfortable if they are positioned so that they do not directly face the "audience.") For example, seated in the first row of staff may be the occupational therapist, speech therapist, social worker, teachers, and other staff people who have direct involvement with this particular child and family. In the second row, farther from the center of focus, are the staff members who have had less contact with the child and his family, such as the psychologist or audiologist. In the next row may be visiting observers at the center, students, and other peripherally concerned persons. The row to which an observer is assigned depends on his/her degree of involvement with the family.

Involvement of the family (including the child, if old enough) with the staff should precede the arena interview so as to clarify roles; the responsibilities of the team facilitator should be clearly explained and every effort should be made to ensure that the parent and child are comfortable about the situation. Ordinarily, one primary facilitator is in charge and will be with the child and parent in the center of the arena, working directly with them as the child's abilities are checked and progress noted; comments and suggestions from the parent and from those seated in the successive rows will be directed to the facilitator. Preceding exposure to the arena, the parent and child have usually been interviewed by, and become acquainted in individual sessions with, at least one of the staff seated in the first row, and had an initial relationship with them. But this is not always the case; the arena may be the first evaluation.

In no existing center does the arena model constitute the entire service delivery process. Most commonly, an arena arrangement is used for evaluation and for professional staff training demonstrations. It has some distinct advantages: it enables the parent to be involved with the whole staff; and it permits an entire staff to be involved with the child and keep up to date with his progress without having each one handle him; and it helps foster transdisciplinary approaches to caregiving.

Obviously there are also risks with such a procedure. The parent and the child can easily be overwhelmed by the number of people present. The arena method of diagnosis and service delivery needs to be handled extremely sensitively, so as to blend the contributions of the various people present without making the family feel overwhelmed. The primary facilitator has to be highly supportive of the parent as well as very knowledgeable about the staff and its potential contributions to the particular case. He/she has to be keenly aware of the other professionals and know when to bring them in, when to demonstrate without additional help. Centers that include appropriately sensitive individuals on their staff may wish to try the procedure—perhaps with the arena limited to two rows at first—particularly for periodic reevaluation sessions.

The procedure can also be used, perhaps in reduced form, for demonstration sessions with parents—either for the parent to demonstrate an acquired skill or for the parent to be helped to learn some new approach or concept relating to the child. When these sessions are handled sensitively, under the control of a primary facilitator who is known to the child and the parent and with whom they are comfortable and at ease, a blending of recommendations and advice from several staff people can be accomplished. In the process, participating staff members will gain a better understanding of the expertise of their peers, and gradual movement toward full transdisciplinary participation may be achieved.

In some centers a one-way observation booth may be used for staff members other than the primary facilitator. However, use of the open arena system can promote a feeling of competence in the parents and a true team colleagueship among staff—when all participating are not merely comfortable and accepting of the arena but also welcome the opportunities it provides. The young child usually is not discomfited by the presence of others and is spared excessive and inconsistent handling. Naturally the arena is not recommended in those cases where the child is not sufficiently secure even in the presence of his parent and is disturbed or frightened by the presence of others.

THE ARENA—AN ILLUSTRATION

Situation	Ten-month-old infant; spastic right hemiplegia; normal intelligence; beginning to bear weight.
Concerns	Some evidence of increased spasticity on right side. Question of visual tracking. Previous difficulty in feeding and dietary patterns.
Goals	■ To obtain further evaluation of increased spasticity.
	■ To assess feeding pattern.
	■ To assess value of continued home visits by public health nurse.
	■ To assess current home–clinic therapy program and provide for new input.

■ To assist family in developing alternative techniques for management of child.

Plan

■ *Physical therapist* will assume the role of primary facilitator. With mother, will carry out a reevaluation of the child to assess possible increased spasticity. Will demonstrate pivoting activities by having the child work to attain toys out of reach. Will demonstrate to mother how to encourage weight bearing on both feet. Will discuss with mother activities to encourage child to reach toward her with both hands. (Occupational therapist will have instructed physical therapist in how to assess visual regard.)

■ *Occupational therapist* will suggest activities to increase tactile stimulation on right side, which primary facilitator will then demonstrate to mother.

■ Primary facilitator will have mother demonstrate feeding.

■ *Speech therapist* will discuss feeding problem. Will arrange with public health nurse to monitor feeding problem during home visits.

■ *Social worker* will observe behavior during demonstrations and join in the dialogue if indicated. Will arrange for individual conference with parent.

■ *Public health* nurse will be asked prior to the demonstration to share insights and findings from her home visits. Will provide reinforcement and support for the parent if indicated during the session. Will counsel, as appropriate, regarding the fit of the evolving program plan, in the light of the family's life style.

■ *Seating:* The professionals named above are seated in the first row. The second row has the psychologist, early childhood educator, and physician.

Comment
This method was chosen because of the age and diagnosis of the child. The physical therapist was selected as the primary facilitator because of her competency in handling hemiplegics. The visual problems could be better observed by the rest of the team from a distance.

Intelligence and medical diagnosis were already established; the physician, psychologist, and teacher were therefore assigned to the second row.

The Consultation

In dealing with young atypical children, medical surveillance is of critical importance. The basic health status of such infants may be precarious. There are dangers in excessive or inconsistent handling. Such infants are also quite vulnerable to intercurrent illnesses. However, this does not imply that a center's service should be restricted to a medical model, nor that there should be medical dominance of all facets of center programs. What it does imply is an ever-present need for the consistent incorporation of medical counsel and judgment in the overall program design and implementation.

There are certain functions of medically related staff members working at the center (such as therapists and nurses) that can be carried out within their respective professional competencies without a specific medical referral or order. However, in certain cases where nursing services or therapy treatments are to be provided for the infant, there is a need for specific medical referrals or orders.

The term *consultation* is used here to refer to two types of medical review. One is in conjunction with the child's primary physician where the latter is not a member of the center staff but continues to see the child routinely at his office and to prescribe and monitor all medically related aspects of the center program as these are integrated within the center's overall services for the child. The consultation with the primary physician may then be part of the regular program of pediatric surveillance or an extra visit (initiated by the parent, staff, or physician him/herself) in advance of the next routinely scheduled visit.

The other type of medical review is consultation with a specialist (e.g., neurologist, psychiatrist, orthopedist), which may be initiated by the primary physician or requested by the center staff seeking special guidance (for instance, following their observation of a change in the child's condition).

At times, the consultation may lead to referral to a person who is not a physician but an expert in the field of psychology, genetics, nursing, social work, or some other area of special expertise, to meet apparent needs of the child or his family and to provide guidance for the staff. The primary physician may wish to have the specialist's report come directly to his office, or he may request that the report be directed to the center and a copy sent to his office. In either case, arrangements will need to be made for the physician to discuss the findings with the staff and guide them as to the implications for program implementation. The physician will also convey the findings of the report to the family and advise them accordingly.

In some centers there is a physician who serves on a full- or part-time basis as a member of the center staff. Under these circumstances a primary physician may request the staff physician to take major responsibility for the medical aspects of the center program on behalf of his patient, including referrals for special medical consultation, and he may reserve as his role only the routine monitoring of the child's basic health, prophylactic inoculations, and direct care during periods of intercurrent illness. In such instances, the staff physician may be the chief liaison person in maintaining communication with the primary physician and in exercising the appropriate professional ethics involved in all such matters.

Regarding the medical aspects of a center's services, there is a vital need for preplanning, clearly delineated lines of communication, and mutually agreed upon allocation of responsibility. It may be the center's program coordinator, social worker, or director who is vested with primary responsibility for medical arrangements. Or it may be the team facilitator working most directly with the infant and family. Whatever the center's policies regarding medical procedures, they should be clearly defined and agreed upon by all concerned.

The parent also should have the right to initiate a consultation. In a soundly administered transdisciplinary approach, with clear focus upon the parents as members of the team, parents are encouraged and enabled to discuss their concerns in medical as in other pertinent matters, and are always included, with the primary physician, in the decision-making process. When parents are able to present their own child at center staff conferences or on clinic days at the center, these presentations provide opportunities for the exchange of ideas and the planning of such medical initiatives.

Once the need for a doctor's visit is established, related concerns need to be addressed. If the consultation (whether with physician or specialist) is initiated by the primary physician or by the center staff, several questions need to be asked. Does the family concur? Do they need help in financing such a visit? Is other assistance needed, such as transportation or a baby-sitter for other siblings? Who will be responsible for relaying the findings to the family and to the center staff? What safeguards have been established in the event that there is some conflict with regard to the diagnosis or with regard to subsequent implementation of the program planned at the center for that child?

Some specialists have a sound perspective of total child and family needs. But others may concentrate their findings and recommendations very precisely within the boundaries of their own segregated area of expertise. Who will interpret the findings to the family? If there are any conflicting recommendations or other resulting problems, how shall these be resolved with regard to the family's concerns and the center's total program design for the infant and his family? These are some of the eventualities that must be planned far in advance, some of the safeguards that must be built in, clearly delineated, and mutually agreed upon by all those concerned, when the model of the consultation is defined.

There are many positive values to this model, primary among which is the spectrum of skill and competence that can be brought to bear on behalf of the baby, his family, and the center staff operation. It must also be recognized that the status of a center and of its staff is enhanced when acknowledged experts in the community are known to be involved in contributing to quality service design and implementation. Awareness in advance of the possible confusions or conflicts that might ensue, and sound advance planning to deal with them, can lead to optimal utilization of this valuable model.

THE CONSULTATION—AN ILLUSTRATION

Situation
Two-year-old child; spastic left hemiplegia. Near normal intelligence. Only child. Suspected seizure disorder.

Concerns
Subtle and fleeting symptoms observed by staff may be evidence of seizures. Parents feel child does not need specialized therapy treatment since her gait and use of affected hand are improving. They do not fully understand diagnosis or its implications and feel child just "doesn't pay attention." Parents do not carry out home program in any consistent manner.

Goals
■ To evaluate possible seizure activity.

■ To prepare parents for the possibility that neuromuscular abnormalities may become more apparent as child becomes older.

■ To emphasize importance of treatment and periodic medical reevaluation.

■ To formulate program recommendations appropriate to child's needs, age, and abilities.

■ To provide guidance for the center staff members relative to program implementation from the medical point of view.

Plan
■ Discuss the need for consultation with both the family and their physician. With physician's concurrence, refer child to pediatric neurologist for evaluation and establish who will interpret the findings to the family. Inform family about details of the consultation (e.g., time, place, cost).

■ Alert specialist's office that consultation should include providing general information about cerebral palsy and emphasizing the importance of continued therapy. (Be sure that time is provided for parents to ask questions and have them answered by the neurologist.)

■ Provide family physician with copy of neurologist's report and recommendations. Plan for physician's continued cooperation and help in implementing recommendations.

■ Provide staff members with copy of neurologist's report.

■ Plan for medical member of staff to discuss implications of the findings with other staff members and the family.

■ Arrange for social worker from center to provide periodic follow-along contacts and any additional explanation or support family needs.

■ Refer to evaluation team at center for reappraisal of child's developmental status and any program changes that may be indicated.

■ Alert staff about need to integrate findings into the various kinds of service delivered to the child.

■ All staff members to be sensitive to the problems faced by the child and family and recognize the need to encourage, motivate, and commend the family for their important contribution toward the child's progress.

Comment   Since the center was providing the major care of the infant, staff members needed specialized confirmation about what appeared to be seizures in order to understand the child's needs more completely. Parents needed an in-depth interpretation by an expert of the child's medical problem and prognosis, and had to be convinced of the importance of following through with these recommendations.

The Slot Machine

In the slot-machine model, the child is escorted (usually by the parent) sequentially to a series of professionals (one or more physicians, therapists, psychologists), each of whom sees the child individually. Often the parent is not present with the child during the session with each professional but waits outside or returns to collect the child at a designated time.

There is nothing in this arrangement that precludes parental involvement; parents could accompany their child during each session and have information and suggestions shared with them. But most commonly the slot-machine arrangement occurs within settings that are heavily medical in orientation and in which there is little tradition of including parents in the therapeutic process.

There are occasions in most centers, whatever their overall organization, in which some version of the slot machine may be needed, as when a child must be seen by an outside expert of some kind. But, where possible, it is highly desirable to have the consultant come to the center to see the child, rather than sending child and parent to an unfamiliar office situation. It should be emphasized that a slot-machine type of service delivery does deliver service. The child is seen by the assorted professionals, some direct therapy is given, and parents may be given suggestions. However, when other types of service delivery are feasible for a center, then those other options are clearly preferable. The negative aspects of the slot-machine model are obvious. There is extensive handling of the child by many individuals; there is no development of a single contact person with whom the parent may feel confident; there is no supportive therapist or interpreter of procedures or unfamiliar terms. Instead, the parent must adjust to the many different professional personnel involved.

In the slot-machine model the parent is usually far too little involved. He or she can be involved with each of the professionals separately, but, in the absence of a single person to interpret findings and correlate services, this may produce confusion. The model is of value when the individual requiring care lives in an isolated area without local facilities, or when local facilities are available but "fractured," requiring trips to several different locations.

THE SLOT MACHINE—AN ILLUSTRATION

Situation   Nine-month-old infant; diagnosis not yet confirmed. Convulsions? Hearing loss? Retardation?

Concerns   Family resides in rural mid-America. No facilities for adequate diagnosis. No provision for treatment or follow-along care. Limited supportive services for family.

Goals

■ To obtain a comprehensive medical review.

■ To instruct family in home care regime on
the basis of the medical review.

■ To provide for continued home visits by
county nurse.

Plan

■ Family physician to refer child to nearest
medical center (80 miles from family home)
and set up appropriate clinic appointments with
pediatrician, neurologist, audiologist, psychologist—some or all requiring more than one visit.
Primary clinic at medical center may set up
additional evaluations.

■ Public health nurse to set up appointments
for essential therapy evaluations at the medical
center.

■ Provide transportation if needed by the
family.

■ Nurse (or home visitor) to work with parents
in home.

Comments

The slot-machine model (in combination with
the home-call model—see next section) is appropriate because distance is a major factor in this
situation. Copies of reports from the medical
center should be made available to the home
visitor, and he/she must be alert to possible
variations in advice from diverse medical personnel—which may result in confusion—and be
able to help the family reach some understanding. If the home visit were to take place in isolation from the medical center, it could become
just another slot in the slot-machine model.

The Home Call

For most of the centers participating in the collaborative
project, the home call, or home visit, was included as just one

procedure in overall program design. In only one of the centers was it the major focus of service. However, home-call programs do of course exist outside of the collaborative project; professional persons go from one family to the next, offering advice and training for parents, and providing equipment and follow-along care.

Where the home visit is integrated into the center's overall program for child and family, the home visitor sees families—primarily the families of very young babies—perhaps as often as once a week. The home visitor—who may be a social worker, nutritionist, therapist, nurse, or other practitioner—then often serves as a facilitator for the team. Emotional support is provided for the parents and close personal relationships often develop with the mothers visited. The visitor works with the mother to cope with the infant's daily needs, instructs her in appropriate types of play and stimulation for the child, answers questions, and serves as a public advocate for the family where needed.

In some programs, the home visitor is not a full-time member of the team but is recruited from a general community service for families in special need. For example, the public health nurse from the city, county, or state health department, or from a private visiting-nurse service, may make home calls at the request of center staff, either to deal with a specific problem or for follow-along service.

The role of the visitor is a demanding one; it requires someone who is able to combine the many needed skills, one who can recognize the primary needs of the family and deal with them effectively. The home visitor needs to be versatile and flexible, and adept in establishing rapport with a wide variety of people. Any center that has such a person on its staff (and many do) should seriously consider including home visits in its programs. Home visits are expensive, but they can be enormously effective, particularly in cases of severe handicap, in which the parents may be greatly discouraged or depressed and in which practical home management problems may require on-the-spot solutions. Opportunity for other staff to accompany the visitor as required to assist in meeting special needs should be built into a home-visiting program.

The home-visitor role need not be restricted to one member of the team. Dependent on the changing needs of the infant and family, practitioners of different disciplines may have the greatest potential to help at different times. Rapport between the family and the worker, as well as the worker's skill, are ever important considerations.

Administratively, safeguards must be set up to protect the visitor in travel as well as in service delivery. While the costs of travel and of time consumed often preclude this type of program, it should be considered, if at all feasible, since it is an important component of a comprehensive program. In addition to the financial difficulties, not all families are readily accepting of a visitor in the home, looking on this as an intrusion. When this type of program is in effect, visitors must be aware of the cultural and ethnic background of families; they must be prepared to adjust to the mores of the group and take care not to alienate the family.

One of the great advantages of this design is that it permits visitors to adjust time schedules and to visit during periods when the father may be at home—and father involvement is something that is often difficult to arrange in other models. If home visits are included in the program, administrators must allow time for these visits to include informal experience sharing; coffee-drinking time, for example, must be viewed as a very important part of the total care of the infant.

THE HOME CALL—AN ILLUSTRATION

Situation Six-week-old infant—premature delivery, birth weight 2 pounds. Severely involved, with convulsive disorders, weak suckle reflex. Life expectancy very limited, sleeps a great deal; when held has a constant fretful cry.

First baby of very young parents, frightened yet realistic, needing support. Parents isolated from any extended family support. Transportation to local center, complicated and expensive, as well as hazardous for baby.

Concerns Parents need help in sustaining baby's life as adequately as possible.

Goals ■ To assess response to medication for convulsions.

■ To evaluate feeding techniques and diet.

■ To assess sleeping arrangements and possibility of need for change.

■ To give support to parents.

Plan   ■ Home-call program to be undertaken by nurse on the center staff. After checking on medication, arrange for visit to physician if indicated; provide transportation if needed. Nurse may transport and accompany family if it appears necessary.

■ Demonstrate feeding techniques that may result in better food intake.

■ Note crib placement, determine means for change if warranted.

■ Allow ample time to stay and visit with parents.

■ Make positive arrangements for return visit.

■ Provide opportunity for parents to contact nurse in an emergency.

Comment   Since it is doubtful if infant will live beyond a few weeks, it is essential that major support be given to parents, with least possible hassle. Need to provide nursing–nurturance care for the sake of parents' morale as well as for infant's life expectancy.

Group Settings

Six of the models involve a group setting: the octopus, the three-ring circus, follow the leader, the great circle, stop and go, and the four winds. Important variables to consider in these programs are:

1. *Geographic area* from which children are drawn—whether a small, compact area or spread-out rural communities.
2. *Space available*—whether limited or spacious, convenient or inaccessible, available for limited periods of time or all day.
3. *Equipment*—whether appropriate and plentiful or generally inadequate; storage problems.

4. *Time constraints*—program given once a week, once a day; intermittent or repeated regularly.

5. *Attendance*—depends somewhat on geographic area but also on parents' commitment to attend; also on the health, physical problems, and age of children served.

6. *Staff*—available full time or shared; full complement of therapists and teachers versus one or two major program facilitators; purchased service of some staff members from other agencies.

7. *Parent participation*—required, requested, or variable, depending on program activity.

8. *Paraprofessionals*—availability; utilization will depend on need for (and center's ability to provide) supervision, in-service training.

The Octopus

This system is commonly found in residential care settings, schools, or hospitals, but not often with very young children. It provides a core area for the child, usually with some peer interaction, as a base from which he is sent or taken for various therapies or medical examinations. For example, he "goes out" for physical therapy, then returns to the home room. The system has many negatives; treatment is in isolated disciplines or areas, staff members work independently of one another, and there is usually no parent with the child. It has one advantage, namely, the child's interrelationship with his peer group at the base operation. Unless the child is old enough or has enough mobility to get to and from the various outposts, it also requires extra personnel to convey the child to the service.

THE OCTOPUS—AN ILLUSTRATION

Situation	Three-year-old child; athetotic; "trainable" mentally retarded; nonambulatory.
Concerns	Child is approaching age level necessitating placement elsewhere. Is presenting feeding problems, largely emotionally based. Has developed some mild "seizure" activity, etiology unknown. Parents are cooperative but anxious about the future.

Goals

■ To determine present level of intellectual ability.

■ To establish feeding regime beginning at center then introduced at home.

■ To refer for neurological review.

■ To explore community resources for further placement.

■ To confer with parents in developing future plans.

Plan

■ From a group care program base, child to be evaluated by various staff professionals.

■ Child to be seen by clinical psychologist for reevaluation.

■ Child to be seen by speech or occupational therapist for assessment of feeding problem.

■ Child to be seen by neurologist for evaluation of seizure activities.

■ Social worker to confer with family and community agencies regarding future placement.

■ Staff of center, including social worker and psychologist, to confer with parents on child's present developmental status and specialists' recommendations.

Comment

The main advantage of the octopus model in this situation is that four mornings a week the child has a "home base"—his group program resembling the home room common to many orthopedic school rooms. From this base he is seen by the center's speech therapist, psychologist, etc., leaving his room for therapy, or medical review, but returning to a familiar peer group for interaction and competition. Unlike the slot-machine model, all family services are clearly integrated at the final point. Planning for future placement is shared by and with staff—

family is not sent off alone to search for resources. Also, respite is provided to the family
four mornings a week.

The Three-Ring Circus

This model requires ample space if it is not to become chaotic.
In each of the "rings" a type of activity is undertaken—for example, movement in one, water play in another, and eating in a
third. A large number of children, grouped according to their
abilities, can be treated in one time period with minimum staff.
Parents handle their own children, under tutelage of the therapist, teacher, or nurse. Each mother can become a "teacher" for a
time and demonstrate her child's skills. However, the area must be
sufficiently large to enable the children and parents to shift easily
from one group to the next.

The three-ring-circus model provides an opportunity for the
child to demonstrate his strengths. For example, a child who is
quite immobile may have good speech and be able to compete
favorably in the speech activities. It enables the parent to see the
levels of ability of the child and to get some positive reinforcement
when the child is able to perform at a higher level in one activity
than in another. It affords an opportunity for the child to have a
variety of contacts with peers and the professional staff. And the
staff member has many children to demonstrate to parents a particular skill at varied levels.

The three-ring circus also lends itself to an educational focus,
since one or more of the "rings" may involve speech or early cognitive skills, as well as physical or occupational therapy. From the
point of view of parent participation, the three-ring circus has
many advantages. It is also valuable in preparing the child for
further (preschool) educational experiences.

One of the disadvantages of the model is that it does not involve staff members with one another during the session, and it
separates, rather than integrates, the several facets of the child's
functioning. As the program develops, staff members could begin
to shift their roles through mutual transdisciplinary teaching.

To function optimally the model is highly dependent on the
majority of the children being able to attend the majority of the
time. Care should be exercised that each child has some oppor-

tunity for success—this may require a change in format or an added piece of adaptive equipment. Each child should be allowed some choice in activity, and staff should try, within limits, to respect those choices.

THE THREE-RING CIRCUS— AN ILLUSTRATION

Situation

Group of eighteen children, aged 18 months to 3 years, varying degrees of disability; all have well-established diagnoses; all are on home therapy regimes. The majority of parents are able to carry out individual therapy; transportation to and from the center is available by family or can be arranged. Center is able to provide adequate space and equipment.

Concerns

Most of the children have limited opportunities for peer group relationships. Parents have few opportunities to observe their children in situations of interaction—find it difficult to assess improvement or change. Staff time is limited.

Goals

■ To provide opportunities for the *child* to have multiple experiences in the gross motor, fine motor, language, personal–social, and cognitive domains, in a wide variety of situations.

■ To provide opportunities for the *parent* to observe his/her child in a variety of experiences, including some in which he is successful.

■ To provide a variety of *media* for play activities that stimulate cognitive, language, and movement goals and that might be adapted to home use.

■ To provide *staff* with an opportunity to observe the children in a variety of situations that include interaction and some competition— which is not possible in individual therapy.

Plan

■ Three activity areas to be designed:

A. Obstacle course
    1. Place the following pieces of equipment

in one portion of the room, separated so that play with one does not hamper play with another.

    a. Large, open-ended, rug-lined barrel.

    b. Small, closed, rug-covered barrel.

    c. A 3-step staircase placed parallel to and against the wall (to provide some support) and a large mat on the floor (to alight upon).

    d. Walking board, 8 feet long by 6 inches wide, raised at one end and attached to the second rung of a stationary climbing ladder.

2. Each mother to supervise own child. Instruct mothers that each child should try four out of several activities, using the equipment as suggested, but also allowing the child to explore other safe alternatives.

    Activity possibilities:

    a. *Open barrel:* climbing through; lying in (on stomach or back) and rocking (or being rocked).

    b. *Covered barrel:* straddling like a horse; lying over barrel and rolling forward on abdomen, keeping balance when rocked.

    c. *Stairs:* climb up and down; climb up and jump off onto mat.

    d. *Walking board:* walk up, step off; walk up, turn around, walk down; walk up, climb ladder.

    e. *Ladder:* climb up and down; climb up, over the top, and down.

B. Water Play

1. Staff member to act as leader; parents take a secondary, supportive role.

2. Small plastic swimming pool containing 3 inches of water.

3. Children find places on the floor where they can comfortably reach into pool (corner seats, prone boards, or other adaptive equipment might be used by some—see Appendix A).

4. Children push up their long sleeves.

5. Toys include floating objects, containers, baby dolls to wash, etc.

6. As children are playing, adult attempts to stimulate conversation, for example as to which things float or sink. Social awareness of group can be developed by discussing the specific activity in which each child is involved.

C. Snack Time

1. Arrange for seating at low table (s), with each parent appropriately seated at table with own child. See that children are appropriately positioned. Provide utensils to fit each child's special need.

2. Provide opportunity for hand and face cleaning.

3. Encourage discussion about the food— taste, smell, texture, and child's familiarity with it; give child opportunity for choices.

4. Staff members help parents to develop regime for each child as appropriate to child's level of feeding skills.

5. Those children who are able to contribute can be assigned small tasks—pouring juice, passing food, setting and clearing table.

Comment The children, their families, and the center all fit the criteria for this model: a large number of children each accompanied by an adult; the center able to provide ample space but limited staff. The model meets the children's need to socialize and provides opportunity for child and parent to experience success in one or other activity. Parents should be encouraged to comment on child's successes or failures and to relate the home experiences that have led to, or developed as a result of, the child's activity in the group. Where individual therapy needs are apparent, they can be met through the home program and/or through some other mode of service delivery.

Follow the Leader

This model closely approximates what is frequently seen in nursery school settings, except that in the centers of the collaborative project the children are supported by the presence of parents.

The "leader" and primary facilitator is usually a teacher skilled in recognizing cognitive abilities and varying attention spans and levels, as well as appropriate positioning requirements. The teacher must be familiar with each child's needs and abilities. He or she must know how to assist parents to position the children, so that all may participate in the activity, and know which roles or actions are suited to which child. (For example, while the teacher may offer a child a "choice" of musical instruments to play in the band, in reality the child's choice is between two instruments that have been suggested by therapists as relating to the nature of the handicap—such as instruments requiring *two hands* for the hemiplegic.) The leader must also pace the activity, taking note of readiness, attention, and participation, and stopping the activity as the children's needs indicate. The leader must have an extensive repertoire, so that the activity does not become dull through repetition. In some instances, a parent or a child may serve as leader.

The teacher–leader must be well trained in the transdisciplinary approach and be able to maintain the status of the primary facilitator *throughout the activity*. This requires considerable preplanning and interchange of skills and knowledge. Since the duration of the activity has to be somewhat open-ended, other staff members will need to remain flexible—ready to pick up individual children for therapy if the session should stop abruptly, or willing to wait for a longer period if the group activity is at a high peak and not able to be cut off at the specified time. Thus, although only one staff member may be actively involved during the session, support from other staff members before, during, and after the session is essential.

The follow-the-leader model provides a format in which a wide variety of children can participate. It is a form of activity with which people are generally familiar. Parents feel relatively less restrained about participating, since the choice of roles and actions is such that every child is able to enjoy some success. It also permits parents to learn from one another; to "exchange" children and view their own child from the other side of the circle; and to learn about variables in muscle tone, varying abilities in gross and fine motor areas, differences in the social–emotional domain, and so on. For the "nonactive" staff members (who may move on the periphery of the circle to help with positioning), it provides an opportunity to note each child's successes and failures; to observe the children and parents in an informal setting, particularly parent–child interaction; and to note problems with which they may wish to deal later in individual sessions.

FOLLOW THE LEADER—AN ILLUSTRATION

Situation Five children (or any suitable number depending on size of area) who have some approximation in age and skill level. All have opportunity for individualized therapy, as needed, at other times. Majority of parents are able to accompany children to center. Major input from a suitable early childhood educator is available.

Concerns A majority of the parents have little knowledge of early childhood educational standards, principles, techniques, and measures. The children have little chance for interaction outside of immediate family. Staff members need an extra dimension by which to evaluate each child's potential, especially in deciding future placement.

Goals
- To provide nonthreatening activities that will allow parents to participate without unnecessary anxiety.

- To provide children and parents with a wide variety of peer contacts.

- To provide opportunity for staff to observe, participating where indicated.

Plan
- Arrange for play area that will provide space for selected number of children to sit comfortably in a semicircle, with parents sitting on the floor behind them (or staff member, if parent not in attendance). All face the teacher. Time and duration of the session will be determined by age of children and average length of attention span.

- Teacher will preplan with therapy staff, assessing each child's needs, so that during the group activity the child will be adequately positioned (using adaptive equipment if required) and be offered the activity that will complement his therapy program and enable him to participate to the fullest extent.

- Teacher will assemble a variety of educational materials for each selected activity, as well as provide resources to take advantage of new experiences that may arise serendipitously. Some of the experiences should correspond with the child's family background (e.g., songs that are well known to the group and snacks that are commonly used by families). Others should be experiences that are new to the child and his parent, to increase their awareness of the outside world.

- Teacher will encourage parents to participate in songs and finger play. Therapists will assist with positioning where necessary, but this assistance must be rendered as unobtrusively as possible so as not to interfere with teacher–child–parent interactions.

■ Activities selected by teacher will involve gross and fine motor areas and will also stimulate language and promote cognition. Opportunity should be provided for children and parents to experience some interaction with other participants.

Comment Choice of this model over others fulfills needs of children and parents for experiences relating to early childhood education.

The Great Circle

In this model, parents, children, and staff sit together in a circle. The parents have been given individualized instructions prior to the group session. Now the parent serves as the primary therapist and programmer, with supportive interventions from staff as to treatment procedure or management techniques. Parents interact with one another, as do the children, in the course of the session. When outside consultants (physicians, psychologists, nutritionists) are brought in to see the child or to evaluate progress, the child or child–parent pair is not sent to a separate room, nor does the staff member take over. Rather, the parent is given the opportunity to discuss the child directly with the consultant, demonstrate the child's skills, and express areas of satisfaction or concern.

The circle time is divided into segments—for gross motor activities, fine motor activities, and free play. The session usually ends in a competitive game. Language, cognitive, motor, health, and social–emotional goals are integrated throughout the whole session. The social worker, as well as other staff members, rotate around the circle, sensitive to evidences of need that often surface as parents relate to one another in congenial and free discussion. This is reported to be of equal or sometimes greater value than the more formal social worker–parent conferences that take place in an office or at home.

The obvious strength of this model is the heavy parent involvement. The parents recognize that they are the central "therapists" and caregivers, and the parent group itself develops important dynamics. Usually, a circle arrangement also helps foster good transdisciplinary staff involvement. The several staff who participate in the parent–child group sessions move about the circle giving individual suggestions to parents, trying out new possibilities with the infant, and serving as model and interpreter. For staff members to fill this role effectively they should have a fairly wide knowledge in several disciplines, since the needs of individual infants in the group may vary considerably.

Another advantage of the circle method is that the session can be carried out in a relatively small area and at relatively low cost. (However, adequate floor space and a supply of simple toys and equipment are essential.) If the child–parent group meets for 1 to 1½ hours several times a week, with each parent continuing the therapy at home, several different groups of parents can be served at different times of the day, utilizing the same space. In addition, the space remains free for other uses during the remaining part of the week. Since all activities involve the whole group, there is less need for separate consulting rooms (although at least one is essential). Since the group does not ordinarily meet for protracted periods, there is less need for much ancillary space. Staff members may be employed only part-time and may in fact be "borrowed" from other agencies or from other programs under the same roof. This type of infant program can be fitted into a program for older atypical children without great cost and can provide some service to quite a large number of families.

There are some risks involved in the great circle arrangement which should be recognized ahead of time by any center contemplating the use of this model of service delivery. A prerequisite of success is that the staff members involved be very skilled, very transdisciplinary in their approach, and highly sensitive to group processes. The various mothers and children have widely differing needs and have to be offered very different kinds of suggestions and assistance. Staff also have to be aware of the possibility that parents may teach one another inappropriate things. Also, the parent whose child is progressing slowly may find it discouraging to see the more rapid progress of other infants in the group. There are difficult decisions to be made about the composition of the several groups, and such decisions may affect the whole course of the group process. While a well-functioning model of the great circle can achieve wonders, less well executed versions may have serious limitations and may in fact provide a lesser amount of service—less instruction, less therapy, less support to the parent— than alternative models.

The staff cannot sit back and let the parents run the group entirely, even though that may be the appearance of the group functioning. There must be good preplanning and subtle, continuous involvement of staff members throughout the group session. Therapists must be aware of variations in physical disabilities of children in the group and must provide for these. Parents may want to know why certain procedures are not applicable to their child, and continual explanation of therapies will be necessary.

The great circle is one model that allows for parent–parent interaction and continued parent education, while still allowing for professional input and supervision. It works well within a fairly limited geographic area, where transportation is less of a problem. Circles can meet two or three times each week and do not require consistency of attendance.

THE GREAT CIRCLE—AN ILLUSTRATION

Situation

Seven children (although the number may be slightly larger or smaller) with varying degrees of physical and mental abilities ranging from mildly to moderately retarded. Chronological ages of children are from 11 months to 2 years of age. All are nonambulatory. Most of the children have some speech sounds.

Concerns

The children have had limited opportunity to play with their peers. Most will relate to others only from the security of their mother's arms. In some cases the parents have allowed the child to control the family, unaware that not all aspects of the child's behavior can be attributed to his handicap.

Goals

■ To encourage correct positioning appropriate to each child's developmental age and capacities.

■ To provide some peer relationships.

■ To encourage children's use of language.

■ To encourage mothers to use speech and language for more than punitive control.

■ To encourage group discussions on child management.

Plan

■ Arrange for group to meet twice weekly.

■ Allow mothers ample opportunity to practice recommended positions and activities.

■ Demonstrate to mothers ways to communicate with children through play.

■ Encourage mothers to praise children's efforts and be sensitive to their needs but to set limits on excessive demands.

■ Encourage verbal interaction and feedback between mothers and children. Provide opportunities for parents to talk to one another and observe one another's ways of handling child.

Comment

While providing individual therapeutic assistance for each child, this model meets the needs of children and parents for socialization and peer relationships. It provides a relaxed atmosphere in which to relate to and learn from others who face similar problems. Frequent meetings of the small group foster closeness, confidence, and mutual concern.

Stop and Go

This model, which in some ways resembles the great circle model, was developed to handle the twin problems of involving parents and making do with limited space. There are many possible modifications of the basic concept, but the core group is a set of parents and children working with staff. At the outset, half of the parent–child pairs (or triads when both mother and father are present) meet together with the staff—to demonstrate progress, receive new instructions, get questions answered and, perhaps, stimulate the children in specific ways—as in the great circle model. Then the parents leave the room and the first group of infants is joined by the infants of the other half of the families. Thus, in the middle segment of time, all the children are together. During this session the children have an opportunity to interact together and staff members have an opportunity to provide individual or group experiences designed to foster each child's overall development.

Meanwhile, all the parents are together in another room meeting with a group worker, social worker, or psychologist for counseling, further educational input, and the discussion of concerns. At the end of this hour, parents in the initial group collect their children and leave. The second group of parents and children now meet together with staff for a similar session as was offered during the first segment of time.

In the parent–child segments there should ideally be one primary evaluator for each child. As with the great circle model, sensitivity on the part of the staff members is crucial in this setting. If staff become too didactic, useful opportunities for parent–parent interaction may be lost; if staff are too laissez-faire, opportunities to instruct parents in new stimulative skills may be lost or parents may copy one another inappropriately. The all-child segment of this model is a setting common to many centers. It facilitates more concentrated therapy for individual children and permits the staff to keep more fully in touch with each child's progress, so that appropriate suggestions may be made to the parents and activities planned for future sessions.

There are some clear advantages to this model, especially since it is very flexible and permits quite a number of modifications. The parents are heavily involved and can be helped to develop a feeling of confidence about their handling of the child. Parents have an opportunity to share experiences, which creates a bond among them and provides emotional support for each. There is opportunity both for individual work and for group work with the children. Also, the model encourages the transdisciplinary involvement of staff, because the one or two staff members present during the all-parent sessions will be called upon to provide information and guidance across the whole range of specialties.

In any center with insufficient space for all parents and children to meet simultaneously, the stop-and-go system may be a very good option. (However, bear in mind that a second room will be needed for the parent meetings.) The model does not require continuity of attendance, although this is desirable; neither does it restrict the level of ability of the child. It does require a well-trained transdisciplinary-oriented staff.

STOP AND GO—AN ILLUSTRATION

Situation

Twelve children (although the number may be larger or smaller, depending on available staff) with a wide variety of physical and intellectual abilities, ages range from newborn to 24 months. The majority of parents have had little or no assistance in providing adequate care through a home regime. All families have (or can obtain) transportation on a fairly regular basis.

Concerns

Children need therapy that is not generally available in the area. Children are isolated in individual homes, without peer interaction. Parents need help in carrying out home regime, understanding implications of physical disability, and planning for the future. Staff need recurring opportunity to assess child's' developmental progress and outline future home programs. Space and staff are limited.

Goals

■ To provide individualized therapy and reassessment, with cooperation of parent.

■ To provide group counseling of parents.

■ To enable staff to introduce new therapy regimes, including language, cognitive, and personal–social goals.

■ To make optimum use of limited space and staff, and thus increase number of children seen.

Plan

■ Preplanning to enable all staff members to act as primary facilitators for a given child, with input from all other staff.

■ At 9:00 A.M., six children and their parents (or caregivers) arrive at the center. Each family is assigned to a therapist or trained aide. Parents report on successes or failures since last meeting. Staff person demonstrates suggested changes in home program, allowing ample time for parent to practice. During this time, it is possible for all staff to observe all the children, while working directly with only one child.

■   At 10:00 A.M., six other children and their parents arrive at the center. Children from this new group join the children of the 9:00 A.M. group in the large room, while the parents of both groups leave the room. The children may be divided into small activity groups, according to their level of competency. Physical therapist, occupational therapist, or speech therapist may continue to work with individual children on specific tasks; teacher may develop some group activities; speech therapist could utilize snack time for developing feeding skills, etc.

■   At 10:00 A.M., the parents of both groups of children meet in a second room with social worker, psychologist, or other appropriate personnel for group discussion. This may take the form of parent education, group counseling, or group therapy, depending on needs of the group and the skills of available staff. A therapist might lead discussion if several parents have questions about a specific area, e.g., feeding, care of braces. This meeting should be informal, with parents and staff seated in a circle or semicircle.

■   At 11:00 A.M., all parents return to infant room. The parents and children who arrived at 9:00 A.M. now leave the center. The parents and children who arrived at 10:00 A.M. stay on for a program that follows the format of the 9:00 to 10:00 session.

■   Sessions to be held weekly; attendance to be as regular as possible.

Comment   This model incorporates the advantages of the great circle but provides more opportunity for parent education and group counseling.

The Four Winds

This model was specifically designed to focus on parent involvement in the habilitative process. While the format has remained the same, there have been changes in implementation since it was initially conceived. Originally, activities were action oriented, for example, finger painting or block building; later they became purpose-oriented, for example, "to increase fine motor coordination" or "to promote language acquisition." Staff members set up the activities in the four corners of the room. One staff member usually stays with one activity throughout the time period. Where possible, videotapes are used, as a method for recording mothers' teaching styles and providing them with a means to assess their own performance. If tape is not available, observers may record behaviors from a position outside the activity, and these can be reviewed during the discussion session.

The four-winds model is best used when the parents are familiar with the center's educational approach and able to assist in planning the program. Time should be set aside at the end of the session for parents and staff to review and evaluate the child's performance during the session and to plan for the next session. Home follow-up can also be discussed at this time.

This program design provides a change of pace, incorporates an important element of choice for parents and children, and allows staff members a quiet period with each parent. It also provides an opportunity to help parents play with the child, gain pleasure from his success, and evaluate his lack of success in relationship to his disability.

THE FOUR WINDS—AN ILLUSTRATION

Situation   Six children (age range 12 to 18 months): two spastic quadriplegia, mentally retarded; one spastic hemiplegia, normal intelligence; two mildly mentally retarded, ambulatory, with only minimal physical involvement; one athetoid, moderately involved, above normal intelligence.

Concerns Parents feel isolated and express a need to meet other parents with disabled young children. They desire a better understanding of what is developmentally appropriate when interacting with their child. Limited staff does not permit individual scheduling of every child for all aspects of program.

Goals ■ To provide various opportunities for participation of each child. To provide opportunity for child and parent to experience success in selected activities.

■ To design activities that will allow for a range of functional performance levels.

■ To assist parents and staff in evaluating child's successes as judged by his performance.

■ To allow child to make choices of activities on repeated occasions.

Plan ■ Children and parents to attend four-winds session two mornings a week. Parents to act as programmers, with limited staff intervention.

■ Preconference about all the children's needs by staff to ensure that all are aware of functioning level and program goals for each child.

■ Design four areas of activity, using bubbles, variously textured materials, cone of colored rings, and balloons. Maintain some distance between areas, allowing space for child to roll, crawl, or walk from one to another if possible.

■ Parents to decide among themselves the sequence in which each child will be brought to each area of activity.

■ Child will be allowed to explore the specific activity; will be encouraged by mother to try for higher performance level as he becomes familiar with each medium.

■ Therapists will monitor positioning, hand functioning, and speech production in each area.

■ Time allocation for each activity will be pre-determined, but cueing for change will be monitored, so that child is not automatically removed from activity if interest level is still high or if he is reaching toward success.

■ Whenever feasible, within restrictions of time and space, each child will be in each of four activities during the one-hour session.

■ One staff member or volunteer will be assigned to each activity area and be provided with a list of functional performance levels (as shown below).

■ Time for all parents and staff to meet together for joint discussion, review, and selection of next session's activities will follow the session.

FUNCTIONAL PERFORMANCE LEVELS:

A. *Bubbles:*

   1.   Visually focuses on bubble

   2.   Visually tracks bubble

   3.   Makes generalized motoric response to bubble

   4.   Reaches for bubble

   5.   Reaches for bubble and "catches" it

   6.   Reaches and catches with one hand and/or with two hands, on command

   7.   Attempts to blow bubble by exhaling

   8.   Attempts to blow bubble by pursing lips

   9.   Attempts to blow bubble by pursing lips and exhaling

   10.   Vocalizes in response to sight or touch of bubble

B. *Textures (using variously textured pieces of fabric):*

   1.   Visually regards fabric

   2.   Touches fabric

   3.   Scratches fabric

4. Picks up with hand (s)

5. Manipulates fabric

6. Manipulates fabric and makes verbal response

7. Transfers fabric from one hand to the other

8. Holds fabric to arm or other body part

9. Holds fabric to face

10. Rubs face with fabric

11. Begins to distinguish between rough and smooth textures

12. Vocalizes while handling fabric

C. *Cone of Colored Rings:*

1. Visually regards colored cone

2. Picks up cone from base and dumps rings

3. Takes rings off one by one

4. Attempts to replace rings

5. Replaces rings without regard to size gradation

6. Replaces rings with relative awareness of size gradation

7. Replaces rings in correct order through trial and error (i.e., corrects initial error)

8. Replaces rings correctly with full awareness of size gradation

9. Attends until reaches completion of activity

D. *Balloons:*

1. Visually regards balloon

2. Visually tracks balloon

3. Makes generalized motoric response to balloon

4. Reaches for balloon

5. Touches balloon

6. Touches balloon and makes vocal response

7. Throws balloon

8. Attempts to catch balloon by extending arms in general direction

Comment   In the review and planning period, the parents have an opportunity to exchange views and experiences. Analyzing activities according to functional performance levels teaches the parents the developmental sequence for acquiring mastery of the task.

Residential Care

No discussion of alternative modes of service delivery for the atypical child is complete without some mention of residential care—the "home away from home" model. While, for a variety of reasons, residential care is the least desirable option, in many situations it is the only option. For example, in sparsely populated rural areas, the children to whom service is to be delivered may be so scattered and inaccessible that regular therapy, either in individual or in group sessions, is impossible. The families of some atypical infants are unable to have the child at home for any of a number of reasons: the parents live in as domestic servants, or all adults in the family have to work full-time to support the family, or there is a lack of appropriate parental figures. Or the atypical child may be an orphan. Where foster placement or adoption proves impossible, residential care may be the only option. Whatever the reasons for residential care having to be resorted to, it is to be hoped that the child can maintain regular contact with, and periodically return to, his parental home.

The primary drawback of residential care is the difficulty for the child in establishing a close relationship with his parents or in developing a sense of security in any human relationship. There is also a danger of a too hospitalized atmosphere—one that emphasizes the child's "sickness" and provides too little enrichment for perceptual and cognitive development. These are not inevitable characteristics of residential systems. It is possible to design residential environments that overcome these tendencies, and it is of the utmost importance to do so.

First, it is important that the actual caregiving staff—often persons with minimal preparation—share the knowledge of professional staff members and be familiar with their goals. Caregivers should be helped to understand the need for each aspect of the program, be alert to opportunities to motivate exploration, and be fully aware of the child's need for some emotional constancy in relationships. The number of caregivers should be adequate, so that each has primary responsibility for only a few infants and the infants can form a primary attachment to their caregiver.

Second, the environment in which the children live should be as rich and varied as possible and appropriately full of color, light, and varied texture, with toys and materials designed to foster exploration and cognitive growth (without overstimulating the child).

Third, the professional staff needs to avoid adopting a slot-machine or octopus model, in which the child is removed from the home environment for each separate kind of service—diagnosis, therapy, treatment. Where possible, the therapy should be carried out in the living section of the residential center and involve the primary caregiver. Where this is not possible, the child should at least be accompanied by his major caregiver.

Regular "going out" of the home room—as for play outdoors and visits to the store, in the normal way that these might occur in the family home—is important for normative childhood experiences and should be incorporated into the residential care setting.

Finally, every effort should be made to include the real or foster parents in the educational–habilitative process and to provide them with as much information as can be managed, especially in those programs where the child is in residence for only brief periods of time because of service lacks in the home community.

The components of residential care (staffing patterns, support systems, etc.) vary depending on the duration of time the child is away from his parental home and the reasons for such separation.

Home Away from Home (Short Term)

Short-term residential care would include nursery care for a newborn considered to be at risk, hospitalization of a child for diagnostic purposes (i.e., to carry out such medical procedures as electroencephalograms, blood studies), hospitalization to establish seizure control, or temporary full-time care to provide respite service for the parents. A further category of need is surfacing: immediate care of the abused or neglected child who must be removed from his parental home until professional services for the family determine the possibility of his return.

HOME AWAY FROM HOME (SHORT TERM) —AN ILLUSTRATION

Situation

Eighteen-month-old, hyperactive, visually handicapped boy with seizure patterns. Mother is pregnant with her third child. Father is a military career man. Family is quartered on the base.

Concerns

Medical staff on the post see a need for

1. The extent of visual acuity to be clarified
2. The seizure pattern to be reassessed
3. A drug therapy plan to be established

Goals

■ To facilitate exploratory diagnostic procedures.

■ To enable these procedures to be completed prior to mother's confinement.

Plan

■ Short-term hospitalization at a special children's medical center will be arranged.

■ Pediatrician from the base hospital will contact the appropriate staff at the selected hospital to arrange for admission.

■ Parents review and give permission for all past pertinent information about the child to be sent by base hospital to the children's hospital.

■ Parents will make appointment with social worker at children's hospital to discuss procedures, provide complete background data, and clarify financial arrangements.

■ An informing conference with medical staff and parents will be held at the pediatric hospital before discharge; with parents' consent formal reports will be forwarded to the base hospital.

Comment   This service delivery model is uniquely appropriate to meet the family's special needs (mother's impending confinement) and provide services not available at the center where the child is being followed.

Home Away from Home (Long Term)

Long-term residential care is less and less frequently resorted to as community resources are developed. In the past, severely involved and/or severely retarded children were frequently placed in large residential settings as the only recourse. With increased day care centers and early intervention programs in the child's community, admission of the young child to large residential settings is decreasing. More children now remain in their family setting.

Distance from an accredited treatment center formerly was a factor influencing families to consider placing children for long-term care. Increased mobility of society, improved transportation systems, and the development of programs in rural or less populated areas are further factors contributing to a decrease in residential placement.

Long-term care away from the family poses many problems and should be resorted to as infrequently as possible. Selection of this method should be undertaken with caution, considerable family input, and only after examination of all other possibilities for providing the needed services from within the community. When it does become the method of choice, safeguards to provide for parental contact can be built in. Plans can also be made to provide financial assistance for such care, so that the strain on the family's resources will not be too severe.

Professionals who find this the only feasible method of providing the needed service must remain alert to possibilities for developing community resources that will allow the child to remain in his own home or to return to his home as soon as possible. If the child has no family, or if the family is unable or unwilling to nurture the child, foster home care in a community where the needed services are available should be sought as a far preferable alternative to institutional placement during infancy and childhood. In cases where the family is able and willing to have the child at home but lives in an area remote from needed services, temporary foster care may be an alternative.

HOME AWAY FROM HOME (LONG TERM)
—AN ILLUSTRATION

Situation

Three-year-old girl, spastic quadriplegic. Child's all-round potential is good, providing she receives proper therapy on a daily basis. Family includes six other children and lives on a large farm in a remote rural area of the state. Nearest rehabilitation center to home is the residential center (300 miles).

Concerns

Child's needs cannot be met in the home, and there are no facilities or programs within the community. However, staff members are concerned about the impact of separation on the family–child attachment.

Goals

■ To provide for the therapeutic and other special needs of the child that will enable her to develop to her full potential.

■ To provide for continued parental input into care of child as frequently and as intensively as is feasible.

■ To provide for surrogate parental nurturing during time that child is away from her own family.

Plan

■ Child's admission to the residential center will be arranged.

■ Financial support for child's full-time, long-term care will be provided through private or public funds, as needed.

■ A variety of therapists, nurses, educators, social workers, and psychologists, as well as specialists in various medical fields, will be involved. There will be some group programming, as well as individualized sessions or treatments.

■ A parent surrogate will be provided to maintain consistent contact with the child.

■ To maintain the family attachment, a 24-hour-a-day telephone "hot line" between the parents and a designated staff member will be available. Family will be encouraged to take the child home two weekends per month.

■ While the child is in residential care, the social worker serving the county in which the family lives will begin a community organizational approach with the educational and the health and mental health agencies responsible for designing and implementing programs for handicapped children. This direct advocacy role should result in programs for handicapped children nearer their homes via a home service worker and mobile programs that include medical, social, psychological, and educational components.

Comment   Long-term care away from home appears, in this case, to be the only way in which the child's potential can be developed to the full.

APPENDICES

ADAPTIVE EQUIPMENT

The furniture and equipment regularly used by the normal child under 3 years of age often does not meet the specific needs of the young child with developmental disabilities. In such cases, the modification of available items or the construction of new equipment is necessary. The utilization of adaptive equipment can aid the child's motor development and functional abilities during his daily activities. However, assistive devices should be used only temporarily, as an interim step until the child can master the task independently. The infant's development should be continually reassessed to ascertain whether the modifications are still necessary or can be eliminated.

The following examples of adaptive equipment have been employed with success in numerous settings. This is a representative listing; it is not to be regarded as comprehensive in coverage. Additional items are briefly mentioned in "Selected Sources" at the end of this appendix.

Examples of Adaptive Equipment

Hammock

A hammock provides a desirable sleeping position for young children with two types of problems: (a) the child with a strong extensor pattern causing him to pull back the head and arms, arch the back, and possibly scissor the legs and (b) the infant with low muscle tone who assumes a froglike posture when lying supine. The hammock encourages proper body alignment and decreases the likelihood of the child assuming an abnormal posture. The hammock can be made of canvas, with wooden dowels along the edges to provide support. Finnie (1975) provides a discussion of hammock design and construction.

The major contributors to this appendix are Margaret H. Jones and G. Gordon Williamson.

Bolster (Figure A.1)

A roll, or bolster (Bergen, 1974), serves multiple purposes (e.g., under a prone-lying child's chest to facilitate head lifting and back extension; or as a seat to be straddled by a child who tends to scissor his legs). For smaller bolsters, carpet tubing can be used as the center core (4 to 6 inches in diameter). Hard cardboard tubes of larger diameter, which normally serve as casings for poured cement, are manufactured by Sunoco Corporation under the brand name "Sonotube" and can be obtained from construction companies. Bolsters can also be purchased commercially (see list of sources at the end of this appendix).

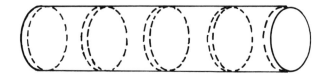

FIGURE A.1 *Bolster.*

The following points should be borne in mind when constructing a bolster:

1. If cement casings are used, they should be reinforced by wedging and nailing plywood discs, 1 foot apart, throughout the roll and at each end.
2. Extra firm foam (2 to 3 inches thick) can be used to pad the outer surface of the tube.
3. The entire unit should then be covered with a machine-sewn, waterproof vinyl sleeve, which can be either purchased or made at home.
4. An outer cover of washable fabric will add to comfort and cleanliness.

Side-Lyer Designed by Suffolk Rehabilitation Center (Figure A.2)

The side-lying position is particularly helpful for severely involved children who have a strong asymmetrical tonic neck reflex, a tonic labyrinthine reflex, and/or a marked extensor pattern of the total body. On his side, the child may have less spas-

Figure A.2 *Side-lyer designed by Suffolk Rehabilitation Center.*

ticity and a greater ability to bring his hands together in the midline. Thus visual–motor coordination is encouraged. The side-lyer (Levine, 1974) maintains the young child in a position that inhibits abnormal patterns of movement and posture.

A piece of ½-inch plywood 46 inches long and 12 inches high is covered with vinyl but not padded. In order to stabilize the board in a near-vertical position, two flat blocks are made for the board to be inserted into, one at each end. A slanted groove is cut into each block so that the board fits into it at an angle of about 80°. (The angle will depend on the child's needs; but it should be noted that, as the board approaches an angle of 90° to the floor, extensor tone may increase, accompanied by retraction at the shoulders.)

Four-inch webbing is stapled to the back of the board and passed under the child and across his chest, the webbing fitting just under the armpit. It is then passed through a slit made low in the board so that the angle of pull is downward against the lateral surface of the child's rib cage, rather than against the front of his chest, which would tend to flatten it. The webbing is then passed under and pulled over a bar that is attached to the back of the board (a simple towel rack may be used) and fastened to the board with velcro. A similar slit and webbing combination is made at the other end of the board, so that the setup can be reversed and the child can lie on either side.

The child is positioned with his back placed firmly against the board to prevent thrusting into extension. The extensor pattern can be further inhibited by placing a small pillow or folded towel behind his head to keep it in slight flexion. Another pillow or towel may be placed under the lower side of the head to maintain proper alignment with the body. If necessary, a rolled towel may be placed between his legs to keep them in abduction (spread apart).

Corner Chairs

A corner chair can be employed to improve head and trunk control, increase intercostal breathing, and assist visual-motor coordination.

CORNER CHAIR DESIGNED BY UCLA (Figure A.3). A cardboard grocery carton is used for construction of the corner chair designed by UCLA. Two sides and the top are cut out and stapled to the remaining two sides and the base for reinforcement and greater stability. The inside surface is covered with a shag carpet to increase comfort. The sides are approximately 14 inches high; the base about 14×14 inches. A second grocery carton, with a cutout to fit around the child, can serve as a table. It is approximately 8 inches high, with an area 13×13 inches, and is covered with a self-adhesive decorating paper (e.g., Contact).

THREE-CORNER CHAIR (Figure A.4). It is often difficult to create a comfortable sitting position for the child who tends to have an abnormal, total extensor pattern. Extensive strapping

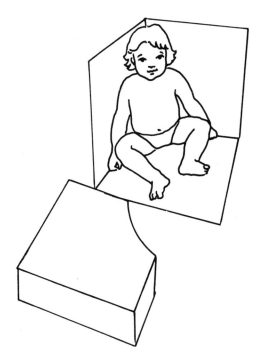

FIGURE A.3 *Corner chair designed by UCLA.*

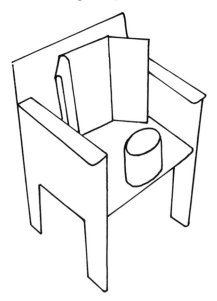

FIGURE A.4 *Three-corner chair.*

imposes limits on both mobility and attempts at balance. One solution is a seat with a three-sectioned back, which encourages curling the shoulders forward (protraction) as part of the desired flexed position (Bergen, 1974). With proper placement, the child seated in this chair may have greater use of his head and arms. An abduction post maintains the legs apart and helps to keep the hips properly flexed. The seat can be utilized on the floor, on a wooden chair, or in a stroller, high chair, wheelchair, or car.

The seat back is constructed of $\frac{1}{2}$-inch plywood, measured to reach mid-scapula height. The three sections are reinforced at the top and bottom by angle irons to maintain a 120° angle. When the seat back has been adequately positioned, measurements are taken for placement of the abduction post, which is a well-padded block covered with fabric and screwed into position on the base.

Chair with Pelvic-Tilt Backrest (Figures A.5, A.6)

The requirements for good sitting posture are true hip flexion with an anterior tilt of the pelvis and correct foot placement with adequate knee flexion. The back should be in comfortable extension with slight low-back lordosis and upper-back kyphosis. The chair with a pelvic-tilt backrest (Staller, 1973) facilitates the appropriate postural adjustments needed for good sitting, without being overly supportive. Moreover the design offers adjustability to the needs of different children.

The seat height should be adjusted to allow the feet to be flat on the floor. (This can be determined by using the measurement from behind the child's knee to the heel.) The seat depth should be measured along the thigh from at least 2 or 3 inches behind the flexed knee to behind the back. A broad base of support encourages better weight bearing.

The back of the chair is a vertical beam from seat to shoulder height. Two parallel slots are cut vertically into the beam, so that two adjustable, firmly padded bars can then be mounted horizontally on the beam. Each bar is 2 inches high and 2 inches deep. The bars are held to the vertical beam by means of bolts and wing nuts inserted into the slots. This assembly allows the bars to be vertically adjustable.

The lower bar makes contact at the crest of the pelvis, creating a push forward. A seat belt is attached at the junction of the beam and seat. The belt is positioned to pull the hips straight back and to position the pelvis in contact with the bar. Combination of the two forces creates hip flexion with an anteriorly tilted pelvis.

The upper bar is positioned at the inferior angle of the scapula (shoulder blade). The bar keeps the child from leaning backward. The resistance between the upper and lower bars facilitates extension in the back and discourages shoulder retraction. Raising the upper bar to a higher position prevents extensor thrusting.

An abduction post, to discourage hip adduction, is placed at the center front edge of the chair seat, exerting pressure at the knee and up to 3 inches proximally onto the thigh. Placing the peg in this position minimizes sensation on the medial thigh, which may stimulate adduction. This placement of the peg also allows easy sitting and rising from the chair. If there is strong adduction, the position may cause internal rotation, in which case the peg must be placed at mid-thigh.

For children with some trunk control, straight bars are recommended. For children without trunk control, contoured bars provide some lateral support. The backrest and bars (without the

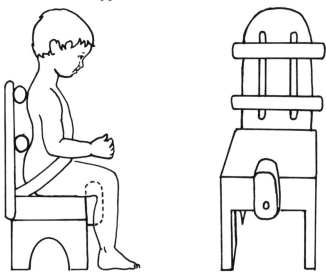

FIGURE A.5 *Chair with pelvic-tilt backrest (side view).*

FIGURE A.6 *Chair with pelvic-tilt backrest (front view).*

chair seat) can be used separately as an insert for a wheelchair, stroller, or high chair.

Sawhorse Chair (Figure A.7)

A sawhorse chair or bench aids the sitting balance of a child who tends to sit with his legs pulled together. By straddling the bench his legs are abducted and externally rotated. This provides him with a wider base of support, which increases trunk stability. The child should be properly positioned on the sawhorse chair— symmetrical alignment, adequate hip flexion, and a straight spine. A short backrest can be provided. If trunk control is precarious, children should not be left unattended on the bench. The correct height of the bench is obtained by measuring from below the knee flexed at 90° to the sole of the foot.

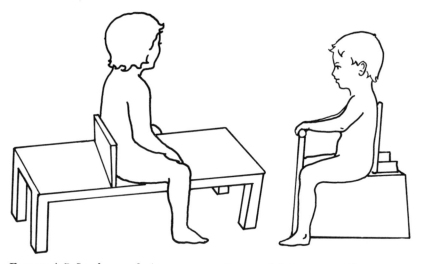

FIGURE A.7 *Sawhorse chair.*   FIGURE A.8 *Box type floor potty.*

Box Type Floor Potty (Figure A.8)

Young physically handicapped children who are too small for a standard toilet seat often present a positioning problem. Traditional adapted seats may have back and armrests but usually do not have footrests. On the standard seat the child usually has to sit on his lower spine with a rounded back, legs extended and adducted, and feet pointed. In this uncomfortable position, balance is poor. The child may become fearful and increasingly spastic.

Sitting posture is enhanced if the legs are abducted and flexed at the hip. Therefore the box type floor potty seat is designed so that the child straddles a box. A handle is provided in front for the child to grasp for stability. A back support adds to the feeling of security. No side panels or restraints are required. Since spasticity and fear are reduced, it is easier for the child to use the toilet. Bergen (1974) provides procedures for constructing the potty chair.

Prone Board (Figure A.9)

A padded board, sometimes referred to as a prone board, was devised in Switzerland to provide the handicapped child an opportunity to stand with proper body alignment. If the footboard is elevated and padded, the prone board can also be used for kneeling. This piece of equipment can be constructed in various designs depending on the needs of the child. It is also available commercially (see list of sources at the end of this appendix).

Footholders (foot plates) attached by set screws to slots on the standing board may be added to permit the feet to be turned out-

FIGURE A.9 *Prone board.*

ward or inward and at whatever distance apart is desired (not illustrated in Figure A.9). Velcro can be applied around the foot-holder and strapped over the shoe. Another strap across the but-tocks maintains hip extension and provides security. Knees rest against the lower cross bar; axillae (armpits) should be 1 inch above the upper padded area (chest board).

Using prone boards, several children can be placed around a table simultaneously, for play or for feeding. This equipment helps to prevent contractures from developing at the hips, knees, and ankles, and at the same time places the child in a more opti-mal position for various activities.

Wedged Scooter Board with Abduction
Triangle (Figure A.10)

Spastic children often use their arms to drag themselves along the floor. The effort necessary for this activity may create overflow of spasticity into the legs causing adduction and extension (scis-soring). Scooter boards offer these children mobility, but modifica-tions must be made to ensure optimal positioning and to decrease the possibilities of deformities (Bergen, 1974):

1. Shoulder blocks (A) are employed to discourage asymmetrical positioning of the trunk.
2. An abduction triangle (B) maintains the child's legs in abduc-tion, extension, and external rotation.
3. Front wedge (C) facilitates extension.
4. Hip strap inserted in slots (D) maintains alignment and ex-tension at the hips.

The scooter board is built of ¾-inch plywood (width: should-der width plus 4 inches; length: axilla-to-heel distance). Place the child in position on the plywood board and mark for location of shoulder blocks (blocks should be close to the trunk at scapula level), the abduction triangle (positioned to achieve maximum normal abduction; the feet should hang free to allow normal dorsi-flexion), and slots for the hip straps (slots should be close to the body line). For a small child, the hip strap can be fastened to the outside edge of the board. Install well-padded shoulder blocks (A). Cut slots for the hip straps (D). Glue wedge-shaped piece of foam (C) to the surface of the board to raise it at the front end.

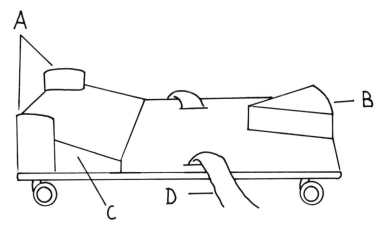

Figure A.10 *Wedged scooter board with abduction triangle.*

The abduction triangle (B) is made of foam 2 inches thick glued to a piece of ¾-inch plywood cut to triangle size. Long screws are used to fasten the abduction triangle onto the scooter board. Cover the entire scooter board with vinyl so that it is washable and waterproof. If Shephard casters are used, the scooter board will roll easily on all floor surfaces.

Table Top with Peg Handle (Figure A.11, A.12)

The extra effort a cerebral palsied child expends during table activities may cause an associated overflow of movement into other areas of the body. Depending on the severity and consistency of the movements (which tend to become ingrained and stereotyped for that child), deformities may result.

Table height is often significant. Normally the table surface should be at a height that permits the forearms to rest naturally on it. However, for a child with increased flexor tone, a table at nipple height, with or without a cut-out, can lessen trunk flexion. Pegs can be placed on the table for the child to hold (Bergen, 1974). The pegs will encourage shoulder external rotation, elbow extension, forearm supination, and a cylindrical grasp. For a child who tends to pull into an asymmetrical posture, holding a peg with one hand while engaged in a unilateral activity with the other will enhance normal, symmetrical body alignment.

The peg consists of a wooden dowel 4 inches in length, with a piece of threaded rod screwed into the end (the diameter of the

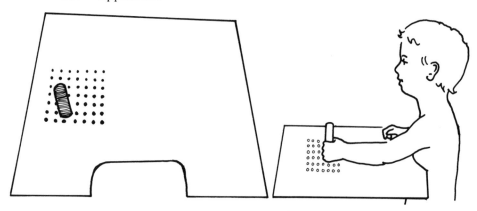

Figure A.11 *Table top with peg handle.*

dowel depends on the size of the child's hand; usually it measures 1 to $2\frac{1}{2}$ inches). If 1 inch of the rod is left exposed, it will fit through the table top and accept a wing nut on the underside. For maximal adjustability, the table top should have a matrix of holes at 1-inch intervals (see Figure A.11). The hole into which the peg is fitted for the specific child should be located under the child's hand when the arm is nearly or fully extended.

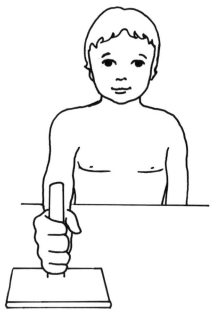

Figure A.12 *Peg handle device with suction base.*

Another design for a peg handle allows attachment to any table surface. A 5-inch wooden dowel is screwed or nailed into the center of a ½-inch board (4×6 inches), which serves as a base (see Figure A.12). Suction cups are secured on the underside of the base to anchor the peg device to the table ("little octopus" rubber soap holders may be used for a firm hold, since they have numerous suction cups). The peg handle device can be placed anywhere on the table and is easily removed.

Adapted Tricycle (Figure A.13)

Tricycle riding provides an opportunity for the child to develop sitting balance, hand reach and grasp, reciprocal leg motion, and a knowledge of spatial relations through steering. However, for some children, attempts to hold regular handlebars while pedaling the tricycle may tend to increase flexor tone. The spasticity creates a rounded sitting posture with an abnormal flexor pattern of the arms (flexion, pronation, and ulnar deviation). Often the child will pedal with the legs in an adducted, internally rotated position. His feet may frequently slip off the pedals.

To improve the arm and trunk posture, the handlebars should be converted to a vertical position (Bergen, 1974). The child will then grasp with arm extension, external rotation, and

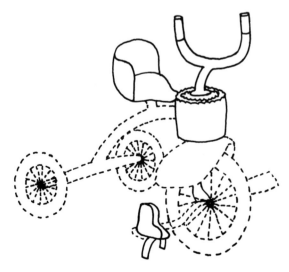

FIGURE A.13 *Adapted tricycle.*

supination. If the tricycle has a one-piece handlebar, the shaft bar can be bent until the handles become vertical. If the tricycle has a two-piece handlebar-shaft unit, it is possible to rotate the handlebars into a vertical position with a simple screw adjustment.

If additional leg correction is required to avoid adduction and internal rotation, a corrective "drum" should be attached around the handlebar shaft. Remove the top and bottom from a metal coffee can and slit along the seam. Place the can around the handlebar shaft and rejoin the seams, using internal wooden cross pieces to secure it in position and to maintain the correct diameter. Pad the outside of the tin, including the upper and lower edges, and cover with vinyl so that the child's legs slide easily over the surface.

An adaptation to assist trunk control is commercially available through the Preston Corporation (Tricycle Body Support, PEC 4749; see list of sources at the end of this appendix). However, a homemade unit can be constructed using a section cut from a heavy plastic wastepaper basket. This is screwed onto the back of the tricycle seat to provide back and lateral support. Or the pelvic-tilt backrest described earlier can be attached to the tricycle seat.

It is possible to use old shoes for pedal modifications by removing the laces, tongue, and front portion of the shoe. Velcro straps are then attached to act as closures. The shoe is held to the pedal in two places with nuts, bolts, and washers; it should be positioned in the center of the pedal. (The Preston Corporation has special pedals, in assorted sizes, in its catalogue.)

Selected Sources for Adaptive Equipment

☐ **Adaptive Equipment Company**
11443 Chapin Road
Chesterland, Ohio 44026

An *adaptive chair* is available in 3 sizes with additions of tilt control, lap board, and head and trunk supports if necessary. *Prone boards* (not free-standing) come in three sizes. *Bolsters* with hard cores are available in two lengths (2 or 4 feet) and three diameters (6, 8, or 10 inches).

☐ **Bobby Mac Company, Inc.**
95 Morris Lane
Scarsdale, New York 10583

The company makes a *high chair* that converts to a *car seat, floor seat,* or *infant carrier.* It is made of high-impact plastic and is washable.

☐ **CBA Custom Wood Products**
P.O. Box 105
Fort Collins, Colorado 80522

The company markets an *adjustable standing prone board*. It will adjust for a maximum 60° angle to a table or counter top height of 29 to 40 inches.

☐ **Community Playthings**
Rifton, New York 12471

The company manufactures wooden toys and furniture for use by young children, including *chairs* that readily accept adaptations. The wooden *toy carriage* (#D12) is sturdy, has large wheels, and can be easily weighted for the beginning walker. *Toys and trucks to ride on* are made of polished wood with large rubber-treaded wheels that roll easily.

☐ The General Motors *car seat* provides support and safety for infants and preschoolers. It comes in two models according to the child's weight (Infant Love Seat, #994259; Child Love Seat #9677326). The seats are available at most local General Motors dealers.

☐ **Gerico, Inc.**
Box 998
Boulder, Colorado 80302

The company is one of many that make lightweight, portable umbrella strollers, with a seat surface of vinyl. The *Gerry Carry-Free stroller* is indicated for the floppy infant with poor head and trunk control or one who tends to stiffen into extension (it maintains the infant in a flexed posture). As soon as the child has achieved greater balance against gravity, he should graduate to a standard stroller that has a firm seat for right-angled sitting.

☐ **Ha Si Sicher Leits-Kindermobel**
Friedrich Havenstein KG
8 Munchen-Neuaubing 66
Freinfelsstrasse 20a, West Germany

This firm's catalogue of German-made equipment contains many interesting items. Several of the adaptations can be fabricated by a professional or by a skilled do-it-yourselfer.

☐ **ICTA Information Centre**
FACK
S-161 03
Bromma 3, Sweden

The *Aids for Children* catalogue and subsequent fliers contain many useful pieces of equipment.

☐ **L. Mulholland and Associates**
985 Ann Arbor Avenue
Ventura, California 93003

This company has developed a *wheelchair* that is custom-made to suit individual needs. It is expensive, but it provides head and trunk alignment for individuals with severe motor problems, especially children with athetosis.

☐ **J. A. Preston Corporation**
71 Fifth Avenue
New York, New York 10003

The firm's catalogue lists an extensive array of adaptive equipment for adult and child rehabilitation.

☐ **Skill Developmental Equipment**
Vantel Corporation
Box 6590
Orange, California 92667

The vinyl-covered, *foam rubber equipment* manufactured by this firm offers many possibilities for seating, mobility, and therapy. Since it is colorful and tough, it is well suited for children.

☐ **Wallace Davis Company**
Hamden, Connecticut 06518

The *"Baby Anchor" bath seat* (Deluxe Model #112) may be used for infants 6 months to 2 years or up to 40 pounds.

☐ *Selected Equipment for Pediatric Rehabilitation*
Compiled by Adrienne Bergen
Blythedale Children's Hospital
Valhalla, New York 10595

A *booklet on adaptive equipment* that clearly describes the purposes of each item and offers construction details with ample photographs. Supplements that fit readily into the booklet are sent out periodically to keep it up to date.

ADVISORY COUNCIL, STAFF, AND CONSULTANTS FROM SPECIAL PROJECTS, NATIONAL COLLABORATIVE INFANT PROJECT JULY 1, 1971, TO JUNE 30, 1974

Kathryn E. Barnard
Professor of Nursing
Department of Maternal–Child
  Nursing
University of Washington
Seattle, Washington 98195

Gwen Bell Brooks
Physical Therapist
Fresno Association for Mentally
  Retarded
Infant Development Program
Lincoln School
651 "B" Street
Fresno, California 93706

Gloria R. Burgess
Consumer Representative
11585 Brookford Lane
Bridgeton, Missouri 63044

Mary Carroll
Former Program Representative
UCPA Midwest District Office
2400 East Devon Avenue, Suite 170
Des Plaines, Illinois 60018

Susan Collins
Director
Agency for Infant Development
1030 Sir Francis Drake Boulevard
Kentfield, California 94904

Frances P. Connor
Professor and Chairman
Department of Special Education
Teachers College
Columbia University
New York, New York 10027

Eric Denhoff
Medical Director
Meeting Street School
667 Waterman Avenue
East Providence, Rhode Island 02914

Helen Bee Douglas
Consultant in Developmental
  Psychology
UCPA, Inc.
Route 1, Box 2
Eastsound, Washington 98245

Nancy D'Wolf
Executive Director
Meeting Street School
667 Waterman Avenue
East Providence, Rhode Island 02914

Eric Erickson
Research Associate
Technical Assistance Development
  System
Frank Porter Graham Center
University of North Carolina
Chapel Hill, North Carolina 54220

Una Haynes
Director
National Collaborative Infant
  Project
UCPA, Inc.
66 East 34th Street
New York, New York 10016

Alfred Healy
Medical Director
University Hospital School
Iowa City, Iowa 52240

Elsie D. Helsel
Coordinator of Special Education
College of Education
McCraken Hall 119-B
Ohio University
Athens, Ohio 45701

Dorothy J. Hutchison
Associate Professor
Department of Nursing
Health Sciences Unit
University of Wisconsin-Extension
Manitowoc County Campus
705 Viebahn Street
Manitowoc, Wisconsin 54220

Margaret H. Jones
Professor Emeritus of Pediatrics
Medical Center
University of California
1000 Veteran Avenue
Los Angeles, California 90024

Sara W. Kelley
Director of Public Relations
UCPA, Inc.
66 East 34th Street
New York, New York 10016

David Lillie
Director
Technical Assistance Development
  System
Frank Porter Graham Center
University of North Carolina
625 West Cameron Avenue
Chapel Hill, North Carolina 54220

Joan Meisel
Project Evaluator
National Collaborative Infant
  Project
UCPA, Inc.
500 Redwood Road
San Anselmo, California 94960

Sherwood A. Messner
Former Director
Professional Services Program
  Department
UCPA, Inc.
66 East 34th Street
New York, New York 10016

Marie L. Moore
National Advocacy Coordinator
UCPA, Inc.
66 East 34th Street
New York, New York 10016

Gary Nielsen
Former Chief
Special Problems Unit
Marin County Community Mental
  Health Services
Agency for Infant Development
1030 Sir Francis Drake Boulevard
Kentfield, California 94904

Gene Patterson
Consultant in Program Services

National Association for Retarded
Citizens
2709 Avenue E, East
Arlington, Texas 76011

Clara (Freddie) Pincus
Coordinator
United Cerebral Palsy of Greater
New Orleans, Inc.
1739 Bordeaux Street
New Orleans, Louisiana 70115

Raymond R. Rembolt
Medical Director
University Hospital School
Iowa City, Iowa 50010

Sylvia O. Richardson
Assistant Director
Learning Disabilities Program
Children's Neuromuscular Diagnostic
Clinic
University of Cincinnati
Medical Center
Cincinnati, Ohio 45219

Margaret Schilling
Program Consultant
UCPA, Inc.
1210 Astor Drive
Apartment 1413
Ann Arbor, Michigan 48104

Boyd V. Sheets (deceased)
Former Deputy Chairman

Department of Speech Pathology–
Audiology–Speech and Hearing
Science
Brooklyn College
City University of New York
Brooklyn, New York 11210

John M. Siepp
Educational Consultant
Professional Services Program
Department
Associate Director
National Collaborative Infant Project
UCPA, Inc.
66 East 34th Street
New York, New York 10016

Leon Sternfeld
Director
UCP Research and Educational
Foundation, Inc.
66 East 34th Street
New York, New York 10016

G. Gordon Williamson
Consultant in Occupational Therapy
and Special Education
United Cerebral Palsy Associations,
Inc.
Department of Special Education
Teachers College,
Columbia University
New York, New York 10027

ROSTER OF PARTICIPATING CENTERS NATIONAL COLLABORATIVE INFANT PROJECT

First Phase Centers

Agency for Infant Development
1030 Sir Francis Drake Boulevard
Kentfield, California 94904
Susan Collins, Director

Meeting Street School
667 Waterman Avenue
East Providence, Rhode Island 02914
Nancy D'Wolf, Executive Director

Program for Infants and Young Children with Developmental Disabilities
Medical Center
University of California
1000 Veteran Avenue
Los Angeles, California 90024
Judy Howard, Medical Director

United Cerebral Palsy of Greater New Orleans, Inc.
1739 Bordeaux Street
New Orleans, Louisiana 70115
Clara (Freddie) Pincus, Coordinator

University Hospital School
Iowa City, Iowa 52240
Alfred Healy, Director

Second Phase Centers

Cerebral Palsy Center of Middlesex County
Roosevelt Park
Edison, New Jersey 08817
Mary Witherspoon, Program Director

Infant Development Center
12510 West 62 Terrace
Shawnee, Kansas 66203
Lee Ann Britain, Director

Nisonger Center
Room 446, McCampbell Hall
Ohio State University
1580 Cannon Drive
Columbus, Ohio 43210
Lynn Allen, Coordinator

Special Children's Center
Tomkins County
Community Health Center
1287 Trumansburg Road
Ithaca, New York 14850
Frances Berko, Former Director

Suffolk Rehabilitation Center
United Cerebral Palsy of Suffolk County

159 Indian Head Road
Commack, New York 11725
Richard Lash, Former Director

United Cerebral Palsy of Detroit
10 Peterboro Street
Detroit, Michigan 43201
James Simpson, Director

United Cerebral Palsy of Lehigh Valley
3144 Linden Street
Bethlehem, Pennsylvania 18017
Mary Colkett, Project Coordinator

United Cerebral Palsy of Miami
1411 N.W. 14th Avenue
Miami, Florida 33215
John T. Horan, Former Director

United Cerebral Palsy of Nassau County
380 Washington Avenue
Roosevelt, New York 11725
Sal Gullo, Former Program Director

United Cerebral Palsy of Pittsburgh
House Building
4 Smithfield Street
Pittsburgh, Pennsylvania 15222
Molly Brickenstein, Coordinator of Infant Services

United Cerebral Palsy of Polk County
716 East Bella Vista Street
Lakeland, Florida 33801
Jim Sawyers, Director

United Cerebral Palsy of Rochester
1000 Elmwood Avenue
Rochester, New York 14620
Winnifred Fletcher, Former Executive Director

University of Hawaii
School of Public Health
1960 East-West Road
Honolulu, Hawaii 96822
Setsu Furuno, Director

Third Phase Centers

Agency for Infant Development
Alameda County
41450 Roberts Avenue
Fremont, California 94538
Cathy Lusson, Director

Alameda County Association for the Mentally Retarded
1120 East 14th Street, Suite C
P.O. Box 982
San Leandro, California 94577
Alta Kelly, Director

Children's Hospital of Akron
Buchtel and Bowrey Streets
Akron, Ohio 44308
Kathleen Austin, Team Coordinator

Chinatown Child Development Center
1007 Kearny Street
San Francisco, California 94133
Sue Louie, Senior Counselor

Crippled Children's Hospital and School
2501 West 26th Street
Sioux Falls, South Dakota 57105
Harvey Vogel, Director

Delaware Curative Workshop, Inc.
1600 Washington Street
Wilmington, Delaware 19802
Celeste Ryan, Coordinator, Early Childhood Education

Division for Disorders of Development and Learning
Child Development Center
Box 523
North Carolina Memorial Hospital
University of North Carolina
Chapel Hill, North Carolina 27514
Nancy Johnson, Infant Team Coordinator

Downeast Health Services
Pre-School Development Project
5 Oak Street
Ellsworth, Maine 04605
Daphne Rosenzweig, Home and
Community Services

Early Intervention Program, Inc.
41 Main Street (Route 520)
Holmdel, New Jersey 07733
Jane D. Chazkel, Program Director

Easter Seal Rehabilitation Center
226 Mill Hill Avenue
Bridgeport, Connecticut 06610
Diane Lombardi, Project Director

Easter Seal Rehabilitation Center
80 Tarrytown Road
Manchester, New Hampshire 03103
Carol Fryer, Director, Infant Program

**Easter Seal Society for Crippled
Children and Adults of San
Francisco, Inc.**
6221 Geary Boulevard
San Francisco, California 94121
Jone Ubbenga, Director of Infant
Program

Easter Seal Society of Polk County
2920 30th Street
Des Moines, Iowa 50310
Jean Linder, Occupational Therapist

Ellisville Baby Project
Preventorium Child Development
Center
Box 98
Sanitorium, Mississippi 39112
Olive Jones, Infant Project
Coordinator

**Ira Allen Early Essential Education
Center**
Fletcher Place
Burlington, Vermont 05401
Lois Holbrook, Administrator and
Project Director

**John W. Simpson Cerebral Palsy
Center**
2430 11th Avenue, North
Birmingham, Alabama 35234
James L. Dill, Director

**Poplar Center for Educational
Development**
515 East Poplar
San Mateo, California 94401
Karen Campbell, Director of Early
Child Development Program

Rehabilitation Center, Inc.
3701 Bellemeade Avenue
Evansville, Indiana 47715
Spiro B. Mitsos, Director

**San Diego County Association for
the Retarded**
3035 G Street
San Diego, California 92102
Irene Sharpe, Coordinator of Infant
Programs

**Sonoma County Agency for Infant
Development**
886 Second Street
Santa Rosa, California 95404
Sue Powell, Director

**United Cerebral Palsy of Akron and
Summit County**
93 West Exchange Street
Akron, Ohio 44308
Keith Penman, Program
Administrator

**United Cerebral Palsy of Central
Arizona**
2904 East Roosevelt Street
Phoenix, Arizona 85008
John L. Riddle, Director

**United Cerebral Palsy of New York
City**
Staten Island Developmental Center
777 Seaview Avenue
Staten Island, New York 10305
Rhona Hanshaft, Director

United Cerebral Palsy of the
North Shore Area
5 Borad Street
Salem, Massachusetts 01970
Peg Ruggeri, Project Director

United Cerebral Palsy of Orange
County, Inc.
3020 West Harvard Street
Santa Ana, California 92704
Patricia Meidell, Program Services
Coordinator

United Cerebral Palsy of Schuylkill,
Carbon, and Northumberland
Counties
210 South Center Street
Pottsville, Pennsylvania 17901
Mal Weaver, Director

United Cerebral Palsy of Western
New York, Inc.
100 LeRoy Avenue
Buffalo, New York 14214
John G. Spindler, Program Director

United Services for Handicapped
Developmental School
178 West Buchtel Avenue
Akron, Ohio 44302
Ruth B. Fischer, Director

University Affiliated Center for
Human Development
51 Smith Street
Athens, Ohio 45701
Loyd Inglis, Director

Walton Development Center
Stockton Unified School District
4131 North Crown Avenue
Stockton, California 95207
Jean Wilson, Team Leader,
Early Childhood Education

Weaver School
89 East Howe Road
Tallmadge, Ohio 44278
Jill Wolf, Home Training Supervisor

CURRICULUM TASK FORCE
NATIONAL COLLABORATIVE
INFANT PROJECT

Ellen Anderson
Teacher
Program for Infants and Young Children with
   Developmental Disabilities
Medical Center
University of California
1000 Veteran Avenue
Los Angeles, California 90024

Frances P. Connor
Professor and Chairman
Department of Special Education
Teachers College
Columbia University
New York, New York 10027

Patricia Keesee
Speech Pathologist
University Hospital School
University of Iowa
Medical Center
Iowa City, Iowa 52240

Elaine Lieberman
Speech Pathologist
Meeting Street School
667 Waterman Avenue
East Providence, Rhode Island 02914

Gary Nielsen
Former Chief
Special Problems Unit
Marin County Community Mental Health Services
Agency for Infant Development
1030 Sir Francis Drake Boulevard
Kentfield, California 94904

Carol Porter
Physical Therapist
United Cerebral Palsy of Greater New Orleans, Inc.
1739 Bordeaux Street
New Orleans, Louisiana 70115

SAMPLE FORMS EMPLOYED BY PARTICIPATING CENTERS IN DEVELOPING AND MONITORING INDIVIDUALIZED PROGRAM PLANS

Center A

Name: Code:

Diagnosis: Chronological age:

Description of child:

Problem:

1. Goal:

2. Behavioral objective:

3. Method:

4. Materials:

5. Staff:

6. Indiv. or group:

7. Location:

8. Rx. begun:

9. Accomplished:

10. Not accomplished:

11. Comments:

Center B

Date:

Name:

Problem: Birth date:

Goal:

Behavioral objective:

Dates	Methods	Frequency	Materials

Location: Accomplished:

Staff and others: Not accomplished:

Treatment begun:

No. of treatments given:

Comments:

Center C

Child study no. ____

Goal or area:

Behavioral objectives: _____

Materials: _____

Method: _____

Outcome: _____

People involved: Date:

Center E

Name:

Date:

Developmental description:

Coding	Objectives	Procedures	Extensions and/or modifications

Center D

Name:

Birth date:

Description of Child:

Area	Problem	Needs	Program
Motor			
Language			
Cognition			
Pre-speech			
Personal and social			

Center F

Client's name and number: _____   Child's birth date: _____

Code no. _____   Date program initiated: _____

Name of programmer: _____

BEHAVIOR Problem	PROCEDURE Behavior/activity	STIMULUS Educational aids	RESULTS Consequences for behavior

Center G

Name: _____   Date: _____   Case no. _____

Assessment Needs	Goals	Methods	Materials	Staff and other	Location	No. RX.	Date			Comments
							Rx. begun	Report		
								Accomp.	Not accomp.	

378

APPENDIX F

CONTRIBUTORS AND COLLABORATORS

Maureen Keenan Abell
Senior
Physical Therapy Department
Blythedale Children's Hospital
Valhalla, New York 10595

Ellen Anderson
Teacher
Program for Infants and Young
 Children with Developmental
 Disabilities
Medical Center
University of California
1000 Veteran Avenue
Los Angeles, California 90024

Judy Johnson Ayers
Former Director
Early Intervention Program, Inc.
41 Main Street (Route 520)
Holmdel, New Jersey 07733

Kathryn E. Barnard
Professor of Nursing
Department of Maternal–Child
 Nursing
University of Washington
Seattle, Washington 98195

Ellis I. Barowsky
Assistant Professor

Department of Curriculum and
 Teaching
Programs in Special Education
Hunter College
466 Lexington Avenue
New York, New York 10017

Adrienne Bergen
Assistant Director
Physical Therapy Department
Blythedale Children's Hospital
Valhalla, New York 10595

Frances Berko
Education and Training Specialist
Suffolk Developmental Center
P. O. Box 788
Melville, New York 11746

Lois L. Bly
Director
Physical Therapy Department
Blythedale Children's Hospital
Valhalla, New York 10595

Gloria Boylan
Teacher
University of Hawaii
School of Public Health
1960 East-West Road
Honolulu, Hawaii 96822

Molly Brickenstein
Coordinator of Infant Services
United Cerebral Palsy of Pittsburgh
House Building
4 Smithfield Street
Pittsburgh, Pennsylvania 15222

Lee Ann Britain
Director
Infant Development Center
12510 West 62 Terrace
Shawnee, Kansas 66203

Linda Buch
Clinical Supervisor
Teachers College Speech and
  Hearing Center
Columbia University
New York, New York 10027
Program Director
Unit 6
United Cerebral Palsy of New York
  State
Willowbrook Developmental Center
2760 Victory Boulevard
Staten Island, New York 10314

Susan Collins
Director
Agency for Infant Development
1030 Sir Francis Drake Boulevard
Kentfield, California 94904

Frances P. Connor
Professor and Chairman
Department of Special Education
Teachers College
Columbia University
New York, New York 10027
Chairman, Curriculum Task Force
  of the National Collaborative
  Infant Project

Maxine Conway
Clinic Director
United Cerebral Palsy Association of
  Western New York, Inc.
100 LeRoy Avenue
Buffalo, New York 14214

Leslie Faye Davis
Boyd Sheets Fellow 1975
United Cerebral Palsy Associations,
  Inc.
Education and Training Specialist
Suffolk Developmental Center
Box 788
Melville, New York 11746

Eric Denhoff
Medical Director
Meeting Street School
667 Waterman Avenue
East Providence, Rhode Island 02914

Sylvia Brooklyn Denhoff
Teacher of Cooking and Nutrition
Governor Center School
Providence, Rhode Island 02906

Helen Bee Douglas
Consultant in Developmental
  Psychology
United Cerebral Palsy Associations,
  Inc.
Route 1, Box 2
Eastsound, Washington 98245

Nancy D'Wolf
Executive Director
Meeting Street School
667 Waterman Avenue
East Providence, Rhode Island 02914

Bruce Ettinger
Teacher
Blythedale Children's Hospital
Valhalla, New York 10595

Carol Fortunato
Illustrator
481 Washington Avenue
Nutley, New Jersey 07110

Lynn Freer
Former District Program
  Representative
United Cerebral Palsy Associations,
  Inc.
66 East 34th Street
New York, New York 10016

Mary Garrigan
Teacher
United Cerebral Palsy of Lehigh
  Valley
3144 Linden Street
Bethlehem, Pennsylvania 18017

Sue Gelber
Director of Speech Pathology
Suffolk Rehabilitation Center
United Cerebral Palsy of Suffolk
  County
159 Indian Head Road
Commack, New York 11725

Donna Hanson
Physical Therapist
Harlem Hospital Center
135th Street and Lenox Avenue
New York, New York 10037

Una Haynes
Associate Director
Professional Services Program
  Department
Director
National Collaborative Infant Project
United Cerebral Palsy Associations,
  Inc.
66 East 34th Street
New York, New York 10016

Elsie D. Helsel
Coordinator of Special Education
McCracken Hall 119B
College of Education
Ohio University
Athens, Ohio 45701

Helen Hoffman
Psychologist
Suffolk Rehabilitation Center
United Cerebral Palsy of Suffolk
  County
159 Indian Head Road
Commack, New York 11725

Carol Hosaka
Teacher
University of Hawaii

School of Public Health
1960 East-West Road
Honolulu, Hawaii 96822

Ann Johnson
Occupational Therapist
Medical Center
University of California
1000 Veteran Avenue
Los Angeles, California 90024

Margaret H. Jones
Professor Emeritus of Pediatrics
Medical Center
University of California
1000 Veteran Avenue
Los Angeles, California 90024

Patricia Keesee
Speech Pathologist
University Hospital School
University of Iowa
Medical Center
Iowa City, Iowa 52240

Shari Stokes Kieran
Assistant Professor in Special
  Education
Eliot-Pearson Department of Child
  Study
Tufts University
Medford, Massachusetts 02155

Nancy Kinney
Physical Therapist
Suffolk Rehabilitation Center
United Cerebral Palsy of Suffolk
  County
159 Indian Head Road
Commack, New York 11725

Claire Lapidakis
Program Coordinator
United Cerebral Palsy of Lehigh
  Valley
3144 Linden Street
Bethlehem, Pennsylvania 18017

Shirley Joan Lemmen
Nurse
Child Development and Mental
  Retardation Center

Clinical Training Unit
University of Washington
Seattle, Washington 98105

Mark Leventhal
Speech Pathologist
Brooklyn Developmental Center
8888 Fountain Avenue
Brooklyn, New York 11208

Billie Levine
Director of Physical Therapy
Suffolk Rehabilitation Center
United Cerebral Palsy of Suffolk
County
159 Indian Head Road
Commack, New York 11725

Elaine Lieberman
Speech Pathologist
Meeting Street School
667 Waterman Avenue
East Providence, Rhode Island 02914

Miriam Lowry
Consultant in Developmental
Disabilities
Agency for Infant Development
1030 Sir Francis Drake Boulevard
Kentfield, California 94904

Sharon McDermott
Occupational Therapist
Lexington School for the Deaf
26-26 75th Street
Jackson Heights, New York 11370

Joan Meisel
Project Evaluator
United Cerebral Palsy
Associations, Inc.
National Collaborative Infant
Project
500 Redwood Road
San Anselmo, California 94960

Sherwood A. Messner
Former Director
Professional Services Program
Department
United Cerebral Palsy Associations,
Inc.

66 East 34th Street
New York, New York 10016

Joan Day Mohr
Pediatric Therapy Consultant
332 Concord Street
Cresskill, New Jersey 07626

Gary Nielsen
Former Chief
Special Problems Unit
Marin County Community Mental
Health Services
Agency for Infant Development
1030 Sir Francis Drake Boulevard
Kentfield, California 94904

Laureen B. Place
Physical Therapist
Brookdale Hospital
Linden Boulevard and Rockaway
Parkway
Brooklyn, New York 11212

Carol Porter
Physical Therapist
United Cerebral Palsy of
New Orleans, Inc.
1739 Bordeaux Street
New Orleans, Louisiana 70115

Sylvia O. Richardson
Assistant Director
Learning Disabilities Program
Children's Neuromuscular Diagnostic
Clinic
University of Cincinnati Medical
Center
Cincinnati, Ohio 45219

Claire Salant
Principal
New Interdisciplinary School
370 Snedecor Avenue
West Islip, New York 11759

Barbro Šálek
Physical Therapist
Suffolk Rehabilitation Center
United Cerebral Palsy of Suffolk
County

159 Indian Head Road
Commack, New York 11725

Margaret Schilling
Program Consultant
United Cerebral Palsy Associations,
Inc.
1210 Astor Drive
Apartment 1413
Ann Arbor, Michigan 48104

Lillian Shapiro
Assistant Professor
Department of Special Education
Teachers College
Columbia University
New York, New York 10027

John M. Siepp
Educational Consultant
Professional Services Program
Department
Associate Director
National Collaborative Infant Project
United Cerebral Palsy Associations,
Inc.
66 East 34th Street
New York, New York 10016

Dorothy M. Smith
Home Service Director
Coordinator, Infant Project
Staten Island Developmental Center
United Cerebral Palsy of New York
City
777 Seaview Avenue
Staten Island, New York 10305

Jerry Staller
Director
Physical Therapy Department

Mental Retardation Institute
Valhalla, New York 10595

Leon Sternfeld
Director
United Cerebral Palsy Research and
Educational Foundation, Inc.
66 East 34th Street
New York, New York 10016

Janice Tessier
Teacher
Blythedale Children's Hospital
Valhalla, New York 10595

Ethel Underwood
Director
Professional Services Program
Department
United Cerebral Palsy Associations,
Inc.
66 East 34th Street
New York, New York 10016

G. Gordon Williamson
Assistant Chief
Occupational Therapy Department
Robert Wood Johnson Jr.,
Rehabilitation Institute
John F. Kennedy Medical Center
Edison, New Jersey 08817
Department of Special Education
Teachers College
Columbia University
New York, New York 10027

Doris Woodward
Educational Director
United Cerebral Palsy of Western
New York
100 LeRoy Avenue
Buffalo, New York 14214

REFERENCES

Abeson, A. *A continuing summary of pending and completed litigation regarding the education of handicapped children*. Washington, D.C.: Council for Exceptional Children, Report No. 6, 1973.

Ainsworth, M. D. S. The development of infant–mother interaction among the Ganda. In B. M. Foss (Ed.), *Determinants of infant behavior* (Vol. 2). New York: Wiley, 1963.

Ainsworth, M. D. S. Patterns of attachment behavior shown by the infant in interaction with his mother. *Merrill–Palmer Quarterly,* 1964, *10.*

Ainsworth, M. D. S., & Bell, S. M. Some contemporary patterns of mother–infant interaction in the feeding situation. In A. Ambrose (Ed.), *Stimulation in early infancy*. London: Academic Press, 1969.

Ainsworth, M. D. S., & Bell, S. M. Attachment, exploration, and separation: Illustrated by the behavior of one year olds in a strange situation. *Child Development,* 1970, *41.*

Ainsworth, M. D. S., Bell, S. M., & Stayton, D. J. Individual differences in the development of some attachment behaviors. *Merrill-Palmer Quarterly,* 1972, *18.*

Aird, R. B., & Cohen, P. Electroencephalography in cerebral palsy. *Journal of Pediatrics,* 1950, *37.*

Altschule, A. M. *Proteins, their chemistry and politics*. New York: Basic Books, 1965.

Ambrose, J. A. (Ed.) *Stimulation in early infancy*. London: Academic Press, 1969.

American National Red Cross. *American Red Cross first aid textbook* (4th ed. rev.). Garden City, N. Y.: Doubleday, 1957.

Andrews, B., Banks, H., Blumenthal, E., Freeman, R., & Taft, L. Cerebral palsy: My baby is slow. *Patient Care,* 1972, *21.*

Arganian, M. Sex differences in early development. In J. C. Westman (Ed.), *Individual differences in children*. New York: Wiley, 1973.

Ayres, A. J. *Sensory integration and learning disorders.* Los Angeles: Western Psychological Services, 1972.

Baird, H. W. Convulsions in infancy and childhood. *Pediatric Clinics of North America,* 1963, *10.*

Barnard, K. E., & Powell, M. *Teaching the mentally retarded child: A family care approach.* St. Louis: Mosby, 1972.

Barness, A., & Pitkin, R. M. Symposium on nutrition. *Clinics in Perinatology,* 1975, *2* (2).

Battaglia, F. C. Intrauterine growth retardation. *American Journal of Obstetrics and Gynecology,* 1970, *106.*

Battle, C. U. Disruptions in the socialization of the handicapped child. *Rehabilitation Literature,* 1974, *35.*

Bax, M. Terminology and classification on cerebral palsy. *Developmental Medicine and Child Neurology,* 1964, *6.*

Beal, V. A. On acceptance of solid foods and other food patterns of infants and children. *Pediatrics,* 1957, *20.*

Bee, H. L., Van Egeren, L. F., Streissguth, A. P., Nyman, B. A., & Leckie, M. S. Social class differences in maternal teaching strategies and speech patterns. *Developmental Psychology,* 1969, *1.*

Beintema, D. J. *A neurological study of newborn infants* (Clinics in Developmental Medicine, No. 28). London: Heinemann Medical Books, 1968.

Bell, R. Q. Conributions of human infants to caregiving and social interaction. In M. Lewis & L. Rosenblum (Eds.), *The effect of the infant on its caregiver.* New York: Wiley, 1974.

Bell, S. M. The development of the concept of object a related to infant–mother attachment. *Child Development,* 1970, *41.*

Bergen, A. *Selected equipment for pediatric rehabilitation.* Valhalla, N. Y. Blythedale Children's Hospital, 1974.

Berlyne, D. C. Laughter, humor, and play. In G. Lindzey & E. Aronson (Eds.), *Handbook of social psychology.* New York: Addison-Wesley, 1970.

Berry, M. *Language disorders of children.* New York: Appleton-Century-Crofts, 1969.

Berry, M., & Eisenson, J. *Speech disorders.* New York: Appleton-Century-Crofts, 1956.

Birch, H. G., & Gussow, J. D. *Disadvantaged children: Health, nutrition, and school failure.* New York: Harcourt, Brace, & World; Grune & Stratton, 1970.

Black, F., Bergstrom, L., Downs, M., & Hemenway, W. *Congenital deafness: A new approach to early detection of deafness through a high risk register.* Boulder: Colorado Associated University Press, 1971.

Blehar, M. P. Anxious attachment and defensive reactions associated with day care. *Child Development,* 1974, *45.*

Bloom, B. S. *Stability and change in human characteristics*. New York: Wiley, 1964.

Bobath, B. The very early treatment of cerebral palsy. *Developmental Medicine and Child Neurology*, 1967, *9*.

Bobath, B. *Adult hemiplegia: Evaluation and treatment*. London: Heinemann Medical Books, 1970.

Bobath, B. *Abnormal postural reflex activity caused by brain lesions* (2nd ed.) London: Heinemann Medical Books, 1971.

Bobath, B., & Bobath, K. *Motor development in the different types of cerebral palsy*. London: Heinemann Medical Books, 1975.

Bobath, K. *The motor deficit in patients with cerebral palsy* (Clinics in Developmental Medicine, No. 23). London: Heinemann Medical Books, 1966.

Bobath, K., & Bobath, B. An analysis of the development of standing and walking patterns in patients with cerebral palsy. *Physiotherapy*, 1962, *48*.

Bobath, K., & Bobath, B. Cerebral palsy. In P. H. Pearson & C. E. Williams (Eds.), *Physical therapy services in the developmental disabilities*. Springfield, Ill.: Thomas, 1972.

Bosley, E. Development of sucking and swallowing. *Cerebral Palsy Journal*, 1965, *26* (6).

Bosma, J. (Ed.). *Symposium on oral sensation and perception*. Springfield, Ill.: Thomas, 1967.

Bosma, J. *Fourth symposium on oral sensation and perception*. Bethesda, Md.: National Institute of Health, 1973.

Bower, T. G. R. The visual world of infants. *Scientific American*, 1966, *251* (6).

Bower, T. G. R. *Development in infancy*. San Francisco: Freeman, 1974.

Bowlby, J. *Maternal care and mental health* (World Health Organization Monograph No. 2). Geneva: World Health Organization, 1951.

Bowlby, J. *Attachment*. New York: Basic Books, 1969.

Brasel, J. A. Newer tools for the diagnosis of malnutrition. *Pediatric Annals*, 1973, *2*.

Brazelton, T. B. Psychophysiologic reactions in the neonate. *Journal of Pediatrics*, 1961, *58* (4).

Brazelton, T. B. Observations of the neonate. *Journal of the American Academy of Child Psychiatry*, 1962, *1* (1).

Brazelton, T. B. The early mothering adjustment. *Pediatrics*, 1963, *31*.

Brazelton, T. B. Visual responses in the newborn. *Pediatrics*, 1966, *37*.

Brazelton, T. B. *Infants and mothers*. New York: Delacorte Press, 1969.

Brazelton, T. B. *Neonatal behavioral assessment scale* (Clinics in Developmental Medicine, No. 50). London: Heinemann Medical Books, 1974.

Brazelton, T. B., Koslowski, B., & Main, M. The origins of reciprocity: The early mother–infant interaction. In M. Lewis & L. Rosenblum (Eds.), *The effect of the infant on its caregiver.* New York: Wiley, 1974.

Bridges, K. A genetic theory of the emotions. *Journal of Genetic Psychology,* 1930, *37.*

Bridges, K. *The social and emotional development of the pre-school child.* London: Routledge, 1931.

Bridges, K. Emotional development in early infancy. *Child Development,* 1932, *3.*

Brodbeck, A. J., & Irwin, O. C. The speech behavior of infants without families. *Child Development,* 1946, *17.*

Brody, S. *Patterns of mothering.* New York: International University Press, 1951.

Broussard, E. R., & Hortner, M. S. Further considerations regarding maternal perception of the first born. In J. Hellmuth (Ed.), *Exceptional infant: Studies in abnormalities* (Vol. 2). New York: Brunner-Mazel, 1971.

Brown, J. R., Dorley, F. L., & Gomeg, M. R. Disorders of communication. *Pediatric Clinics of North America,* 1967, *14* (4).

Bruner, J. S. Play is serious business. *Psychology Today,* 1975, *8.*

Bruner, J. S., Olver, R. R., & Greenfield, P. M. *Studies in cognitive growth.* New York: Wiley, 1966.

Bühler, C. *The first years of life.* New York: John Day, 1930.

Burch, G. E. Fat cells, nutrition, and obesity. *American Heart Journal,* 1971, *82.*

Caldwell, B. The effects of psychosocial deprivation on human development in infancy. *Merrill-Palmer Quarterly,* 1970, *16.*

Chase, W. P. Color vision in infants. *Journal of Experimental Psychology,* 1937, *20.*

Chess, S., & Thomas, A. Temperament in the normal infant. In J. C. Westman (Ed.), *Individual differences in children.* New York: Wiley, 1973.

Chomsky, N. *Syntactic structures.* The Hague: Mouton, 1957.

Chomsky, N. *Language and mind.* New York: Harcourt, Brace, Jovanovich, 1968.

Crickmay, M. C. *Speech therapy and the Bobath approach to cerebral palsy.* Springfield, Ill.: Thomas, 1970.

Cronbach, L. J. Heredity, environment, and educational policy. *Harvard Educational Review,* Spring 1969.

Crothers, B., & Paine, R. S. *The natural history of cerebral palsy.* London: Oxford University Press, 1959.

Dale, P. *Language development: Structure and function.* Hinsdale, Ill.: Dryden Press, 1972.

Dargassies, S. Neurological maturation of the premature infant of 28–44 weeks gestational age. In F. Falkner (Ed.), *Human Development*. Philadelphia: Saunders, 1966.

Dayton, G., & Jones, M. Analysis of characteristics of fixation reflex in infants by use of direct current electro-oculography. *Neurology,* 1964, *14.*

Dekaban, A. *Neurology of infancy*. Baltimore: Williams & Wilkins, 1959.

Denhoff, S. Any child can cook. *Providence Sunday Journal,* March 14, 1976.

Denney, N. W. A developmental study of free classification in children. *Child Development,* 1972, *43b* (a).

Denney, N. W. Free classification in preschool children. *Child Development,* 1972, *43d* (b).

Dennis, W. Causes of retardation among institutional children: Iran. *Journal of Genetic Psychology,* 1960, *96.*

Dewey, J. *The child and the curriculum*. Chicago: University of Chicago Press, 1902.

Dreyfus, B. C. Organization of sleep in prematures: Implications for caregiving. In M. Lewis & L. Rosenblum (Eds.), *The effect of the infant on its caregiver*. New York: Wiley, 1974.

Drillien, C. *The growth and development of the prematurely born infant*. Baltimore: Williams & Wilkins, 1964.

Dubowitz, V. *The floppy infant* (Clinics in Developmental Medicine, No. 31). London: Heinemann Medical Books, 1969.

Egan, D. F., Illingworth, R. S., & MacKeith, R. C. *Developmental screening 0–5 years* (Clinics in Developmental Medicine, No. 30). London: Heinemann Medical Books, 1969.

Eisenberg, R. The development of hearing in man: An assessment of current status. *American Speech and Hearing Association,* 1970, *119.*

Elliott, H. C. *Textbook of the nervous system*. Philadelphia: Lippincott, 1947.

Erikson, E. Growth and crises of the healthy personality. In C. Kluckhorn & H. A. Murray (Eds.), *Personality in nature and society, and culture and education*. New York: Knopf, 1953.

Erikson, E. *Childhood and society* (2nd ed.). New York: Norton, 1963.

Escalona, S. K. *The roots of individuality: Normal patterns of development in infancy*. Chicago: Aldine, 1968.

Eyzaguirre, C. *Physiology of the nervous system*. Chicago: Year Book Medical Publishers, 1969.

Fantz, R. L. Pattern vision in newborn infants. *Science,* 1963, *140.*

Faulkender, P. J., Wright, J. C., & Waldron, A. Generalized habituation of concept stimuli in toddlers. *Child Development,* 1974, *45.*

Feingold, B. F. *Why your child is hyperactive*. New York: Random House, 1974.

Finnie, N. R. *Handling the young cerebral palsied child at home* (2nd ed.). New York: Dutton, 1975.

Fiorentino, M. R. *Normal and abnormal development: The influence of primitive reflexes on motor redevelopment.* Springfield, Ill. Thomas, 1972.

Flavell, J. H. *The developmental psychology of Jean Piaget.* Princeton: Van Nostrand, 1963.

Food and Agriculture Organization of the United Nations. *Amino-acid control of food and biological data on protein.* Rome: United Nations Publications, 1970.

Fraiberg, S. *The magic years.* New York: Scribners, 1959.

Fraiberg, S. Parallel and divergent patterns in blind and sighted infants. *Psychoanalytic Study of the Child,* 1968, 22.

Frailberg, S. Blind infants and their mothers: An examination of the sign system. In M. Lewis & L. Rosenblum (Eds.), *The effect of the infant on its caregiver.* New York: Wiley, 1974.

Fraiberg, S., Siegel, B. L., & Gibson, R. The role of sound in the search behavior of a blind infant. *Psychoanalytic Study of the Child,* 1966, 21.

Freedman, D. C. Heredity control of early social behavior. In B. M. Foss (Ed.), *Determinants of infant behavior* (Vol. 3). New York: Wiley, 1965.

Freud, S. *Beyond the pleasure principle* (Standard Edition, Vol. 18). London: Hogarth, 1955.

Furth, H. G. *Thinking without language.* New York: Free Press, 1966.

Gardner, D. B. *Development in early childhood: The preschool years.* New York: Harper & Row, 1964.

Gardner, E. *Fundamentals of neurology* (6th ed.). Philadelphia: Saunders, 1975.

Gerwitz, J. L. A program of research on the dimensions and antecedents of emotional dependency. *Child Development,* 1956, 27.

Gerwitz, J. L. Mechanisms of social learning: Some roles of stimulation and behavior in early human development. In D. A. Goslin (Ed.), *Handbook of socialization theory and research.* Chicago: Rand McNally, 1969.

Gesell, A. The ontogenesis of infant behavior. In P. H. Mussen (Ed.), *Carmichael's manual of child psychology* (3rd ed.). New York: Wiley, 1970.

Gesell, A., Halverson, H. M., Thompson, H., Ilg, F. L., Costner, B. M., Ames, L. B., & Amatruda, C. S. *The first five years of life: A guide to the study of the prechool child.* New York: Harper, 1940.

Gesell, A., & Thompson, H. *Infant behavior.* New York: McGraw-Hill, 1934.

Gibson, E. J. *Principles of perceptual learning and development.* New York: Appleton-Century-Crofts, 1969.

Goodenough, F. L. *Anger in young children*. Minneapolis: University of Minnesota Press, 1931.

Goodenough, F. L. Expression of the emotions in a blind–deaf child. *Journal of Abnormal and Social Psychology*, 1932, 27.

Goodman, L. S., & Gilman, A. *The pharmacological basis of therapeutics*. New York: Macmillan, 1965.

Gray, P. H. *Theory and evidence of imprinting in human infants* (Center for Health Administration Studies, Research series Vol. 1). University of Chicago, 1957.

Guthrie, H. A. *Introductory nutrition* (2nd ed.). St. Louis: Mosby, 1971.

Guyton, A. C. *Textbook of medical physiology* (3rd ed.). Philadelphia: Saunders, 1966.

Harlow, H. F. The nature of love. *American Psychology*, 1958, *13*.

Hawk, S. S. Moto-kinaesthetic speech training for children. *Journal of Speech and Hearing Disorders*, 1937, *2*.

Hawk, S. S. Moto-kinaesthetic training for children with speech handicaps. *Journal of Speech and Hearing Disorders*, 1942, 7.

Hebb, D. O. The organization of behavior: A neuropsychological theory. New York: Wiley, 1949.

Herron, R. E., & Sutton-Smith, B. (Eds.). *Child's play*. New York: Wiley, 1971.

Hess, R. D., & Shipman, V. C. Early experiences and the socialization of cognitive modes in children. *Child Development*, 1965, *36*.

Hess, R. D., & Shipman, V. C. Cognitive elements in maternal behavior. In J. P. Hill (Ed.), *Minnesota Symposia on Child Psychology* (Vol. 1). Minneapolis: University of Minnesota Press, 1967.

Hess, R. D., & Shipman, V. C. Maternal influences upon early learning: The cognitive environments of urban preschool children. In R. D. Hess & R. M. Bear (Eds.), *Early education*. Chicago: Aldine, 1968.

Hirsch, J. Cell number and size as a determinant of subsequent obesity. *Current Concepts in Nutrition*, 1975, *3*.

Hixon, T., & Hardy, J. Restricted motility of the speech articulators in cerebral palsy. *Journal of Speech and Hearing Disorders*, 1964, *29*.

Holt, K. S. Facts and fallacies about neuromuscular function in cerebral palsy as revealed by electromyography. *Developmental Medicine and Child Neurology*, 1966, *2*.

Holzel, A., Schwarz, V., & Sutcliffe, K. W. Defective lactose absorption causing malnutrition in infancy. *Lancet*, May 30, 1959.

Horton, K. Infant intervention and language learning. In R. L. Schiefelbusch & L. L. Lloyd (Eds.), *Language perspectives: Acquisition, retardation, and intervention*. Baltimore: University Park Press, 1974.

Hunt, J. M. *Intelligence and experience*. New York: Ronald Press, 1961.

Hutt, C. Exploration and play in children. In R. E. Herron & B. Sutton-Smith (Eds.), *Child's play*. New York: Wiley, 1971.

Hymes, J. L., Jr. *A healthy personality for your child* (Department of Health, Education, and Welfare, Children's Bureau Publication No. 3337). Washington, D.C.: U.S. Government Printing Office, 1952.

Ilg, F., & Ames, L. B. *Child behavior.* New York: Harper & Row, 1955.

Illingworth, R. S. *The development of the infant and young child: Normal and abnormal* (4th Ed.). Baltimore: Williams & Wilkins, 1970.

Ingram, T. T. S. Muscle tone and posture in infancy. *Cerebral Palsy Bulletin,* 1959, *1* (5).

Ingram, T. T. S. The new approach to early diagnosis of handicaps in children. *Developmental Medicine and Child Neurology,* 1962, *2.*

Inhelder, B. Some aspects of Piaget's genetic approach to cognition. *Monographs of the Society for Research in Child Development,* 1962, 27 (2).

International Study Group. *Hemiplegic cerebral palsy in childhood and adults* (Clinics in Developmental Medicine, No. 4). London: Heinemann Medical Books, 1961.

Jenson, A. R. How much can we boost IQ and scholastic achievement? *Harvard Educational Review,* Winter 1969.

Jersild, A. T. *Child psychology* (4th ed.). New York: Prentice-Hall, 1954.

Johansson, B., Wedenberg, E., & Westin, B. Measurement of tone response by the human fetus. *Acta Oto-laryngologica,* 1964, *57.*

Jones, M., Sands, R., Hyman, C., Sturgeon, P., & Koch, F. Study of the incidence of central nervous sytem damage following erythroblastosis foetalis. *Pediatrics,* 1954, *14.*

Kagan, J. *Change and continuity in infancy.* New York: Wiley, 1971.

Kagan, J. Do infants think? *Scientific American,* 1972, *226* (12).

Kagan, J., & Lewis, W. Studies of attention in the human infant. *Merrill-Palmer Quarterly,* 1965, *2.*

Kearsley, R., Snider, M., Richie, R., Crawford, J. D., & Talbot, N. B. Study of relations between psychologic environment and child behavior: A pediatric procedure. *American Journal of Diseases of Children,* 1962, *104.*

Kennell, J., Jerauld, R., Wolfe, H., Chesler, D., Kreger, N. C., McAlpine, W., Steffa, M., & Klaus, M. H. Maternal behavior one year after early and extended post-partum contact. *Developmental Medicine and Child Neurology,* 1974, *16.*

Kessen, W., Haith, M. M., & Salapatek, P. H. Infancy. In P. H. Mussen (Ed.), *Carmichael's manual of child psychology* (3rd ed.). New York: Wiley, 1970.

Klapper, Z., & Birch, H. G. *A fourteen-year follow-up study of cerebral palsy: Intellectual change and stability.* Paper presented at the annual meeting of the American Orthopsychiatric Association, San Francisco, 1966.

Klaus, M., & Kennell, J. Mothers separated from their newborn infants. *Pediatric Clinics of North America,* 1970, *17* (4).

Knittle, J. L. Obesity in childhood: A problem in adipose tissue cellular development. *Journal of Pediatrics,* 1972, *81.*

Kohlberg, L. A cognitive-developmental analysis of children's sex role concepts and attitudes. In E. E. Maccoby (Ed.), *The development of sex differences.* Stanford: Stanford University Press, 1966.

Köng, E. Very early treatment of cerebral palsy. *Developmental Medicine and Child Neurology,* 1966, *8.*

Korner, A. F. Individual differences at birth: Implications for early experience and later development. In J. C. Westman (Ed.), *Individual differences in children.* New York: Wiley, 1973.

Kubler-Ross, E. *On death and dying.* New York: Macmillan, 1969.

Langlois, A. *Respiratory patterns in infants aged six to thirteen months.* Unpublished doctoral dissertation, Teachers College, Columbia University, 1975.

Lappe, F. M. *Diet for a small planet.* New York: Ballantine Books, 1971.

Leifer, A., Leiderman, P., Barnett, C. R., & Williams, J. A. Effects of mother–infant separation on maternal attachment behavior. *Child Development,* 1972, *43.*

Lemmen, S. J., & Add, C. K. *Group education with mothers of infants with Down's syndrome.* Paper presented at the annual meeting of the American Academy of Mental Deficiency, Atlanta, 1973.

Lenneberg, E. H. On explaining language. *Science,* 1969, *164.*

Leventhal, A. S., & Lipsitt, L. P. Adaptation, pitch discrimination, and sound vocalization in the neonate. *Child Development,* 1964, *35.*

Levine, B. The Kathy side-lyer. *Neuro-developmental Treatment Newsletter,* 1974, *7* (2).

Lewis, M. *How children learn to speak.* New York: Basic Books, 1959.

Lewis, M., & Rosenblum, L. (Eds.), *The effect of the infant on the caregiver.* New York: Wiley, 1974.

Lipsitt, L. P. Learning in the human infant. In H. W. Stevenson, E. Ḥ. Hess, & H. L. Rheingold (Eds.), *Early behavior: Comparative and developmental approaches.* New York: Wiley, 1967.

Lipsitt, L. P. Pattern perception and information seeking in early infancy. In F. Young & D. Lindsley (Eds.), *Early experience and visual information processing in perceptual and reading disorders.* Washington, D.C.: National Academy of Sciences, 1970.

Logan, W., & Bosma, J. Oral and pharyngeal dysphagia in infancy. *Pediatric Clinics of North America,* 1967, *14* (1).

Logan, W., Kavanagh, J., & Wornall, A. Sonic correlates of human deglutition. *Journal of Applied Physiology,* 1967, *23.*

McCandless, B. R. *Children and adolescents: Behavior and development* (2nd ed.). New York: Holt, Rinehart, & Winston, 1967.

Maccoby, E. E., & Feldman, S. S. Mother-attachment and stranger-relations in the third year of life. *Mongraphs of the Society for Research in Child Development.* 1972, *37* (1).

McGraw, M. B. *The neuro-muscular maturation of the human infant.* New York: Hafner, 1963.

McNeill, D. *The acquisition of language.* New York: Harper & Row, 1970.

Major, D. R. *First steps in mental growth.* New York: Macmillan, 1906.

Manocha, S. L. *Malnutrition and retarded human development.* Springfield, Ill.: Thomas, 1972.

Mathews, S. S., Jones, M. H., & Speiling, S. C. Hip derangements seen in cerebral palsied children. *American Journal of Physical Medicine,* 1953, *32* (3).

Mayer, J., & Ramsey, J. How to eat to feel your best. *Family Circle,* 1975, *87.*

Menyuk, P. *The acquisition and development of language.* Englewood Cliffs, N.J.: Prentice-Hall, 1971.

Milani-Comparetti, A., & Gidoni, E. A. Pattern analysis of motor development and its disorders. *Developmental Medicine and Child Neurolgy,* 1967, *9.*

Miranda, S. B., & Fantz, R. L. Visual preferences of Down's syndrome and normal infants. *Child Development,* 1973, *44.*

Miranda, S. B., & Fantz, R. L. Recognition memory in Down's syndrome and normal infants. *Child Development,* 1974, *45.*

Morrow, G. Nutritional management of infants with inborn errors of metabolism. *Clinics in Perinatology,* 1975, *2.*

Mueller, H. Facilitating feeding and prespeech. In P. H. Pearson & C. E. Williams, (Eds.), *Physical therapy services in the developmental disabilities.* Springfield, Ill.: Thomas, 1972.

Mueller, H. *Prespeech and language therapy with the cerebral palsied child.* Course offered at the Special School for Cerebral Palsied Children in Zurich, Switzerland, March 1973.

Mueller, H. Feeding. In N. R. Finnie, *Handling the young cerebral palsied child at home* (2nd ed.). New York: Dutton, 1975.

Murphy, L. B. Infant's play and cognitive development. In M. Piers (Ed.), *Play and development.* New York: Norton, 1972.

Mysak, E. Dysarthria and oropharyngeal reflexology: A review. *Journal of Speech and Hearing Disorders,* 1963, *28.*

Mysak, E. *Neuroevolutional approach to cerebral palsy and speech.* New York: Teachers College Press, 1968.

Nelson, K. Some evidence for the cognitive primacy of categorization and its functional basis. *Merrill-Palmer Quarterly,* 1973, *19.* (a)

Nelson K. Structure and strategy in learning to talk. *Monographs of the Society for Research in Child Development,* 1973, *38* (1). (b)

Northern, J., & Downs, M. *Hearing in children.* Baltimore: Williams & Wilkins, 1974.

O'Donnell, P. A. *Motor and haptic learning.* Belmont, Cal.: Dimensions Publishing Co. in association with Fearon Publishing Co., 1969.

Oppé, T. Risk register for babies. *Developmental Medicine and Child Neurology,* 1967, *9.*

Paine, R. S. The future of the "floppy" infant: A follow-up study of 133 patients. *Developmental Medicine and Child Neurology,* 1963, *5.*

Paine, R. S. The evaluation of infantile postural reflexes in the presence of chronic brain syndromes. *Developmental Medicine and Child Neurology,* 1964, *6.*

Paine, R. S. Cerebral palsy: Symptoms and signs of diagnostic and prognostic significance. *Current Practice in Orthopedic Surgery,* 1966, *3.*

Paine, R. S., & Brazelton, T. B. Evolution of postural reflexes in normal infants and in the presence of chronic brain disorders. *Neurology,* 1964, *14.*

Paine, R. S., & Oppé, T. *Neurological examination of children.* Philadelphia: Lippincott, 1966.

Palmer, M. F. Speech therapy in cerebral palsy. *Journal of Pediatrics,* 1952, *40* (4).

Peiper, A. *Cerebral function in infancy and childhood.* New York: Consultants Bureau, 1963.

Perlstein, M. A., Gibbs, E. L., & Gibbs, F. A. The electroencephalograph in infantile cerebral palsy. *Proceedings of the Association for Research in Nervous and Mental Disorders,* 1947, *26.*

Phelps, W., Hopkins, T., & Cousins, R. *The cerebral-palsied child.* New York: Simon & Schuster, 1958.

Piaget, J. *Play, dreams, and imitation in childhood.* New York: Norton, 1963.

Piaget, J. Development and learning. In C. S. Lavatelli & F. Stendler, (Eds.). *Readings in child behavior and development* (3rd ed.). New York: Harcourt, Brace, Jovanovich, 1972.

Piaget, J., & Inhelder, B. *The psychology of the child.* New York: Basic Books, 1969.

Polani, P. E. The natural history of choreoathetoid cerebral palsy. *Guy's Hospital Reports,* 1959, *32.*

Prechtl, H. Prognostic value of neurological signs in the newborn infant. *Proceedings of the Royal Society of Medicine,* 1965, *58.*

Prechtl, H., & Beintema, D. *The neurological examination of the full term infant* (Clinics in Developmental Medicine, No. 12). London: Heinemann Medical Books, 1964.

Provence, S., & Lipton, R. C. *Infants in institutions: A comparison of their development with family reared infants during the first year of life.* New York: International Universities Press, 1962.

Razran, G. Observable unconscious and inferable conscious in current Soviet psychophysiology. *Psychological Review,* 1961, *68.*

Rheingold, H. L. The effect of environmental stimulation upon social and exploratory behavior in the human infant. In B. M. Foss (Ed.), *Determinants of infant behavior.* New York: Wiley, 1961.

Rheingold, H. L. The measurement of maternal care. In G. R. Medinnus (Ed.), *Readings in the psychology of parent-child relations.* New York: Wiley, 1967.

Rheingold, H. L. The effects of a strange environment on the behavior of infants. In B. M. Foss (Ed.), *Determinants of infant behavior* (Vol. 4). London: Methuen, 1969.

Rheingold, H. L., Gerwitz, J. L., & Ross, H. W. Social conditioning of vocalizations in the infant. *Comparative Physiological Psychology,* 1959, *52.*

Rheingold, H. L., & Samuels, H. R. Maintaining the positive behavior of infants by increased stimulation. *Developmental Psychology,* 1969, *1.*

Rosso, P., & Winick, M. Relation of nutrition to physical and mental development. *Pediatric Annals,* 1973, *2.*

Rubenstein, J. Maternal attentiveness and subsequent exploratory behavior in the infant. *Child Development,* 1967, *38.*

Rushworth, G. On postural and righting reflexes. *Cerebral Palsy Bulletin* 1961, *3.*

Rutter, M. Psychological development: Predictions from infancy. *Journal of Child Psychology,* 1970, *2.*

Rutter, M. *Maternal deprivation.* London: Penguin Books, 1972.

Salapatek, P., & Kessen, W. Visual scanning of triangles by the human newborn. *Journal of Experimental Child Psychology,* 1966, *3.*

Sander, L. W. The longitudinal course of early mother–child pairs. In B. M. Foss (Ed.), *Determinants of infant behavior,* (Vol. 4). London: Methuen, 1969.

Santulli, T. V., Schullinger, J. N., Heird, W. C., Gongaware, R. D., Wigger, J., Barlow, B., Blanc, W. A., & Berdon, W. E. Acute necrotizing enterocolitis in infancy: A review of 64 cases. *Pediatrics,* 1975, *55.*

Satir, V. *People making.* Palo Alto, Cal.: Science and Behavior Books, 1972.

Scarr-Salapatek, S., & Williams, M. The effects of early stimulation on low-birth-weight infants. *Child Development,* 1973, *44.*

Schaffer, H. R., & Callender, W. M. Psychologic effects of hospitalization in infancy. *Pediatrics,* 1959, *24.*

Schaffer, H. R., & Emerson, P. E. The development of social attachments in infancy. *Monographs of the Society for Research in Child Development,* 1964, *29* (4). (a)

Schaffer, H. R., & Emerson, P. E. Patterns of response to physical contact in early human development. *Journal of Child Psychology and Psychiatry,* 1964, *5.* (b)

Schubert, W. K. Fat, nutrition, and diet in childhood. *American Journal of Cardiology*, 1973, *31*.

Scott, J. P. The process of primary socialization in canine and human infants. *Monographs of the Society for Research in Child Development*, 1963, *28* (1).

Sears, R. R., Maccoby, E. E., & Levin, H. *Patterns of child rearing*. Evanston, Ill.: Row, Peterson, 1957.

Semans, S. The Bobath concept in treatment of neurological disorders. *American Journal of Physical Medicine*, 1967, *46*.

Sheppard, J. J. Cranio-oro-pharyngeal motor patterns in dysarthria associated with cerebral palsy. *Journal of Speech and Hearing Research*, 1964, *7*.

Sheridan, M. The STYCAR Graded-Balls Vision Test. *Developmental Medicine and Child Neurology*, 1973, *15*.

Sherman, J. O., Hamly, C. A., & Khachadurina, A. K. Use of an oral elemental diet in infants with severe intractable diarrhea. *Journal of Pediatrics*, 1975, *86*.

Sherman, M. The differentiation of emotional responses in infants: The ability of observers to judge the emotional characteristics of the crying of infants, and the voice of the adult. *Journal of Comparative Psychology*, 1927, *7*.

Sigman, M., & Parmlee, A. H. Visual preferences of four-month-old premature and full-term infants. *Child Development*, 1974, *45*.

Silverman, A., Ray, C. C., & Cozzetto, F. J. *Pediatric clinical gastroenterology*. St. Louis: Mosby, 1971.

Slobin, D. *Psycholinguistics*. Glenview, Ill.: Scott Foresman, 1971.

Smart, M. C., & Smart, R. C. *Children's development and relationships*. New York: Macmillan, 1967.

Smith, D. *Recognizable patterns of human malformation: Genetic, embryologic, and clinical aspects* (Major Problems in Clinical Pediatrics, Vol. 7). Philadelphia: Saunders, 1970.

Solkoff, N., Yaffe, S., Weintraub, D., & Blase, B. Effects of handling on the subsequent development of premature infants. *Developmental Psychology*, 1969, *1*.

Spock, B. *Baby and child care*. New York: Pocket Books, 1957.

Staller, J. New chair design. *Neuro-developmental Treatment Newsletter*, 1973, *6* (3).

Stechler, G. Newborn attention as affected by medication during labor. *Science*, 1964, *144*.

Steward, D., & Steward, M. The observation of Anglo-Mexican and Chinese-American mothers teaching their young sons. *Child Development*, 1973, *44*.

Stockmeyer, S. A. An interpretation of the approach of Rood to the treatment of neuromuscular dysfunction. *American Journal of Physical Medicine*, 1967, *46*.

Stockmeyer, S. A. A sensorimotor approach to treatment. In P. H. Pearson & C. E. Williams (Eds.), *Physical therapy services in the developmental disabilities*. Springfield, Ill.: Thomas, 1972.

Stone, L. J., Smith, H. T., & Murphy, L. B. (Eds.). *The competent infant*. New York: Basic Books, 1973.

Szasz, T. S., & Hollender, M. H. A contribution to the philosophy of medicine. *Archives of Internal Medicine*, 1956, *97*.

Talbot, N. B., Kagan, J., & Eisenberg, L. *Behavioral science in pediatric medicine*. Philadelphia: Saunders, 1971.

Tanner, J. M. Variability of growth and maturity in newborn infants. In M. Lewis & L. A. Rosenblum (Eds.), *The effect of the infant on its caregiver*. New York: Wiley, 1974.

Thompson, J. Development of facial expression of emotion in blind and seeing children. *Archives of Psychology*, 1941, *37* (264).

Tulkin, S. R., & Kagan, J. Compensatory education for infants. *Child Development*, 1972, *43*.

Van Blankenstein, M., Welbergen, U. R., & de Haas, J. H. *Le développement du nourrisson*. Paris: Presses Universitaires de France, 1962.

Van den Berg, B. J., & Yerushalmy, J. Studies on convulsive disorders in young children. *Pediatrics*, 1969, *3*.

Van Riper, C., & Irwin J. *Voice and articulation*. Englewood Cliffs, N.J.: Prentice-Hall, 1958.

Voss, D. Proprioceptive neuromuscular facilitation. In P. H. Pearson & C. E. Williams (Eds.), *Physical therapy services in the developmental disabilities*. Springfield, Ill.: Thomas, 1972.

Waddle, C. W. *An introduction to child psychology*. Boston: Houghton Mifflin, 1918.

Walsh, G. *Cerebellum, posture, and cerebral palsy* (Clinics in Developmental Medicine, No. 8). London: Heinemann Medical Books, 1963.

Weiner, B., & Goodnow, J. J. Motor activity: Effects on memory. *Developmental Psychology*, 1970, *2*.

White, B. An experimental approach of the effects of experience on early human behavior. In J. P. Hill (Ed.), *Minnesota Symposia on Child Psychology* (Vol. 1) Minneapolis: University of Minnesota Press, 1967.

White, B. *Human infants: Experience and psychological development*. Englewood Clifs, N.J.: Prentice-Hall, 1971.

White, B., Castle, P., & Held, R. Observations on the development of visually directed reaching. *Child Development*, 1964, *35*.

White, R. W. Motivation reconsidered: The concept of competence. *Psychological Review*, 1959, *66*.

Wilder, C. N. Respiratory patterns in infants: Birth to eight months of age (Doctoral dissertation, Columbia University, 1972). *Dissertation Ab-*

stracts International, 1973, *33,* 5052B-5053B. (University Microfilms No. 73-93056).

Wilder, C. N., & Baken, R. Respiratory patterns in infant cry. *Human Communication,* Winter 1974–75.

Willerman, L., Broman, S. H., & Fielder, M. Infant development, preschool IQ, and social class. *Child Development,* 1970, *41.*

Winick, M. Cellular growth during early malnutrition. *Pediatrics.* 1971, *47.*

Winters, R. W. (Ed). *The body fluids in pediatrics.* Boston: Little, Brown, 1973.

Wolff, P. H. The natural history of crying and other vocalization in early infancy. In B. M. Foss (Ed.), *Determnants of infant behavior* (Vol. 4). London: Methuen, 1969.

Yarrow, L. J. Separation from parents during early childhood. In M. L. Hoffman & L. W. Hoffman (Eds.), *Review of child development research* (Vol. 1). New York: Russell Sage Foundation, 1964.

Yarrow, L. J. The development of focused relationships in infancy. In J. Hullmuth (Ed.), *Exceptional infant.* New York: Brunner-Mazel, 1967.

Yarrow, L. J. The crucial nature of early experience. In D. Glass (Ed.), *Environmental influences: Biology and behavior series.* New York: Rockefeller University Press, Russell Sage Foundation, 1968.

Yarrow, L. J., Rubenstein, J. L., Pedersen, F. A., & Jankowski, J. J. Dimensions of early stimulation and their differential effects on infant development. *Merrill-Palmer Quarterly,* 1972, *18.*

Young, E. H. The moto-kinaesthetic method as applied to cerebral palsy. *Cerebral Palsy Review,* May–June 1962.

Zubek, J. P., & Solberg, P. A. *Human development.* New York: McGraw-Hill, 1954.

INDEX

A Preliminary Note

Cited sources: Italicized last names refer to sources cited in the book. Full details are given in the preceding list of references. When a source has two authors, both authors' names are indexed separately; when three or more, only the first is indexed, followed by "et al."

Individually planned programs: The sample program plans (pp. 275-301) have not been indexed, because they are uniquely applicable to the needs of a particular child and because the plans need to be read in their entirety and related to the total context of the particular case.

Cross-references: The reader should, in most cases, consult also the term or concept implied or contained in the key words modifying the entry, e.g., in the entry "Motor devt., and learning," the reader should consult also the entry "Learning."

Abbreviations: The following abbreviations have been used in the index:

devt.—development	quadripl.—quadriplegic
exam.—examination	reqd.—required